American Cooking

TIME
LIFE
BOOKS ®

Foods of the World

American Cooking

by

Dale Brown

and the Editors of

TIME-LIFE BOOKS

photographed by Mark Kauffman

TIME-LIFE BOOKS, NEW YORK

THE AUTHOR: Dale Brown *(left picture, above)* is a staff writer for TIME-LIFE BOOKS
and a former editor of *Holiday*. With his wife, Liet (shown with him), and his two-
year-old daughter, Elisabeth, he traveled across the country sampling the foods of
various regions for this book. He is also author of *The Cooking of Scandinavia* and
American Cooking: The Northwest in the FOODS OF THE WORLD Library.

THE CONSULTING EDITOR: The late Michael Field *(above, right)* was one of America's foremost food experts and culinary teachers and wrote many articles for various
leading magazines. His books include *Michael Field's Cooking School* and *Michael
Field's Culinary Classics and Improvisations.*

THE PHOTOGRAPHER: Mark Kauffman *(on left in left picture, above)*, a graduate of the
photographic staff of LIFE, is a top journalistic and food photographer. His assignment for this book took him to every part of the United States. He also
photographed *The Cooking of Provincial France* for FOODS OF THE WORLD.

THE CONSULTANT: James Beard *(on right in left picture, above)*, the consultant for this
book, has long been recognized as a foremost authority on American cooking and
an accomplished teacher of the culinary arts. His many books include *Delights and
Prejudices, James Beard's Treasury of Outdoor Cooking, The James Beard Cookbook* and
James Beard's Fish Cookery.

THE CHEF: John Clancy *(above, right)*, who was in charge of the preparation and test-
ing of the recipes for this book and the accompanying recipe booklet, has taught
cooking classes since 1959. He has also served as chef at a number of outstanding
restaurants, and as a food consultant for the Green Giant Company.

THE COVER: An old-fashioned strawberry shortcake, one of America's most popular desserts, is topped with cream before serving. The recipe is on page 179.

Contents

Introduction   6

I   From a Cookery to a Cuisine   8

II   America the Plentiful   36

III   The Flavor of the Regions   66

IV   U.S. Choice: Meat and Poultry   106

V   A Delectable Kettle of Fish   132

VI   Dairy Riches and Mountains of Snacks   152

VII   The Joy of Baking   166

VIII   Two Hundred Years in the Kitchen   184

Appendix   *Tips on Outdoor Cooking*   203

Recipe Index   204

General Index   205

Credits and Acknowledgments   208

The Recipe Booklet that accompanies this volume has been designed for use in the kitchen. It contains all the 74 recipes at the ends of the chapters plus 50 more. It also has a wipe-clean cover and a spiral binding so that it can either stand up or lie flat when open.

Take Equal Parts of Bounty, Diversity and Ingenuity

In three and a half centuries American cookery has developed a repertory of enormous diversity and complexity. Its pattern, established by early settlers—the English, Dutch and French—carried over through the 19th Century and into the 20th. Meanwhile, native cooking traditions evolved, with strong regional overtones. And in the great immigration waves of the last century, the numerous ethnic groups that pushed across the country introduced countless new dishes and brought sophistication to American food. Now, after 350 years of inventions and borrowings adapted to please the composite American palate, we are on the way to establishing a cuisine that can truly be called our own.

In addition to a rich heritage of native and foreign dishes, the country is fortunate in the bounty and quality of its food products. We have developed some of the best meat in the world; we have fine dairylands that produce several great cheeses and many good ones; we have excellent fruits and vegetables—and in wide variety, thanks to the genius of such men as Luther Burbank; we have an abundance of good fish, both fresh and cured; and we have created a remarkably fine wine industry. Our marketing techniques bring fresh foods to us from every corner of the country, extending the season of many fruits and vegetables, and making some of them available the year round. Apart from commercially available foods, we can be grateful for the treasure of food still to be found in the wilds—morels, meadow mushrooms and puffballs; huckleberries and strawberries, fiddleheads and pokeweed; catfish, suckers and crappies.

We are an amazingly versatile nation, producing everything from good caviar to good salted peanuts. Out of our prodigious gastronomic wealth it has been the job of the editors of this book to represent American cookery justly. It would have been a partial truth to offer only recipes from Colonial America, or purely regional recipes. Instead the editors have chosen dishes that show the true diversity of American food. Some of the recipes have long histories. A few are nearly as new as this book. Many are traditional—all-time favorites found on menus from coast to coast. All of them are in use today in one section of the country or another. They are authentically American.

The recipes have been adapted for this book in the FOODS OF THE WORLD kitchen through exhaustive testings, and they have been written—and, in some cases, modernized—by Michael Field to make them practicable for today's kitchens. Every effort has been made to search out an honest version of each dish, as free as possible of embellishments, although the editors have provided suggestions for preparing dishes in different ways and for creating variations on traditional themes. It is not always possible to track down an original recipe. Some never existed in writing in their original form and may have been transmitted through several generations before a writer of the 18th or 19th Century decided to set them down—in his own fashion. No one knows the exact original recipe for red-flannel hash, for example. Some people insist that it was made with codfish, beets and potatoes. This is unlikely, and the version accepted today —with beef rather than codfish—is quite good in its way and is therefore worthy of a place in this book.

Recently I spent several hours checking recipes for as simple a dish as hashed brown potatoes. I had seen it made countless times over the years by farm cooks and short-order cooks. I recall, with some delight, how they threw cooked potatoes on a greased griddle, chopped them rapidly with an empty baking-powder can as they turned golden brown, and then, with a quick flip of the spatula, turned them crisp side up onto a plate. It would seem that there could be little room for enhancing so modest and so satisfactory a dish, but what an array of improvements one finds in the books. Some recipes call for milk, some for cream; some use butter; others, bacon. One cookbook devoted exclusively to the potato offered five different versions of the dish, each substantially different.

As a consequence, the task of our researchers and editors in sifting through recipes was formidable. No doubt we shall be questioned about the authenticity of some of our recipes, and we are certain to have omitted the favorite family recipes of many readers. But because this is perhaps a more personal and more lived-in book than others in the series, we have felt less constrained to abide by tradition alone. We have had to use our individual tastes in making selections. We believe we have gathered a stimulating collection of recipes. And Dale Brown, the author, inspired by repeated trips through various regions of the country to taste food, talk food and discover food, has complemented the recipes with a text that evokes the American past and takes a fresh look at the vigor and variety of American food today.

—*James A. Beard*

I

From a Cookery to Cuisine

American cooking, like the country that it nourishes, is restless, dynamic and constantly changing. American cooks perform in the world's most completely equipped kitchens and are guided by a ceaseless flow of cookbooks that are more explicit, more personal and more helpful than those in any other land. They are blessed with the greatest bounty the world has ever known—almost every conceivable kind of food, including ingredients from tropical, subtropical and Arctic regions. And American technology has gilded these great riches by developing meatier turkeys, hams and chickens, and placing at the fingertips of American cooks an abundance of fruits and vegetables delivered garden fresh over distances of thousands of miles.

Like the Grand Canyon, American cooking is carved out of layers of the past. It begins with the Indians and the English settlers and rises through strata of German, Italian, Czech and other immigrant influences to its present heights of sophistication and complexity. But still, when I think of American food at its most American, I think of farm cooking, the kind my grandmother Brown and her twin sister Ella used to do. It was homey and homely, and often very good. And it was representative, in its own way, of what the greater part of the nation ate in the 19th Century, when 85 per cent of the people dwelled in rural areas and took breakfast and supper in winter by the light—and smell—of an oil lamp.

I consider myself fortunate in having had a grandmother as old as mine. Not only was she old in years, but in time. She brought up behind her the past, and it clung to her as naturally as the strings of her apron.

Acorn squash, one of the most authentic American foods, dates all the way back to the pre-Pilgrim Indians. It is at its most delicious when slowly baked *(page 33)* with cinnamon, cloves, nutmeg and pure maple syrup to lend it an old-fashioned flavor.

8

She had been born on a farm in upstate New York and she spent her married life on a nearby farm, rearing five children. And when, after her husband's death, she moved to town, it was to a town so small, so rural, so unsullied by the 20th Century that the scent of new-mown hay or the warm, billowy odor of barns drifted down in summer from the surrounding hills into the streets.

Grandma's cooking was as honest and as simple as she. One of her favorite dishes was dried-beef gravy. She would uncurl the thin slices of locally cured beef into a frying pan, which she called a spider (the ancient name given to a three-legged frying pan for its presumed resemblance to the insect). Then she would heat the slices with plenty of butter and a little brown sugar and pour in her thickening and some creamy milk, and stir and stir and stir. I have the big silver spoon she used, and it is worn to a slant, almost halfway up the bowl. When the gravy was nice and thick and brown, she would bring it to the table in a big sauceboat, and we would quickly peel our boiled potatoes and crush them with the tines of our forks. A great lump of butter would go onto the crumbled potatoes, and then the rich gravy was poured over them.

Such a meal was not complete without some of Grandma's chunk pickles, the most delicious pickles I have ever eaten and, I suspect, the most time-consuming ever made. I was with her one summer when she put up her chunk pickles, and she was at it well over a week. First she soaked the "cukes" (as she called cucumbers) for three days in a strong brine; after that, she let them sit in clear water for three more days. Then she cut them in chunks and scalded them in diluted vinegar, with some alum and a handful of grape leaves thrown in. Next she "boiled up" (her phrase again) a solution of vinegar, brown sugar, cinnamon sticks, allspice and celery seeds. Patting the chunks dry, she strained the hot solution over them and let them stand for 24 hours. Four more days she worked at the pickles—pouring off the solution each morning, heating it up and pouring it back over the chunks. Then on the last day, her creation done, she bottled them and, like God, she rested.

If there were no chunk pickles to go with the dried-beef gravy, then there most certainly was an aromatic green-tomato relish Grandma called "higdom." I wonder how old higdom is; I have never seen anything with that name in the cookbooks. Higdom, in the best country language of Grandma's recipe, called for "one peck green tomatoes and four onions chopped fine, then add one cup salt and let stand overnight, then drain off and add two quarts vinegar and one quart water, cook fifteen minutes, drain this off, then add two pounds brown sugar (maple preferred), three pints vinegar, one tablespoon white mustard seed, scant tablespoon black pepper, scant tablespoon ginger, one tablespoon powdered cloves, one tablespoon ground allspice. Cook fifteen minutes."

Grandma was best at making pickles, relishes and jams. In a way, it is odd that such spicy and piquant foods should have been her forte while the rest of her table was so plain. But wasn't this to be expected in the America of her day? While farm food may not have been heavily seasoned, the pickles and relishes, the chili sauces and piccalillis and chowchows that went with them were; they—not the food—set the tone for the meal. Long after her five children left home and Grandma had moved to an apartment in town, she continued to turn out pickles and preserves and store them in a closet, and lucky was the family that received a jar of her higdom or rhubarb marmalade *(page 18)*, which contained lemon and orange peel and walnuts, in addition to the rhubarb, which she always referred to as "pie plant."

My grandmother was also a good baker; although she had given up making bread a long time ago, she continued to turn out her oat-flake gems, little muffins made with buttermilk and oatmeal, into which she stirred some maple sugar. She often made johnnycake. When the Otselic Valley Grange, of which she was a member, published a community cookbook in 1946, no less than four recipes for johnnycake appeared in it. (American women are forever jotting down their recipes and putting them together in cookbooks. Some of our best local recipes are preserved this way.) I hadn't known that so simple a hot bread could be so subtly varied; but Gladys Davis' recipe called for a little molasses, Blanche Clough's for buttermilk instead of sour milk, and Etta Angell's for Graham flour as well as cornmeal.

If johnnycake is really a corruption of the word "journey cake," as some people suppose it to be, then I can understand why recipes for it are so prevalent in South Otselic. Most of the people who settled the area came there from New England in the early 19th Century; they journeyed in wagons, with all their household belongings packed inside, and johnnycake was one of the breads they could make most easily at roadside camps. The liking for it—which was probably already well developed—became so ingrained in the settlers that it lasted through several generations. Johnnycake can still be found on many a farm table around South Otselic, though I wonder whether it tastes as good as in the days when people went visiting and had to stay overnight because distances between farms were often too great to cover in a buggy before nightfall. When visitors awakened in the morning, they were served a big breakfast, with steaming pieces of johnnycake on their plates.

My grandmother, of course, ate at home mostly. Eating out for a woman like her was a treat that meant to the end of her life "visiting," or attending a covered-dish affair in the basement of the Methodist church or a pancake supper given by the Masons in their hall above Grandma's apartment. There were no restaurants in South Otselic (population 350) and few, if any, in the adjacent towns, except for what my grandmother contemptuously referred to as "booze joints." Yet she loved going out to eat and the occasion she loved best was a family reunion, held by one group or another in the Grange Hall or on the lawn under the shade of the sugar maples on Aunt Ella's farm. I attended several such reunions, but the one I remember best is the convocation of Neal-Eldredge folks in the Grange. (Grandmother was a Neal before she was married, and her mother was originally an Eldredge.) The families brought their own table services, a knife, fork, spoon and plate, a few sandwiches and a dish to pass. As more and more people crowded the recreation room, the tables set up in two long rows grew heavy with food. There were homemade rolls and bread, jars of pickles and relishes, bowls of scalloped potatoes

Crisp, Homemade
One-Day Pickles

Homemade pickles usually take several days to make, allowing time for brining and ripening. But bread-and-butter pickles can be prepared and eaten in the same day by following these instructions. To prepare them, wash 12 medium-sized cucumbers, cut them into 1/4-inch slices and combine them in a glass or stainless-steel bowl with 1½ pounds of thinly sliced onions and ½ cup of salt. Let the mixture stand for 3 hours, then pour it into a colander to drain. Rinse with cold water and drain again. In an 8- to 10-quart saucepan, combine 3 cups vinegar, 3 cups sugar, ½ teaspoon turmeric, ¼ cup mustard seed, 2 teaspoons celery seed and ¼ teaspoon cayenne pepper. Bring to a boil, then add the drained cucumber and onion slices. Bring just to a simmer and simmer for 2 minutes. Avoid boiling; it would soften the cucumber slices. Cool the pickles you want to serve immediately and pack the rest in hot, sterilized jars. (This recipe makes 4 to 5 pints.)

and baked macaroni, and everyone's favorites, chicken salad and potato salad *(page 59)*. And ranged under cheesecloth, to taunt the flies and tempt the appetites of all, were the home-baked cakes and pies, decorated with or containing the season's berries.

Then after the first cousins, being closest of kin, had had their pictures taken in self-conscious groupings, we all scrambled for places at the tables. As always I looked forward to the dessert, and I was lucky enough to get a large slice of my great-aunt Ella's currant pie, filled with the tiny garnet-colored berries from her garden and so much sugar—to cut back the tartness—that sparkling crystals clung to the inside of the top crust.

It was at this reunion that Grandma's cousin Frank, a dapper man out of Chicago wearing white trousers, received, under unexplained circum-

A world unto itself, this small American farm in upstate New York has been in the author's family for 130 years. Like so many other farms throughout the older sections of the country, it functioned in its busiest days as a completely independent unit. The kitchen garden, concealed behind the hen house to the left, yielded vegetables to be enjoyed in season and canned or preserved for winter use. From apple branches hanging in the foreground and other trees clustered closer to the farmhouse came fine apples for eating and for baking into pies. And in the tangled growth along the edges of the fields there was a special trove, the summer's yearly bonus of berries.

stances, a piece of blackberry pie in his lap. Notwithstanding the purple stain it left, he got up afterward and served as master of ceremonies. He introduced his boyhood friend Enos, a musician who played the violin while Elsie Lamb accompanied him on the upright piano. My aunt Barbara, who has a lovely voice, sang and later there was a general sing, at which my grandmother requested "The Quilting Party." As the local paper used to put it after such occasions, a good time was had by all.

My great-aunt Ella lived only a few miles from my grandmother's place, and many of my memories of eating in upstate New York drift back to Aunt Ella's farm. It sits high above the valley, on the lap of a hill, and is still reached by a dirt road. The white, shingled house is a comfortable one, seeming to rise right out of the lawn that swells in gentle crests around it. It has a front porch and a side porch, and from the arches of the latter dangles a grapevine in green, leafy swags. My father was born in the downstairs front bedroom, as were his mother and her twin sister, Ella.

Little has changed inside the house since the Neal women were girls nearly a century ago. There is even a buffalo-skin rug on a bed upstairs, and in a closet I have seen a carpetbag, as new to the eye as the day it was bought. The kitchen—the room I like best—still has its great wood-burning iron range, into which Aunt Ella, in the lifetime she lived in the house, must have fed a whole forest of maples. A table covered with a shiny oilcloth stands up against the wall, with three captain's chairs drawn up to it and other miscellaneous chairs ranged around the walls. Above the table is a shelf on which ticks a brown, elaborately encased, 1880s-style clock with a rusted face, and from the shelf a pair of scissors hangs by a looped string. The linoleum contains black islands of wear, and is tacked to the wooden floor, which rises and falls in places, and creaks when walked on. Over the door leading into the summer kitchen

Ella Neal, the mistress of the farm shown on the preceding pages, sets about a simple task she pursued throughout most of her 86 years: scraping carrots for supper. Her cooking—like that of so many other Americans of her day—was plain, but occasionally she would allow herself an extra touch such as glazing the carrots with maple syrup.

is a rifle, and from the windows on either side of the room, with their well-washed curtains and wavy panes, can be seen the fields, dropping away into the sky.

In those fields hops used to grow, from which beer was made—although my great-grandfather never touched a drop of alcohol in his life, or so his daughters believed. Aunt Ella laid the failure of the farm—its failure ever to flourish—not to the rocky soil, but to the hops. And as though to mock her, a hop vine would appear every so often by a fence, like the figure of the devil himself, to remind her of the evil of drink and God's curse on the land.

Behind the house is a pond from which the family in winter used to cut its summer ice supply. A broad path winds past the pond up the hill, and on the crest are three wind-blasted apple trees, ancient trees bearing ancient fruit—Belmonts, Northern Spies and Red Astrachans. The apples they produce, although small, tight and often wormy, nevertheless make today's apples seem hopelessly pompous and vain, all polished, pampered blush. Picked hanging cold on the tree, they are full of juice and winy flavor. Tasting them I know the pleasure Grandma and Aunt Ella felt as children, when on a cold winter's night their father went down into the cellar and came back with a pan of russets and the whole family sat around the warm iron stove eating the fruit and telling stories. Beyond the apple trees is a hayfield that rolls down to the sugarbush, the stand of giant maples that for four generations gave the Neals their abundant supply of sugar and syrup.

In a way, the blood of this area is the sap of the sugar maple. It quickens in the trees on a day of thaw and rises up the trunks after a night of frost. Tapped from the trees at this point, it is reduced almost 95 per cent through boiling, and it becomes the syrup that for many living in the Northeastern United States during the 19th Century was the basic sweetener. Gathering the sap from the trees and making syrup in the spring remains one of the most American of experiences, and one that links us with the Indians, who would take the silvery liquid, put it in wooden vessels and reduce it, either by adding hot stones to it (and thus boiling it), or by letting it freeze overnight, removing the ice in the morning and pouring off the syrup that had collected underneath.

When I was a boy, I helped out once at sugaring time on Aunt Ella's farm. We rode the runners of the sap sledge back into the forest, the white horses up front steaming at the nostrils and the lush hemlocks all around trickling cold fingers of ice water down our necks. The snow had begun to melt, and yet the sledge moved easily over the mud. Where the snow had receded, green ferns, trampled and stamped under by winter, lay upon last year's fallen leaves, and the air smelled pungent with leaf mold, an odor that always makes me hungry. We stopped to empty the red tin buckets hanging from spouts driven into the gray, shaggy trunks of the maples. Moving on to the next batch, we listened to the woods come alive with the plunk-plunk sound of the sap dropping from the trees into the drum bottoms of the newly emptied buckets. When the tank on the sledge was full, we drove—the sap, sloshing and foaming from the strainer on top—to the sugarhouse, a rickety structure with

walls of gray, weatherbeaten boards, and a metal roof covered with flaking rust and patches of brown, soaked leaves. We drained off the clear sap into the large boiling pans inside the darkness of the sugarhouse and then started a fire. We let the fire burn all day under the pans as we went out for more sap, and the sweet-smelling steam clouded up the interior and drifted up through a vent in the roof and away through the trees.

When the syrup boiled, we took turns standing by the vats. Someone had to be at hand to see that the volcanic sap did not boil over, and I gained a sense of power in quieting the roiling surface by flicking milk from my fingers into the sticky bubbles and watching them subside instantly. When the first of the syrup was ready, we poured it off into a milk can, straining it through a piece of felt. This was good syrup, the

The pond, from which the Neals cut their year-round supply of ice, is seen on a cold day in early autumn. Recently dug out to a depth of 12 feet, it is to be stocked with brook trout by the descendants of the Neals who spend summers here. The banks will be lined with shrubs and bushes to attract birds and waterfowl.

first run, and people in the valley and on the surrounding farms pay as much heed to a good first run of syrup as do connoisseurs of wine to a good first pressing of grapes. Maple syrup, too, can have its good years and its bad. One day we "sugared off" back at the farmhouse. Aunt Ella took her gray enameled dishpan, went outside and returned with it filled to the brim with packed snow. She had boiled some of the first-run syrup on the stove, and now she trickled it, searing hot, over the snow. Almost immediately it set to a waxy gum, and we forked up long strings of it and chewed it. According to their old habit, the family tempered its sweetness with bites of sour pickles.

Perhaps the outstanding sensory feature of Aunt Ella's house was the odor of maple syrup that pervaded the rooms and clung to them, as well

Grandmother Brown's Recipe for Rhubarb Marmalade

To make 3 pints

2 pounds rhubarb, coarsely chopped
¼ cup orange juice
¼ cup lemon juice
2 pounds sugar
2 oranges, peeled, seeded, sectioned
Grated rind of 1 orange
1 lemon, peeled, seeded, sectioned
Grated rind of 1 lemon
1½ cups walnuts, halved

Combine the rhubarb, orange juice and lemon juice in an enameled or stainless-steel saucepan. Bring to a boil, cover, reduce the heat and simmer for about an hour, or until the rhubarb is soft. Stir in the sugar and, stirring constantly, boil rapidly for about 5 minutes, or until the mixture is translucent and lightly holds its shape in a spoon. Turn off the heat, stir in the orange and lemon sections and rinds, and the walnuts. Still stirring occasionally, let the marmalade cool to room temperature, then pour it into sterilized glasses and seal with paraffin.

it might have after all the sugar-making that had gone on there over the years. Aunt Ella regularly made maple sugar, but not the crystally, rather sandy kind that is produced commercially and sold in maple-leaf forms. Hers was buttery smooth, and she achieved its soothing texture by a simple trick. After boiling the syrup until it haired, that is, fell away from the spoon in long strands, she poured it into bowls and placed them on a cold surface, such as a flat stone. Once the syrup had cooled down, she began to beat it, and gradually, under her insistent urging, it turned color, changing from a honey brown to a creamy tan. Then it was ready, and she poured it into little molds and let it set.

Maple sugar and syrup had multiple uses in my aunt Ella's and grandmother's cooking. They used one or the other in pies, cakes and cookies, in fried cakes (doughnuts) and in custards. They candied sweet potatoes and glazed carrots *(pages 26-27)* with maple syrup, and they spread maple cream —in consistency halfway between sugar and syrup—over their pancakes and ate them as a dessert, with whipped cream spooned on top. But the most delicious use they made of maple sugar was, as is so often the case in cooking, the simplest—they shaved it over fresh wild berries.

Berries were a very important part of Grandma's and Aunt Ella's summer diet, and their winter living as well, since the sisters invariably managed to preserve some for use on their morning toast and lunchtime bread. The best of the berries, by far, were always (and continue to be) the wild strawberries. Their season comes early, in the first surge of summer when daisies and orange and yellow devil's-paintbrushes are in bloom. Aunt Ella always knew where the thickest berry patches lay. We would climb to a deserted pasture, overgrown with crab-apple trees, and she would stalk the landscape, head down, until she came to the place where the best of them grew. Some were tangled in last year's straw, and we had to nuzzle our fingers down into their nests and pull them free; others stood upright, on long, tough stems. I remember kneeling in the patch, parting the devil's-paintbrushes and tugging at the tough stems, which were heavy with tiny, bright-red berries. Soon I had filled my tin bucket to brimming, and the knees of my faded dungarees were spotted pink and my hands were sticky with the juice.

Only one use was made of the first berries of the season, and that was shortcake, the most classic, perhaps, of American desserts *(page 179)*. We would spoon them, crushed and sugared, onto warm biscuits that had been broken open, buttered and closed again; and then we would pour thick cream over the shortcake to soak into the biscuit and mingle with the butter and berry juice.

While I discovered early in life the pleasures of gathering wild strawberries, I also quickly learned the drawbacks to picking blackberries. These grew in profusion at the edge of the sugarbush, and the brakes yielded the big kind my maiden great-aunt, without the trace of a maidenly blush, called "sheeps' tits." The bushes had vicious thorns, and I came away from them scratched and bleeding, and with my fingers purpled. And yet all that would be forgotten at suppertime when my dish of blackberries was set before me.

I remember one such blackberry supper; we had very little else to eat.

I had hiked to the farm with two of my younger cousins, Nelson and Harry, and because a storm was coming up we had been invited by Aunt Ella to sit down and eat with her cousin Frank, his friend Enos and the hired man, Ralph, who had a metal hook for a hand. It was a moody evening, darkening quickly, with a high, cold wind, lightning, thunder and eventually rain.

We ate in the summer dining room, which rarely was used; the table was lit from overhead by a single bulb hanging on a chain. I watched the old people break bread and drop the jagged pieces into bowls of milk to make one of the most basic and the oldest of farmhouse suppers. As I consumed the moist bread, one slice after another to kill the pang of hunger, I hoped that Ella, Frank and Enos would reminisce about old times, and I started them off by telling them, perhaps inappropriately, that on our way to the farm we had stopped in a tiny graveyard to read the inscriptions on the tombstones. I repeated one that I remembered, "My children dear, / Assemble here / A mother's grave to see, / Not long ago, I dwell (sic) with you, / And soon you will dwell with me." There was a fine roll of thunder at that point. Smiling, Frank asked me whether I had heard this epitaph: "Under the sod and beneath these trees, / Lieth the body of Solomon Pease / He is not here, only his pod / He shelled out his spirit / And went up to God." My cousins and I laughed.

Frank turned to Enos, a little white-haired man with a red face, and began —"We were going to school one day. You were there, Enos, I think. We stopped at the graveyard down the corner here. Someone had put a pillow of flowers on the newly dug grave. Written in tinfoil it said: 'Rest in Peace—p-i-e-c-e.'" Enos and Aunt Ella roared, and as I dipped into the sugared blackberries with my spoon, I knew that the reminiscing was off to a fine start.

That night I heard a story that my grandmother's aunt Sally had told about what life was like when the Neals first arrived on this farm and lived in another house. "We used to move Aunt Sally down to our house winters," said Frank, who as a boy had been raised on a farm up the road. "You know that old back room—we used to call it the milk room. She'd stay in there with all her furniture and a stove. We used kerosene lamps but Aunt Sally was afraid of them. She used to have a big old iron swivel candlestick which she'd attach to the back of a chair and swing around beside her. She'd read her Bible by candlelight.

"Well, I used to go in there evenings and get her to tell me about the Indians. She used to tell one story over and over again. In those days the Indians still came up the valley on their hunting trips. It seems Aunt Sally and her mother had been boiling doughnuts in lard over the fireplace. They set them out on the doorstep to cool. When they went to get them, the doughnuts were gone. No one knew what had happened to them. A couple of days later Aunt Sally and her mother found a deer on the doorstep. The Indians had taken the doughnuts and paid for them with a deer."

From eating as simple, but as full in its way as this story-enriched blackberry supper, meals on the farm could range all the way to the plentiful and fairly elaborate Thanksgiving dinner. Actually I spent but one Thanksgiving there, but it imprinted itself on my consciousness, and I know that never again will I experience a celebration quite like it or one quite so American. Half its effect was in the setting—the kitchen with the wood-burning stove—the other half in what we ate. All my uncles and aunts had come, and most of their children as well; we were 20 around the table, which had been expanded to twice its size with a set of leaves. Each of the women had brought a dish of some sort to share and we had all chipped in and purchased the turkey, which Aunt Barbara cooked in the oven, pursuant to Aunt Ella's instructions about how to get a good heat going. The meal stretched all the way down the table, with the turkey in the middle, half blocking the view. On either side of the bird were ranged bowls of creamed onions and mashed butternut squash, with lumps of butter poked down into the orange softness to melt into little golden pools; dishes of sage dressing and cranberry sauce; plates of pickles and higdom and cottage cheese; a platter with someone's colorful (but not very good) gelatin salad gleaming red and green; and baskets of homemade breads—Graham, date and white, the last damp and yeasty. And in good, righteous upstate New York fashion, a glass of spring water stood at each place. No wine here, not ever—except perhaps when the men drank it in the barn.

What amazed me at the time (I had only recently come back from Europe) was not the amount of food served or the haphazard way in which

All over Aunt Ella Neal's farm grow thick-trunked trees like this one, a sugar maple in the full flame of autumn. Chenango County, site of the farm, yields some of the finest maple syrup in the United States. Maples were once so abundant in this region that they were gashed with axes for tapping. If the trees died, there were always plenty more.

the meal had been put together, but the speed with which we ate everything. We raced through it all—through the pumpkin and currant pies on our way to the coffee. And then Thanksgiving on the farm was over; the women got up and did the dishes and the men went out by the barn and down by the pond to talk. Americans still have a hard time lingering over a meal and, sometimes, relaxing. Not until the next day, when a night spent under feather comforters had softened us and the cool country air had cleansed our lungs and oxygenated our blood, did we begin to dawdle, sitting around and even drowsing in the rockers, with as much warmth, boneless ease and good sense as Aunt Ella's four cats, which, I observed, were in the habit of doing it all the time.

My grandmother and Aunt Ella are dead now. Aunt Ella died in 1967, and Grandma but three years before that. In her last letter to me Grandma mentioned how much she was looking forward to the first maple syrup of the new season. The farm has passed on to Aunt Ella's nieces and nephews, and all of us still go there occasionally. No one has bothered, however, to make maple sugar this year, although the house continues to smell of it. Many of Grandma's and Aunt Ella's recipes died with them; some we may try to revive, but I doubt that any of us could make them taste quite the way they did. We of the younger generation are cooking differently, and we drink wine at our tables when the occasion calls for it.

American cooking in general has changed immensely within the past few decades. To some extent, of course, change has always been a distinctive feature of our cooking. George Washington's table with its lukewarm food would be as alien to us today as the pink and green luncheon breads of the 1920s or the single-colored meals of the 1890s.

Even the earliest settlers in the country reluctantly recognized the need for change. At first the food they prepared tended to copy Old World cooking as closely as possible with the materials at hand. The Pilgrims, for example, might have fared better if upon arrival they had eaten more of the indigenous foods instead of trying to grow grain and peas to re-create the dishes they had left behind. Their inability to produce such dishes drove them starving into the woods in search of food and sent them to the Indians for advice. Only after they deigned to use the Indians' cornmeal instead of oatmeal were they able to make their hasty pudding. To their surprise they found that by substituting cornmeal for oatmeal they had improved it.

In subsequent years, later waves of immigrants to this country brought more significant culinary changes. Italians, newly arrived in the 19th Century, cooked the Italian way, creating a national appetite for their food. Chinese, stir-frying the Chinese way, opened restaurants that tempted millions with their combination plates. Germans, saucing and souring their meats, popularized *Sauerbraten* in some parts of the country to the point where it seemed like an old American standby. As a result of these contributions, the melting pot came to have a gastronomic meaning, and Walt Whitman's celebrated line, "I hear America singing, the varied carols I hear," could be modified to read hungrily (if not so poetically), "I smell America cooking, the varied aromas I smell."

Such influences, of course, were immensely important, but it was much later—within my own lifetime—that the pace of change really quickened. America's great affluence and the revolution in communications brought American cooks a profusion of magazines, cookbooks and television programs loaded with enticing recipes and culinary aids. Jet travel enabled them to sample the cuisines of faraway lands, and a bevy of culinary experts inspired them to more daring adventures in the kitchen.

American cooking has now come of age, and in a sense I suppose I have come of age with it. My grandmother and my great-aunt Ella, whose simple cooking I remember so well, represented the rural America of the 19th Century. My mother represented the new cosmopolitanism of the first half of the 20th Century. She was city-born—New York City—and city-bred. She clipped recipes from magazines and pored over cookbooks. Her cooking was very much in the mainstream; there was nothing static about it—it moved along with the times. It was never just fashionable (she had a family to feed), but it was experimental and adventurous, and I realize now that many of our favorites got shunted aside by new favorites. (American recipe files are littered with forgotten dishes.) What ever happened to Mother's walnut fudge? Where did it go? Didn't she use to stir some up every couple of months or so? And now I haven't had it in years; in fact, the last time I encountered fudge was in 1959, in deepest Oregon, where an elderly couple, who used bobcat skins for antimacassars on their overstuffed chairs and couch, kept pressing it upon me. And where did Mother's popovers go? We used to have them often as a kind of Sunday-night supper after the big roast of the afternoon, with a dish of pure maple syrup beside each plate. The recollection of their cocked-hat appearance and of the steaming yellow cavern each concealed (a depository for a golden lump of butter) makes me not only nostalgic today, but hungry. And where are all the other baked goods—the black chocolate cake with mahogany icing; the pale-yellow lemon pie, made from condensed milk, with a stormy sea of brown-tipped meringue on top; and, not to be forgotten, Mother's butterscotch pie, the homemade butterscotch cool and sweet and smooth under its eiderdown quilt of whipped cream?

A couple of our favorites did not die of neglect, but can really be said to have gone with the wind. One year a hurricane blew down their source, the peach tree (raised from a pit) in the back yard of our house in the Bronx, and the cherry tree in the neighbors' yard, from which we were annually invited to pick as many sour cherries as we could use. Mother made grand cobblers from the fruit of both, to be eaten hot, right from the oven, with cream-cheese hard sauce or chilled whipped cream streaming down the biscuit topping. Of the two, my favorite was the cherry cobbler because each cherry was its own little pocket of juice. We often ate the peaches from our tree plain. They were so tender they hardly needed peeling—the skins practically slipped off. And they were delicious sliced, stirred with dark brown sugar and spooned up with sweet cream.

For all her willingness to experiment, Mother felt anxious about too much change in her kitchen, as must a great many other American

women also worried about doing injustice to tradition. I remember how she would come to her brother every once in a while and say, "I found Mother's potato pancake recipe today," or, "I found Mother's recipe for liver dumplings." (Her mother was born in Germany.) She always delivered such a statement in a tone of unspeakable relief, as though she had rescued someone from drowning, and soon, driven by the exhilaration of her discovery she would turn out a batch of crunchy-edged potato pancakes, flecked with parsley and containing the slightest trace of onion juice that her mother always put into them. Mother's anxiety about losing the best of her mother's recipes is manifest in her recipe file, which my wife, Liet, and I now have. Sometimes there are two cards for the same dish, and for a cake called Tropic Aroma there are even three cards, copied and recopied, each a little yellower than the other, indicative of their relative ages. Tropic Aroma had one cocoa-tinted layer and two delicately spiced layers, and although I cannot remember ever having eaten it, I find the recipe for it so tantalizing that I'm sure we will re-create the cake one day soon—our own special form of ancestor worship.

The first sign of spring in upstate New York comes while snow is still on the ground. It is the steam rising from a sugarhouse. In this building clear sap, tapped from the maples in tin buckets, is boiled down to produce syrup.

23

Mother's recipes—when I arranged the entire collection on a table—revealed not only something about her but also, I think, about the trends toward greater sophistication in American cooking over the past 30 or 40 years. The older the recipes, the plainer they are—or the plainer the names for the dishes. "Onion pie," I realized, is none other than *quiche*. I guess few called it by its real name in the '20s and '30s—too foreign-sounding—but as an indication of how sophisticated, in a charming way, we are all becoming, perhaps I should add that recently I heard a Texan in San Antonio call it "keech."

The closer Mother's recipes come to the present the more herbs and seasonings they require. She fell hard for "potherbs" in the late '30s, and pasted into her notebook a layout from a magazine depicting and recommending different flavorings. "This is the closet of magic which transforms mere food into cuisine," says the caption. "Master its sorcery and you will achieve subtleties of taste and aroma that will bewitch all who dine at your table." And yet oddly missing from such sorcery were two herbs that Mother came later to consider indispensable—basil and oregano. I was amused to find penciled in on the very page where she had pasted this "closet of magic" the word *basilico*, spelled out not once but twice, as though she were trying hard to memorize it. *Basilico* is, of course, the Italian word for basil, and how Mother came to hear about the herb—to taste it and to like it—is a whole story in itself.

During World War II, we had a victory garden in the empty lot between our house and the Milones', our Italian neighbors. The Milones used one half the garden and we used the other, and more than a cross-pollination of plants went on there. Kitchens became hybridized too. While we were growing summer squash Mrs. Milone was raising zucchini, as new to us as was our variety to her. Our tomatoes were "beefsteaks"; Mrs. Milone's were pendulous plums. Mother's herb garden was redolent with the odor of sage, thyme and dill; Mrs. Milone's bore the sweet scent of oregano and basil. We nibbled her leaves and she ours, and that's when Mother fell in love with *basilico*.

Mother's and Mrs. Milone's exchanges began to extend to foods themselves. Occasionally on Sundays we were invited in from the garden to dine at her table, with her husband, two daughters and son. This would have been a treat under any conditions: as a butcher Mr. Milone saw to it that his family was amply supplied with meat, rarest of commodities during the War. But the pleasure was rendered even greater for us by Mrs. Milone's excellent Italian cooking; in fact, she fixed in me standards of taste so exacting that I have never been able to find more than a couple of Neapolitan-style restaurants that come close to serving dishes as delicious as hers.

We always began one of Mrs. Milone's meals with a good chicken soup containing tiny *vermicelli*. Next we would have pasta, shells or tubes, coated with a thick tomato sauce in which beef and hot sausages had simmered all morning. After the "macaronis" (as the Milones always called the pasta) came the meat course, the chicken from the soup, the well-cooked sausages bursting from their casings, and the beef, flakily tender and rich with soaked-up tomato sauce. A green salad would follow,

An Easy Way to Preserve Berries

Berry preserves enliven any breakfast or snack and are easy to make. The berries should be ripe but firm and should be stemmed, washed and drained. Only sugar and cooking are required to turn berries into preserves. From ¾ to 1 pound of sugar should be used for each pound of berries. The sugar is added to the berries in either of two ways: layers of berries and sugar are alternated in an enameled or stainless-steel pan, and the mixture should then stand overnight. Or the sugar may be added to the berries in the pan along with a little water, just before cooking begins. In that case the pan should be tightly covered until enough syrup has formed to cover the bottom of the pan. With either method the berries should be cooked on low heat only until they are tender and transparent. Then the preserves that are not going to be used immediately should be poured into sterilized jars and, after cooling, sealed with paraffin.

tossed with yellow olive oil and red wine vinegar. Throughout the meal Italian bread was eaten and red wine was drunk, and even I, the little Protestant boy from next door, was permitted an unwatered glass.

One Sunday at the Milones' we had roast chicken, an herb-blessed chicken tinged with a little tomato paste and red pepper, and kissed with oil and garlic. It was beautiful to see and to eat, and it has grown so excruciatingly appetizing in my memory that I know I shall never see the likes of it again in reality.

Thus early in my life my palate was tempted by a style of cooking other than my mother's, with its slightly German base, and the exposure did me good. It helped me later to approach other cuisines without trepidation. I believe that Americans, or at least some of us, can claim to have been born to a little sophistication in a way that the Scandinavians, for example, living only among Scandinavians and eating only Scandinavian food, cannot. And I was not the only one to benefit from the experience of dining at the Milones'. My mother did, as well, and her recipe file grew and took yet another new direction.

Apart from spicing up our table in new ways, the victory garden performed another service. It revealed to us how incredibly good fresh vegetables, picked at their very peak of ripeness and juiciness, can be; and I for one have hungered for Swiss chard ever since. From our garden also came the first really sweet corn I had tasted, softly tasseled and sheathed in living green. It proved something that my father, born on the farm, had been saying all along, that corn has to be absolutely fresh to be appreciated for the great delicacy it really is. But alas, during our second season the garden was struck by a blight, corn smut—perhaps the first and last time corn smut raged through the Bronx—and we had to wait until after the war and the removal of restrictions on the use of gasoline before we could drive out into the country and buy some fresh corn at a farm.

My mother was a good cook, quick and efficient, but I don't mean to imply that she was a good cook always. She had her misses, especially during the Depression and the war, and I do not suppose she can really be blamed for them. The war dealt her a low blow, as it did every other cook. But food, when it is bad, can be memorable too (what hapless GI will ever forget army chicken with hair on its legs?), and therefore I won't forget easily my mother's mock meat loaf, circa 1943, concocted of ground walnuts and raw potatoes, eggs, onion, bread crumbs, salt, pepper, parsley and sage. But never did her disasters approach the size of her cousin's. Grace was a very sweet maiden lady, a kind woman who had no money but was as generous as she could be with a penny. With her unbridled imagination, coupled with ambitious economy, she expressed all that can be considered worst about American cooking. Her audacity often got her into trouble. She loved to give dinner parties beyond her means and abilities, and these seemed always to be beset by some minor or major disaster, like the day she forgot to turn the oven on, or the two occasions when her gate-leg table gave way, sending the Limoges and the boiled potatoes rolling to the floor. At one of those friendly, but on the whole forgettable, entertainments, she served a dessert that I have not been able to erase from memory—and I was just a small boy at the time. It was a water pudding; Grace dared call it that. It had a pale purply translucence, and it quivered at the bottom of the bowl.

One summer soon after the war we took Grace on a trip upstate in our 1936 Ford. Around lunchtime she reached into her brown paper bag and brought out a sandwich, a *spaghetti* sandwich—two slices of dark brown pumpernickel with undressed spaghetti between them. Never have I seen spaghetti looking paler. Grace's specialty was banana cake. She made it often, and she always brought it to our house for dessert when she came to dinner. She varied the shortening; once, I swear it, she used chicken fat. Imagine my father's astonishment the night he found in his slice of banana cake—a particularly big slice since he is a big man—one of Cousin Grace's hairpins.

Just as my mother's cooking represented a greater sophistication than that of my grandmother Brown or my great-aunt Ella, my wife Liet's cooking represents a further refinement of American cooking, another step toward a fully developed cuisine. While my mother stood for the first half of this century, my wife, I think, represents the greater worldliness of the second half.

My wife is Dutch. She was born and raised in Indonesia, and has lived in Italy, Jordan, Iraq and South Africa, as well as the Netherlands: she cannot help but have a world outlook. She has brought something special to American cooking in our home, and American cooking in its turn has had a special meaning for her. When we first married, Liet approached the stove with diffidence. She confessed that at home she had despaired of ever learning how to cook really well, for, following the European system, ingredients had been measured out on a scale, in grams and kilograms. Is it any wonder that Liet began to feel that cooking required a chemist's soul, rather than an artist's? And while Dutch recipes could be precise in some ways, they were discouragingly vague in other respects, assuming that housewives knew much more about cooking than in fact they often did (Liet grew up in a household where a proud cook brooked no interference in the kitchen).

The United States changed Liet's view of herself as a cook. It gave her interesting recipes she could follow easily; it gave her well-stocked supermarkets in which she could shop for all she needed under one roof, instead of obliging her to wander from store to store. As a newcomer to America, she has helped me in turn to recognize all that is best about our cooking. Growing up with American food, I had taken what I ate for granted. For example, it had never occurred to me that there was anything unusual about having green vegetables and fresh fruits available the year around, or eating meat two or three times a day. But one has only to be Dutch to see the luxury in this: in Holland, leafy vegetables are still largely seasonal gifts, and red meat is usually bought in small, expensive pieces. The great standing rib roast that loads down American tables and sets the mouth watering at mere sight of it is all but unknown there.

My appreciation of American cooking has also been sharpened by the number of Europeans Liet and I have entertained at our table. We try always to give them something different from what they would have at

---

A Touch of Glamor for a Familiar Vegetable

Glazing gives baby carrots a new look and a subtle new flavor. Cook the whole carrots in salted water until they are tender. Then drain and spoon butter and honey or maple syrup over them in the pan. Return the carrots to the heat and turn them over in the glazing liquid until the carrots are well coated.

home, something truly American, which is not so easy in an era when culinary boundaries are tumbling and cooking styles blending and re-emerging, transformed. Unlike President Franklin D. Roosevelt and his wife, who served hot dogs to King George VI and Queen Elizabeth of England when they visited the U.S. in 1939, we strive for a little more refinement and originality in our menus. And yet in doing so, we must take care not to go overboard in our enthusiasm for some foods. For example, no matter how much we may enjoy various lettuces and greens tossed with a garlic dressing in a chilled enameled bowl, with perhaps some creamy slices of avocado, we have found that many Northern Europeans still look down upon salad as rabbit food. Even the Dutch, who gave us *kool sla* (cole slaw) back in the 17th or 18th Century, are not overly pleased with our salad courses. We must be careful, too, not to serve things as exotic to some Europeans as the deliciously American cheesecake. Converts are not made in a day; Liet did not like cheesecake in the beginning either; now she loves it. The same is true of apple pie; it can seem like a strange dish to those who never heard of it before, much less tasted it. Fruit baked between *two* unsweetened crusts? How odd!

The first European we entertained was Liet's cousin Henri, a jolly Dutchman of Belgian extraction, with all the Belgians' love of fine food. The problem of what to serve Henri was solved beautifully by Henri himself. He insisted that we give Liet a night off, and that he take us out to dinner. He wondered whether we would mind having seafood; he had heard, he said, that American seafood was excellent. I remember that it was an extremely cold night; Manhattan's manhole covers were steaming, and this impressed Henri, as it does all Europeans. He said that it made the city look as though it were built right over hell.

We stomped our way into a restaurant, trying to bring the circulation back to our feet, and clapped our hands to get them warm. No sooner were we seated than Henri reached with red, frozen fingers into the pockets of his amply filled vest and brought out a scrap of paper with some scribblings on it. These were the things he wanted to try, he announced. First on the list, he said, was "clam shoulders." "Do you suppose they have clam shoulders here?" Henri asked. Liet and I looked at each other in puzzlement. Clam shoulders? We had never heard of clam shoulders, though I was not surprised that a great *lekkerbek* (gourmet) like Henri had. Could they be the most delicate part of the clam? Before the waiter became involved in our discussion, I asked Henri to show me his note. Clam shoulders, I suddenly realized, looking at the writing, was clam chowder. And that is how we began the meal, with great steaming bowls of New England chowder—thick with tender bits of clams.

Thus warmed, thus fortified in a good, old-fashioned way, Henri was in a position to really answer his aggressive appetite's constant demands, and hungrily he asked whether we had any recommendation for the next course. I urged him to try something he surely could not have in Holland, and not very often outside New York either: sautéed bay scallops, those tender nuggets of purest white meat that are about a quarter the size of the regular sea scallops and twice as tasty. They were presented to us in an American portion, a dozen or more per person, and this pleased

A Sweetening for the Sweet Potato

Candied sweet potatoes, or yams—as one variety is known in the South—are a traditional accompaniment for a Thanksgiving turkey, as well as a year-round substitute for Irish potatoes. First boil them in their jackets until they are tender. Peel them and slice them. Then place them in a casserole, dot them with butter, and top them with honey, maple syrup or—most commonly—brown sugar. Lemon juice, orange juice or crushed pineapple may be added for flavor. Bake the sweet potatoes until they are firmly glazed with the topping, basting them occasionally.

Henri, accustomed as he was to having scallops in Europe as an hors d'oeuvre only, served one or two at a time on a tiny plate. And with the bay scallops came a heaping order of crisp, salty French fries, still blistering hot from the oil. What with the chowder, the scallops and the potatoes, Liet and I were soon full, but Henri, with his appetite demanding that it be fed more, took out his list and consulted it. "Lobsters. Maine lobsters," he said. "How about it?" And with the extravagant generosity of the Belgian-Dutch, he waved the waiter over to our table and ordered us each a lobster. Only then was Henri's appetite placated; it peacefully dozed inside him as Liet and I sat paralyzed over our coffee. Even Henri passed up dessert. He had liked the meal, he said; he had liked it very much. And a couple of nights later, on his own, he sauntered back to the restaurant and had the same seafood dinner all over again.

Liet has another cousin, the head of a large Dutch advertising agency, who comes to see us from time to time when he is in New York. Ton is also a *lekkerbek,* and traveling as much as he does throughout Europe on business, he has plenty of opportunity to indulge his passion for rich cooking and cream-thickened sauces. We decided therefore to give him a simple dinner, and yet serve him the best this country has to offer—namely beef, in the form of a large, thick sirloin steak. Liet had shocked the butcher by asking for well-aged meat (she had been reading in her cookbook about the importance of aging good cuts). He was surprised, he said, because not many of his customers were so specific. With the broiled, rare steak we had fresh string beans, steamed so that their color, flavor and a little of their crispness were all still intact, baked Idaho potatoes, split open and filled with sweet butter, a good loaf of garlic bread (a purely American invention) and an estate-bottled California Burgundy. As I drew the carving knife through the meat, I knew by its glide that this was going to be a deliciously tender steak. The meat glowed pink inside and the juices began to trickle out onto the cutting board. I saw Ton sit up in his chair and take notice.

The dessert was as uncomplicated and as refreshingly direct as the rest of the meal, whole strawberries over which Liet had poured a sauce made by crushing raspberries, sieving out the pulp and juice and adding a little black-currant cassis to it. The recipe had come to us from James Beard, the consultant for this book, and we thought that Ton would be a lot more impressed and pleased by the American phenomenon of fresh strawberries in the dead of winter than by apple pie, as he was. Ton had not one helping of the strawberries but three, and he was unable to resist Liet's offer of some of her home-baked sugar cookies, made from my grandmother's recipe.

It seems to me perfectly natural that a Dutchwoman like my wife should have turned out to be a good American cook. Hasn't it always been so? Isn't the immigrant girl who adapted herself to the ways of this country (and fed her family so wisely and well that they all grew up to be college educators, bank presidents and doctors) one of the heroines of our culture? But for all the Americanization she has undergone, Liet still holds on to the best of her own Dutch and Indonesian dishes, and our kitchen is the richer for it. On our spice rack sit some strange seasonings—

Indonesian lemon grass, *galangal* powder, *tenoe koentji* (a gingerlike spice) and *trassi,* a fermented shrimp paste that, when used in the tiniest of portions, seems to lift the flavors of food. Rarely does Liet use these seasonings in anything but Indonesian dishes, where they add an indefinable something, but in an experimental frame of mind, she is not above sprinkling a little lemon grass into a sauce, or dropping a crumb of *trassi* into chili, which is rather like tincturing dynamite with nitroglycerine. Although our daughter, Elisabeth, at two, is still too young to appreciate all this, one day she no doubt will fall heir to her mother's kitchen wisdom. And perhaps by the time Elisabeth has grown up, American cookery —which has been moving all the while from strength to strength toward something grand—will have become an American cuisine.

Recalling past harvests, Concord grapes, most famous of the native American varieties, hang ripe and juicy from a vine on the side porch of the farm. But with Ella Neal no longer there to turn them into jelly, the grapes now belong to the birds.

The Hearty Perennial of American Feasts

From America's earliest settlement the wild turkey and Thanksgiving have been inseparable. Generally smaller but more succulent and more expensive than the domesticated species, the wild bird is distinguished by its angular bone structure. The one shown here weighs 11¼ pounds, is stuffed with cornbread dressing and accompanied by roast chestnuts and cranberry-orange relish. At the turn of the century wild turkeys were almost extinct in the United States, but careful breeding and conservation have increased their number to around a million today.

The recipes for this chapter make up the menu for an old-fashioned Thanksgiving dinner. Featuring a wild turkey with cornbread dressing and cranberry-orange relish, the dishes include four vegetables and three classic American desserts: apple pie, pumpkin pie and homemade vanilla ice cream, which may be enjoyed separately or à la mode.

Roast Wild Turkey with Cornbread Stuffing

To serve 8 to 10

CORNBREAD STUFFING
10 tablespoons butter
1½ cups finely chopped onion
1 pound well-seasoned sausage meat
The turkey liver
6 cups coarsely crumbled cornbread
   made from cornbread recipe on
   page 179, omitting the sugar
½ teaspoon salt
Freshly ground black pepper
2 teaspoons thyme
¼ cup finely chopped fresh parsley
¼ cup Madeira or sherry
¼ cup heavy cream

TURKEY
A 10- to 12-pound wild turkey
1 teaspoon salt
Freshly ground black pepper
12 tablespoons melted butter (1½
   quarter-pound sticks)
½ cup coarsely chopped onions

GRAVY
3 tablespoons flour
1 cup water or chicken stock,
   fresh or canned
½ cup light cream
White pepper
Salt

CORNBREAD STUFFING: Melt 8 tablespoons of the butter in a large, heavy skillet, add the chopped onions and cook over moderate heat for 6 to 8 minutes, or until they color lightly. Scrape them into a large mixing bowl. Add the sausage to the skillet, now set over medium heat, and break the meat up with a fork as it cooks. When the meat is lightly browned, transfer it to a sieve set over a small bowl and let the fat drain through. Meanwhile, again in the same pan, melt the remaining 2 tablespoons of butter and, when the foam subsides, add the turkey liver. Brown it over high heat for 2 to 3 minutes, then chop it coarsely and combine with the onions in the bowl. Add the drained sausage meat, cornbread crumbs, salt, a few grindings of black pepper, the thyme and parsley. With a large spoon, gently stir the ingredients together, then moisten the stuffing with the Madeira or sherry and cream. Taste for seasoning.

TURKEY: Preheat the oven to 350°. Wash the turkey under cold running water and dry it thoroughly inside and out with paper towels. Rub the inside of the turkey with the salt and a few grindings of pepper, and fill the body and breast cavities loosely with the stuffing, closing the openings with skewers or sewing them with thread. Truss the bird securely. With a pastry brush or paper towel, brush the outside of the turkey with a few tablespoons of the melted butter and sprinkle it with salt. Place the bird on a rack in a shallow roasting pan and scatter the onions around it in the bottom of the pan. Roast the turkey uncovered in the middle of the oven for about 2 hours, basting it every 15 minutes or so with the rest of the melted butter and with the drippings that accumulate in the pan.

To test for doneness pierce the thigh of the bird with the tip of a small, sharp knife. The juice should spurt out a clear yellow; if it is slightly pink, roast the bird for another 5 to 10 minutes. Transfer the turkey to a heated platter and let it rest for 10 minutes before carving.

While the turkey is resting, make the gravy. Pour off all but about 3 tablespoons of fat from the roasting pan and stir the flour into the pan. When the flour is thoroughly absorbed, add the cup of water or stock. Bring to a boil over high heat, stirring constantly with a wire whisk and incorporating into the liquid the brown sediment on the bottom and sides of the pan. When the sauce is quite thick, beat in the cream. If you prefer the gravy thinner, add a little more cream. Taste for seasoning and pour into a heated gravy boat. The gravy may be strained if you like.

NOTE: A domestic turkey may be stuffed and roasted in the same fashion as a wild turkey but may take 15 minutes or so longer to roast. Use the same test for doneness as described above.

Cranberry-Orange Relish

In a 3- or 4-quart saucepan, stir the water, orange juice and sugar together until the sugar is thoroughly dissolved. Add the cranberries, bring to a boil and cook for 3 to 5 minutes, stirring occasionally, until the skins of the berries begin to pop and the berries are tender but not mushy. Do not overcook them.

Remove the pan from the heat and stir in the orange rind. Transfer the mixture to a serving bowl, let cool, and then chill for at least an hour or two before serving.

To make 1 quart

½ cup water
½ cup orange juice
1 cup granulated sugar
1 pound whole cranberries
2 tablespoons grated orange rind

Spiced Acorn Squash

Preheat the oven to 350°. Cut each squash in half and with a teaspoon scrape out the seeds and fibers. In a small bowl combine the brown sugar, cinnamon, nutmeg, cloves, salt and melted butter, and stir them together thoroughly.

Arrange the squash in a shallow ovenproof baking dish that is just large enough to hold them all comfortably. Spoon an equal amount of the spiced butter mixture into the hollow of each squash and over that pour a teaspoon or so of maple syrup. Top with a piece of bacon. Now add boiling water to the baking dish—the water should be about 1 inch deep. Bake in the middle of the oven for about 1 hour, or until the squash can be easily pierced with the tip of a small, sharp knife. Serve at once.

To serve 8

4 medium-sized acorn squash
½ cup dark brown sugar
1 teaspoon cinnamon
½ teaspoon grated nutmeg
¼ teaspoon ground cloves
½ teaspoon salt
8 tablespoons melted butter
   (1 quarter-pound stick)
½ cup maple syrup
Eight ½-inch pieces of bacon
About 2 cups boiling water

Creamed Onions and Peas

Place the onions in a 3- or 4-quart saucepan with enough water to cover them by about an inch. Salt the water lightly. Bring to a boil, then reduce the heat to its lowest point and simmer the onions partially covered for about 20 minutes, or until they show only the slightest resistance when pierced with the tip of a small, sharp knife. Drain the onions in a sieve set over a small bowl and set aside. Reserve the cooking water to use in making the sauce.

Cook the fresh peas by dropping them into 6 or 7 quarts of rapidly boiling salted water. Boil them briskly uncovered for 8 to 10 minutes, or until they are tender. Then drain the peas and immerse them in a bowl of cold water for 2 or 3 minutes. This will stop their cooking and help keep their bright green color. Drain again and put the peas aside with the cooked onions. Frozen peas need not be cooked, merely defrosted.

In a heavy 3-quart saucepan, melt the butter over moderate heat and stir in the flour. Remove the pan from the heat and pour in the 2 cups of the reserved onion-cooking liquid, beating with a wire whisk until the flour-butter mixture is partially dissolved. Add the milk and cream, return the pan to the heat and cook, whisking constantly, until the sauce is smooth and thick.

Simmer for 3 to 4 minutes to remove any taste of uncooked flour, season with the salt, white pepper and nutmeg, then add the cooked onions and the cooked fresh peas or thoroughly defrosted frozen peas. Simmer for 5 minutes, or until the vegetables are heated through. Taste for seasoning and serve.

To serve 8

24 to 28 peeled white onions, about
   1 inch in diameter
3 cups fresh green peas (about 3
   pounds), or 3 packages frozen
   green peas, thoroughly defrosted
4 tablespoons butter
4 tablespoons flour
1½ cups milk
½ cup cream
1 teaspoon salt
Pinch of white pepper
¼ teaspoon nutmeg

Mashed Potatoes

To serve 8

4 quarts water
1 tablespoon salt
4 pounds baking potatoes
½ pound butter, softened
½ to 1 cup cream, preferably heavy
1 teaspoon salt
½ teaspoon white pepper
2 to 4 tablespoons melted butter
   (optional)
1 tablespoon finely chopped parsley,
   chives or dill (optional)

Bring the 4 quarts of water to a boil in a 6- to 8-quart pot. Add 1 table-spoon of salt. Meanwhile peel the potatoes, cut them into halves or quarters and drop them into the boiling water. Boil them briskly, uncovered, until they are tender. Test for doneness by piercing them periodically with the tip of a small, sharp knife. They should show no resistance in the center, but they should not fall apart. Drain them at once in a colander.

Return the potatoes to the pan in which they cooked, or transfer them to a large, heavy skillet and shake them over moderate heat for 2 to 3 minutes until they are as dry as possible. Then purée them into a heated mixing bowl either by mashing them with a potato masher, or by forcing through a potato ricer or through a large, coarse sieve with the back of a spoon.

Now, 2 or 3 tablespoons at a time, beat into the purée, either by hand or with an electric mixer, the ½ pound of softened butter. Heat the cream in a small saucepan and beat it into the potatoes a few tablespoons at a time, using as much as you need to give the purée the consistency that you prefer.

Ideally the mashed potatoes should be neither too wet nor too dry, and they should hold their shape lightly in a spoon. Beat in the salt and the white pepper, and taste for seasoning. Add more salt if you think it is necessary. Serve at once in a heated vegetable dish. If you like, float the melted butter in a well in the center of the potatoes and sprinkle them with one of the herbs.

Pumpkin Pie

To make one 9-inch pie

1¼ cups all-purpose flour
4 tablespoons chilled vegetable
   shortening or lard
2 tablespoons chilled butter, cut in
   ¼-inch pieces
⅛ teaspoon salt
3 tablespoons ice water

FILLING
½ cup heavy cream
½ cup milk
¾ cup dark brown sugar
1 teaspoon cinnamon
⅛ teaspoon ground cloves
½ teaspoon ground ginger
3 eggs, lightly beaten
2 tablespoons applejack
1½ cups puréed pumpkin, freshly
   cooked or canned

In a large mixing bowl, combine the flour, vegetable shortening or lard, butter and salt. Use your fingertips to rub the flour and fat together until they look like flakes of coarse meal. Pour the ice water over the mixture, toss together, and press and knead gently with your hands, only until the dough can be gathered into a compact ball. Dust very lightly with flour, wrap in wax paper and chill for at least ½ hour.

Lightly butter a 9-inch pie plate. On a floured surface, roll the dough out into a circle about ⅛ inch thick and 13 to 14 inches in diameter. Lift it up on the rolling pin and unroll it over the pie plate, leaving enough slack in the middle of the pastry to enable you to line the plate without pulling or stretching the dough. Trim the excess pastry with a sharp knife to within ½ inch of the pie plate and fold the extra ½ inch under to make a double thickness all around the rim of the plate. With the tines of a fork or with your fingers, press the pastry down around the rim. Preheat the oven to 350°.

In a large mixing bowl, combine the cream, milk, brown sugar, cinnamon, cloves and ginger. Stir thoroughly, then add the lightly beaten eggs and the applejack. Stir in the 1½ cups of puréed pumpkin. Carefully pour the filling into the pie shell. Bake for 40 to 50 minutes in the center of the oven until the filling is firm and the center of the pie barely quivers when the pie pan is gently moved back and forth. Serve warm or at room temperature with vanilla ice cream or stiffly whipped cream.

34

Apple Pie

In a large mixing bowl, combine the flour, vegetable shortening or lard, butter and salt. Working quickly, use your fingertips to rub the flour and fat together until they look like flakes of coarse meal. Pour the ice water over the mixture, toss together, and press and knead gently with your hands until the dough can be gathered into a compact ball. Dust very lightly with flour, wrap in wax paper and chill for at least ½ hour.

Lightly butter a 9-inch pie plate and divide the ball of dough in half. On a floured surface, roll out half of the ball into a circle about ⅛ inch thick and 13 to 14 inches in diameter. Lift it up on the rolling pin and unroll it over the pie plate. Be sure to leave enough slack in the middle of the pastry to enable you to line the plate without pulling or stretching the dough. Trim the excess pastry with a sharp knife, so that the pastry is even with the outer rim of the pie plate. Preheat the oven to 375°.

For the filling, combine the sugar, cinnamon, allspice, nutmeg and flour in a large mixing bowl. Add the apples and the lemon juice, and toss together gently but thoroughly. Fill the pie shell with the apple mixture, mounding it somewhat higher in the center. Although the apple filling may appear quite high, it will shrink considerably during the baking. Dot the top of the filling with the 2 tablespoons of butter.

For the upper crust, roll out the remaining half of the dough into a circle the same size and thickness as the bottom crust. Lift it up on the rolling pin and drape it gently over the filling. With a scissors, trim the top crust to within ¼ inch of the pie plate. Tuck the overhanging ¼ inch under the edge of the bottom crust all around the rim and then press down with the tines of a fork to seal the two crusts securely. Brush the pastry evenly with the melted butter and cut two small gashes in the center of the top crust to allow the steam to escape. Bake the pie in the middle of the oven for 40 minutes, or until the crust is golden brown. Serve warm or at room temperature with vanilla ice cream or heavy cream.

To make one 9-inch pie

2½ cups all-purpose flour
8 tablespoons chilled vegetable shortening or lard
4 tablespoons chilled butter, cut in ¼-inch pieces
¼ teaspoon salt
6 tablespoons ice water
1 tablespoon melted and cooled butter

FILLING
6 cups of peeled, cored and sliced Greening apples, about ⅛-inch thick (1¾ to 2 pounds)
1 tablespoon lemon juice
¾ cup granulated sugar
1 teaspoon cinnamon
¼ teaspoon allspice
¼ teaspoon nutmeg
1 tablespoon flour
2 tablespoons butter, cut in small pieces

Old-fashioned Vanilla Ice Cream

In a heavy 1½- or 2-quart enameled or stainless-steel saucepan, heat 1 cup of the cream, the sugar, salt and the vanilla bean over low heat, stirring until the sugar is dissolved and the mixture is hot but has not come to a boil. Remove from heat and lift out the vanilla bean. Split the bean in half lengthwise and, with the tip of a small knife, scrape the seeds into the cream mixture. When the mixture has cooled somewhat, stir in the remaining 3 cups of cream.

Pack a 2-quart ice-cream freezer with layers of finely crushed or cracked ice and coarse rock salt in the proportions recommended by the freezer manufacturer, adding cold water if the directions call for it. Then pour or ladle the cream mixture into the ice-cream container and cover it. Let it stand for 3 or 4 minutes. Then turn the handle, starting slowly at first, and crank continuously until the handle can barely be moved. Wipe the lid carefully, remove it and lift out the dasher. Scrape the ice cream off the dasher into the container and pack down with a spoon. Cover the container securely. Drain off any water in the bucket and repack it with ice and salt. Replace the container and let it stand 2 or 3 hours before serving.

To make about 1½ quarts

4 cups heavy cream
¾ cup sugar
⅛ teaspoon salt
1½-inch piece of vanilla bean

FARMERS MARKET
FRUIT AND PRODUCE
LEE AND ANNA PYATT

II

America the Plentiful

The United States is, in the truest sense, a garden. From its heartland to its four corners and the far-flung states of Alaska and Hawaii, there is hardly a spot where one or another of the world's most important food plants will not thrive. We have a corn belt and a wheat belt, and seas of grass on which our dairy and beef cattle can feed. We have perpetual summer in parts of Florida and California, and we have made our Western deserts arable through irrigation. Our soil, our water, our grasslands and forests, with their still-abundant supplies of game, are among our greatest resources; fully 80 per cent of this country, if the need were to arise, could be put to agricultural use, and in the wild grow thousands of plants that could be tapped for their nutritional energy.

We are the world's greatest agricultural nation, capable not only of feeding ourselves as men have never been fed before, but of exporting the yield of one out of every four of our acres—78 million acres in all. Two thirds of our wheat flows abroad, and in the past 10 years we have given away over 150 million tons of food. We are a land of surpluses in a world of want. And what is perhaps most astonishing about all this is that our agricultural productivity goes on increasing, the result of mechanization and of science helping the farmer. Sixty years ago one farm laborer could produce enough food for himself and seven others; his modern counterpart produces enough for himself and 39 others.

As a people, we have been shaped as much by the foods we have eaten as by democratic ideas; we are taller, stronger, healthier than our ancestors. We are, in a sense, a nation that food has made possible. Never before

America's abundance is exemplified by the beautiful peaches, plums, nectarines, apricots, cherries, melons, oranges and other fruits piled high at the Farmer's Market in Los Angeles. The market is a giant shopping complex that sells more than eight million dollars' worth of food every year.

Two Ways to Cook
Corn on the Cob

Corn on the cob loses its flavor very quickly once it has been picked. It can be kept in plastic bags in a refrigerator for two or three days, but will lose its flavor in a day if unrefrigerated. Most people overcook corn. The best way to cook it is to drop the husked ears into boiling water, bring the water to a boil again, turn the heat off and leave the corn there for five minutes. A pinch of sugar may be added to sweeten the corn, but do not add salt—it will toughen the kernels. To bake corn, pull down the husks, remove the silk and tie the husks back in place with string. Soak the corn in cold water for 10 minutes, then place it on a rack in a baking pan and cook it in a preheated 350° oven for 40 to 45 minutes.

was there a country where there was plenty for all. America, before its settlement, came as close to being Eden as anything this side of Paradise. Everywhere, for the mere plucking, were the commodities so lushly described in the Bible, and much else that was both strange and wonderful, including corn, the true gold of the Americas. Even the plainest, the most taciturn of Anglo-Saxons felt compelled to write home about what they had seen when they stepped ashore, and all that they had subsequently eaten. And had these not been, for the most part, men of character, their descriptions of oysters a foot long, of fish dipped from the water in a frying pan, of roosting pigeons breaking down branches with their combined weight, would have been dismissed as outright fantasy. But seeing is believing, and the forests *were* filled with game, and the streams with fish —and lobsters five or six feet long *did* live in New York Bay, not to disappear until "incessant cannonading" during the American Revolution frightened them away. Indeed, lobsters were once so numerous off the New England coast that gathering them was child's play, and storms would pile them up on beaches in windrows nearly two feet high. But even good things pall. The Pilgrims, the most reverential and thankful of men, a scant two years after their first winter of suffering were feeding clams and mussels to their hogs, for these were but "the meanest of God's blessings."

That most people were amply fed in the early days goes without saying, but how well they cooked their food is another matter. In the beginning, the dishes they prepared were, of necessity, plain: they lacked the proper utensils for fancy cooking, and few seasonings were available to them. And sometimes they had no kitchens. Another deterrent to good cooking was the background of the settlers themselves. They were mostly people off the streets of England's towns and cities or from her farms, and what they sought in their food was nourishment, not refinement. Nor did the dour faith of many encourage them to look upon their food as a source of pleasure.

Yet in a land so bountiful, where everything tasted of freshness and was almost bursting with natural vitality, good cooks were bound to emerge. And they did—in Virginia for one place, where the bounty was almost unlimited. As one of the first settlers wrote in 1607, the colonists' new abode was "nature's nurse to all vegetables," a region where Caribbean plants and English garden seeds thrived. One hundred years later its people were seen living in "so happy a Climate, and [having] so fertile a Soil, that no Body is poor enough to beg, or Want Food, though they have an Abundance of People that are lazy enough to deserve it." But a favorable climate and rich soil do not in themselves bring about good cooking. There must also be prosperity, and taste. Both came to Virginia through the cultivation of tobacco, for which there was a ready market— and ready cash. As fortunes grew, so did peoples' notions of refinement and good living.

Virginians became famous for their hospitality. In so blessed a land, people seemed eager to share their bounty with others—to give it away. An Englishman visiting in Virginia was so touched by the kindness he encountered, reminding him of the old days in England, that he wrote an

article about it for the *London Magazine* of July 1746. He told of breakfast tables with hashed and fricasseed meat, venison pie, coffee, tea,
chocolate, punch, beer and cider, and of dinners with beef, veal, mutton,
venison, turkeys and geese, "wild and tame," fowl, boiled and roasted,
pies, puddings and other desserts. Suppers, he wrote, were like dinners,
"with some small Addition, and a good hearty Cup to precede a Bed of
Down: And this is the constant Life they lead, and to this Fare every
Comer is welcome."

Curiously, there is no mention of vegetables in the Englishman's
account of Virginia dining—perhaps he visited the colony out of season,
or perhaps these were simply taken as a matter of course. But where
he has left the picture blank, John Randolph of Williamsburg, in *A
Treatise on Gardening by a Citizen of Virginia*, penned between 1760 and
1775, charmingly fills in the details. Although Randolph pays little
attention to the beet, sweet potato and watermelon, which emerged
later as staples of the Virginia diet, he does go on at length about a
great many other garden crops. Among these are several vegetables and
herbs that seemed to have been quite common in his day, but that

almost disappeared from the American table, only to appear again in this century. Of one such vegetable, broccoli, he says, "The stems will eat like Asparagus, and the heads like Cauliflower." He praises watercress for its "agreeable warm taste," and he recommends chives because they do not affect the breath, and mint, or *"mentha,* from *mens,* the mind, because it strengthens the mind." About Jerusalem artichokes—which the colonists had obtained from the Indians and which enjoyed wide popularity in Europe until they were displaced by the potato—Randolph is less enthusiastic: "Some admire them, but they are of a flatulent nature, and are apt to cause commotions in the belly."

Reading of the Virginians' rich diet, one wonders how anyone avoided having commotions in the belly. It took people of great cultivation to appreciate the difference between gorging and dining, between good cooking and fine cooking. Thomas Jefferson was just such a person, and one of the first in this country to suggest what an American cuisine might be. All in all, he was an amazing figure, the closest thing no doubt to a Renaissance Man that this country has produced. But his fame as the author of the Declaration of Independence and as third President of the United

States has tended to blur his image as a man, a very real man, fond of food and wine, who loved his wife and children and his home entirely, and who in old age could point to domestic life and literary pursuits as his "first and latest inclinations."

No American seemed more aware of what this country had to offer than Thomas Jefferson; he felt that the New World had been designed for the enjoyment of men. He enthusiastically demonstrated how enormous were the possibilities for fine cooking by utilizing the best of America's overwhelming natural bounty in his kitchen, and marrying it wherever appropriate to the best European recipes. Not only did he grow a wide assortment of vegetables and fruits in his gardens at Monticello, he made sure that his land abounded in deer, rabbits, peacocks, guinea fowl, pigeons, hares "and every other wild animal," excepting predators. In this, and in his table, he was an example, and he continues to be today. His food was talked about by all who dined with him.

It was his assignment to France in 1784 as the American Minister Plenipotentiary to the Court of Louis XVI that opened Jefferson's eyes to the satisfactions of fine cooking and gracious living. In France he encountered

On a farmhouse lawn in eastern Pennsylvania lies an abundant October harvest of pumpkins, including orange Small Sugars and gourdlike Golden Cushaws. Carved into jack-o'-lanterns or baked as rich pies, the handsome pumpkins are a traditional autumn treat.

41

a courtly elegance and a politeness that he wished his countrymen would adopt. And there for the first time he enjoyed real French cooking. He was never again the same man. He considered the French to be far ahead of Americans when it came to the pleasures of the table, and he admired as well the sensible way in which they drank—and especially what they drank, wines rather than spirits. He hired a French chef and a French maître d'hôtel; but he did not neglect to plant in his Paris garden some good American sweet corn. He copied recipes in his own hand, and he pried secrets from cooks. He even designed a silver coffeepot that was inaugurated at a dinner for the Marquis de Lafayette at which Jefferson's daughter Patsy was hostess. His parties became renowned as much for the dishes he served as for the wit and urbanity of the host.

Nothing escaped his notice. He sampled French fruits and vegetables and compared them to our own, preferring their apricots and pears to ours, but ranking all our garden vegetables, except turnips, well above theirs. When traveling, he made a point of entering peasant homes, looking into their kettles and eating their bread. In southern France he tasted oranges all along the route to find out which were the most flavorful, and in Italy he made meticulous notes as he watched Parmesan cheese and butter being made. In Holland, eating waffles for the first time and liking them, he bought a waffle iron.

When he came back home in 1789, dressed in the latest Paris mode, with a topaz ring on his finger, he set about trying to influence American tastes. He had made sure that his maître d'hôtel, Petit, would follow him, and Petit was under strict orders to bring with him a "stock of macaroni, Parmesan cheese, figs of Marseilles, *Brugnoles,* raisins, almonds, mustard, *vinaigre d'Estragon,* other good vinegar, oil and anchovies." Jefferson was immensely fond of salads, and one can only assume that he had salads in mind when he made up this shopping list for Petit. In Petit's wake arrived a French chef, and Jefferson prepared to startle his countrymen with an array of new and delicious dishes and an assortment of fine wines.

Settling down as Secretary of State at the nation's second capital in Philadelphia, Jefferson from time to time put aside state business to ask the U.S. chargé d'affaires in Paris, William Short, to hunt up some ingredient (such as vanilla) unobtainable at home, or to obtain a recipe for a French dish he wanted to re-create. He even had Short make a side trip to Naples to buy a macaroni mold. But the chargé d'affaires found macaroni in Naples to be of a narrower stripe than in Paris, and unwittingly, what he posted to Jefferson was not a macaroni mold at all, but a spaghetti maker. With Petit and Julien Lemaire, the chef, in his employ, Jefferson proceeded to serve his guests macaroni, ice cream, blancmange, macaroons, meringues, *biscuits de savoye.* And for such "gimcracks" as these he was ultimately criticized: Patrick Henry went so far as to call Jefferson a man who had "abjured his native victuals."

When Jefferson became President in 1801 (after having been Vice President for four years), he found it good politics to live simply. He even received ambassadors and other important guests while attired in worn slippers and an old red waistcoat. But there was one area in which he refused to compromise, and this was his table. Here he may have been motivated as much by loneliness as courtesy. He was a widower and the first President to occupy the White House. He was horrified by its emptiness; he called it "a great stone house, big enough for two emperors, one pope and the grand lama in the bargain." He could not be blamed for wanting to warm it up, and he did so by giving dinner parties.

Although such parties were generally small affairs, almost familylike in atmosphere, he made certain that only the finest dishes were served. Even as President, he was not too busy to keep a running list of fresh vegetables available at the Washington market, carefully noting when the first of each variety appeared and when each went out of season. And to the list of French dishes that had become his favorites, he had his chef, Julien, add new ones. A well-fed guest felt moved to remark later that "never before had such dinners been given in the President's House, nor such a variety of the finest and most costly wines. In his entertainments, republican simplicity was united with Epicurean delicacy." But for all this simplicity, Jefferson's expenditures for food, wine and staff ran well ahead of his salary as President; the same problem would beset him at Monticello, where he would be all but eaten out of house and home, and would ultimately die $40,000 in debt.

To serve as White House hostesses for the winter of 1802-1803, Jefferson had his daughters Patsy and Maria come from Virginia. When they went home, the wife of his dear friend James Madison took over. Dolley performed nobly, and her quick-wittedness and tact gained her a lasting reputation as a hostess. She was criticized once by the British Ambassador's wife (a woman with whom almost everyone was on bad terms) for laying out a feast in her own house "more like a harvest home supper than the entertainment of the Secretary of State." Dolley had a ready reply: "The profusion of my table so repugnant to foreign customs arises from the happy circumstances of abundance and prosperity in our country."

Over a lifetime Jefferson sustained an abiding interest in gardening, and he derived some of his greatest satisfactions from plants. He looked to the American wilderness for species that would ameliorate the life of the poor, and he became enthusiastic over such bountiful providers as the Vermont sugar-maple tree and the Illinois "paccan" tree. To his way of thinking, natural America represented an "improved plan," while Europe was nothing but "a first idea, a crude production, before the Maker knew his Trade, or had made up His mind as to what He wanted." But as near to perfection as America may have been in his day, Jefferson saw no reason why it should not be further improved. He firmly believed that no man could do his country a better service than to introduce to it a new and useful plant.

Jefferson set his sights on several Old World plants he was convinced could be of enormous value to the United States once transplanted to these shores. While traveling in Italy, he had risked his life to gather up some grains of Piedmont rice, a special variety that flourished in dry, rather than wet, land, and to carry them out of the country in his pockets; so jealous were the Italians of this strain that they had made stealing its seeds a crime punishable by death. Jefferson's idea was to introduce upland rice to the Carolinas, which he eventually did with success.

Adding Zest to an Indian Dish

The early settlers learned about succotash from the Indians, who not only grew corn and beans together in the same garden patch, but often cooked them in the same pot. The Indians made this dish from dried corn and beans in winter, and from fresh vegetables in summer. The best succotash, to most tastes, is the summer variety, made from fresh whole-kernel corn and freshly shelled baby lima or kidney beans, or a combination of green beans and shelled beans. The best out-of-season substitutes are frozen corn and beans. Cook with salt pork or bacon, and season the succotash with salt, pepper, a little sugar and butter. (The corn should not be added until the beans are almost done and should be cooked not longer than 10 minutes.)

Continued on page 48

Oranges and Artichokes from California's Bounty

California, with its mild climate and fertile valleys, is America's most bountiful state. It is first in the production of avocados, broccoli, asparagus, tomatoes, carrots, eggs, grapes, lettuce, peaches, pears and a cornucopia of other foods. Oranges are always ready for picking in this Eden-like land. Valencias, the variety that grows in groves like those at the left, near Ventura, ripen in spring and summer. And navels, the state's other leading orange, complement Valencias by ripening in fall and winter. So great is California's plenty that it provides the nation's entire crop of artichokes *(below)*. Until fairly recently these thistlelike plants were largely unknown in the U.S. But now California produces some 70 million pounds annually to be eaten hot as separate dishes or enjoyed cold with other ingredients as appetizers and salads *(page 144)*.

Garden-fresh Produce in Seattle's Great Market

The rich soil and abundant rain in the Pacific Northwest produce some of the finest berries, fruits and vegetables in the United States. Every day except Sunday during the growing season, these top-quality foods go on sale at Seattle's Pike Place Market a few hours after they are harvested. The growers bring their produce into the market and arrange the fruit and vegetables before the day starts. When the market opens at 9 o'clock, customers can pick and choose among the red raspberries *(left)* or select vegetables from the beautiful displays *(above and right)*.

The customers can shop for fresh eggs from the nearby countryside or purchase fruits from Washington, California or Arizona. If they need a steak, a roast or seafood they can visit the meat markets and the fish markets where salmon, oysters and Dungeness crab are sold fresh from Puget Sound or the sea. And under the same roof those who are not in a rush can enjoy the Seattle area's fine food in four restaurants while watching the ferries cross the sound or admiring the snow-capped Olympic Mountains.

Jefferson had long wanted to transplant the olive tree to the American South. He considered it to be second only to wheat in importance, and was tempted to rate it even higher since the oil could be used as a condiment to improve and make more palatable a variety of healthful vegetables. He tried to grow olives at Monticello, but a cold spell killed most of the trees. With his Italian friend Philip Mazzei, he attempted also to grow vintage grapes in Virginia, but the Revolution forced him to give up the experiment.

Great as Jefferson's influence may have been in his own day, it was a long time again before it had widespread effect. For the America he left behind him was a growing country, and he had helped make it so through the Louisiana Purchase, an acquisition that enlarged the United States by more than 828,000 square miles that were to become all or part of 13 states in the area between the Mississippi River and the Rocky Mountains.

The westward movement that ultimately was to settle this territory and carry all the way to the Pacific began in the late 18th Century. As new lands opened up, pioneers poured in, halting wherever the soil was best— or wherever they thought they could grow the crops they were most suited to raise. Now the great burning-over began, whole forests yielding to the ax, with the fires from fallen trees blazing high and singeing all that lay within reach of their heat. Sometimes the fires burned with such intensity they left vast depressions in the earth, having eaten their way down into the organic material of the soil. Yet such were the riches of the virgin land and the fertilizing tree ashes that grain would spring up after the first sowing and yield harvests to astonish all.

From the beginning, corn and wheat were the principal crops, and of these, corn was the sturdier and the easier to manage. A man and a boy together could plant a field without laboriously plowing it, the man bringing down his ax to rend the sod, the boy dropping a few kernels in the gash and quickly covering them over. And when a patch of land gave out, the soil was so bountiful that the pioneers simply moved on to another patch or to the next territory.

The westward migration, one of history's great mass-population movements, occurred in stages, leapfrogging from the Mississippi to California in the years 1840 to 1860. In their haste to reach the gold of California and the fine land of Oregon, the pioneers did not pause long enough to settle the Great Plains (they thought that immensely rich area with its low rainfall and its heavily matted topsoil was a desert), or the basin between the Rocky Mountains and the Sierras. During the Civil War other settlers would flow into the basin, and somewhat later, cattlemen would drive their herds north from Texas to fatten on the grasslands of the Great Plains. Still later the inventions of the steel plow and barbwire fencing would open the plains to farming.

With the settlement of the West, the country began to take on a regional character, and an agricultural map began to emerge. The South, with its hot weather, ample rainfall and rich soil, was already established as the land of cotton and tobacco. The Midwest, with its black soil and hot summers, became the great corn- and hog-producing area. The Great Plains, with its low rainfall and cooler weather, became one of the world's great corn- and wheat-producing regions, and the Rocky Mountain basin was given over to grazing and irrigated crops.

On the farthest horizon lay the lushest land and the greatest lure of all: California. People from all over the United States and all over the world would be attracted by its incredibly fertile valleys and its balmy Mediterranean climate. Here was a place where all things would grow. Before the first settlers from the East arrived, Spaniards coming up from the south had fulfilled Mr. Jefferson's design by planting olive trees and high-quality grapes that flourished on American soil. They had also planted citrus fruits—oranges and lemons—that were to number among the bountiful state's most important crops.

At the peak of the westward migration, within the short space of two decades, America almost doubled in population. And despite the early signs of maturity, represented by Jefferson, the United States was now a sprawling, awkward, overgrown youngster of a country. If, unlike Mr. Jefferson, most Americans did not eat elegantly, using their knives as forks, their forks as toothpicks and their fingerbowls as tubs (as one English visitor said they did), at least they continued to eat well. The letters of new arrivals to their families back home were filled with wonders they had encountered, not the least of which was waste. More peaches and apples "than would sink the British fleet" were left rotting in the orchards of Ohio for want of takers, wrote one stunned immigrant. According to another, the wheat left lying in the fields by farmers would "keep a whole parish for a week" in the Old Country. How much this abundance meant to the newcomer is touchingly conveyed by the single statement of an immigrant: "Tell Thomas Arann to come to America; and tell him to leave his strap what he wears when he has nothing to eat in England, for some other half-starved slave. Tell Miriam there's no sending children to bed without supper, or husbands to work without dinners in their bags."

To America flocked not only poor, half-starving immigrants, but well-to-do travelers, curious to see whether it was all true. One such traveler was the Englishwoman Harriet Martineau, who went around the country in 1835-1836 sweeping up information in a big ear trumpet that her deafness forced her to carry with her; although Miss Martineau was basically more interested in the democratic experiment than in American food, she made many charming observations on dishes she was served wherever she journeyed. In Sweet Springs, Tennessee, she feasted on stewed venison, ham, hominy and fruit pies; in Stockbridge, Massachusetts, at the Widow Jones's, she breakfasted on "excellent bread, potatoes, hung beef, eggs and strong tea." (American tea could be so strong that it was known to keep even the English awake.) And at Gloucester she had her first fish chowder, which she found excellent. Tender meat, fresh vegetables, good claret wine and champagne she found welcome provender in Kentucky. Cornbread, buckwheat cakes, buns, broiled chickens, bacon and eggs, rice, hominy, fish, fresh and pickled, and beefsteak were all set before her at breakfast in Montgomery, Alabama. Not surprisingly, she also encountered in her travels much bad food. "The dish from which I ate was, according to some, mutton; to others, pork," she wrote of a meal in Tennessee. "My own idea is that it was dog."

Many of the Europeans who visited the United States and gave their impressions of it when they got home were struck by the tremendous amount of meat that every American man, woman and child consumed. Game was abundantly available, and pigs were allowed to run wild and fatten in the woods, or roam city streets and eat up the garbage. So much salt pork was eaten by so many Americans in the 19th Century that molasses, the most popular of sweeteners, was regularly used to subdue the briny taste. The Duc de Liancourt marveled that even the poorest of settlers had salt meat for breakfast, salt meat or salt fish for dinner, and salt meat again for supper. And he was further amazed that coffee or chocolate should be served at breakfast, and coffee again at dinner. An English observer confirmed this impression, and was alarmed that the people he had encountered never seemed to eat any vegetables, and evidently had an aversion to fresh meat.

In a land where pigs were legion, however, it was only natural that fresh pork should have had an important place. But apparently it was mainly used for special occasions, and then cooked and eaten quickly, before it could spoil. Captain Frederick Marryat, an English writer who visited the U.S., told in *A Diary in America,* first published in 1839, of an astonishing Fourth of July celebration he witnessed in New York City, at which roast pork enjoyed special prominence. Although considered by some at the time to be the London of the New World, New York occupied no more than one third of Manhattan Island, and cooks who wanted sweet cream and fresh butter could still send "to the country" for them, up around where Rockefeller Center stands today. The populace had turned out for the festivities, which included a casual martial review at the Battery, and the streets reverberated with music, firecrackers and shouts. Marryat's eye was caught by the stands and booths along Broadway. These were offering all kinds of food for sale—oysters, clams, pineapples, boiled hams, pies, puddings, candy and a great deal more to eat. "But what was most remarkable," Marryat wrote, "Broadway being three miles long, and the booths lining each side of it, in every booth there was a roast pig, large or small, as the centre attraction. Six miles of roast pig! and that in New York City alone; and roast pig in every other city, town, hamlet, and village in the Union."

However much pork may have been eaten, one thing is outstanding about the American diet from colonial days down through the 19th Century —its protein base, which was unequaled anywhere else in the world. Some people have suggested that the American inventiveness and energy that marked this period can be attributed to the quantities of nourishing meat eaten by all. Certainly protein's effect on growing children could only have been for the good.

Yet, despite this value, Americans ate and drank so much that dyspepsia was almost a national disease, and they were an easy prey for medicine quacks peddling nostrums and elixirs. Whiskey was the American wine (although to be sure, good wine, especially Madeira, continued to be imported after Jefferson's time). Diluted with water, hard liquor was drunk at mealtimes, and in between meals as well. Even ministers and children drank it; boys 12 years of age or less were known to enter stores where whiskey could be had, saunter up to the clerks, "and tip off their drams." Perhaps the American propensity for whiskey in the first half of the 19th Century had something to do with the country's adolescence— the need to feel grown up. But Marryat, for one, blamed it on the rigorous climate, the extremes of winter and summer, and on the availability and cheapness of spirits everywhere. American drinks, he noted, ran all the way from those with ice in them—a luxury the Europeans found themselves admiring—to New Jersey champagne, made from turnip juice, brandy and honey, which, even to a connoisseur like Marryat, tasted not half bad.

Marryat not only approved of these drinks; he found many favorable things to say about American food and cooking in general. He feasted on everything from raccoon and bear to the nation's greatest delicacies, canvasback ducks and terrapin. The meat he found as good as England's, and American markets he considered extremely well supplied. He had been enormously impressed by the New York game market, where he saw 300 deer at one time, plus bears, raccoons, wild turkeys, geese, ducks and an assortment of other birds (75,000 pigeons were once sold in New York in a single day). Suggesting that as anywhere else in the world good cooking depended upon the degree of refinement of the cook or

Freshly picked, part of the 150 million annual United States watermelon harvest awaits buyers at a Pennsylvania market.

the master, Marryat could assure his English readers that they would encounter in American upper-class homes food as fine as they would come across in Paris or London.

From the middle of the 19th Century onward, the variety and freshness of American foods greatly increased. Pineapples, coconuts and bananas began to be imported from the West Indies, Cuba and Central America. Fresh vegetables were shipped from Southern ports like Charleston to Northern cities. As an outgrowth of the Civil War, canning helped to vary the American diet still further; soldiers came home from service requesting that their wives go out and get some of the canned goods they had learned to eat and like in the army. Tomatoes, corn and peas soon led the list of favorites; and this in itself is rather surprising, at least as far as tomatoes are concerned. Only a couple of decades before, many Americans had been afraid to eat "love apples," attributing all sorts of ills to them, including cancer. In 1869 the first carload of fresh fruit from California arrived in New York by rail; barrels of oysters and other perishables packed in crushed ice had already been making the journey in the opposite direction partway, bringing relief to the monotony of an inland diet. And in Vermont, what were probably the first tentative attempts at freezing meat had begun. We know this from Alessandro Filippini, a moustachioed chef at Delmonico's, a restaurant in New York that for several generations meant good food and which contributed a dish still widely popular today, lobster Newburg *(page 150)*.

In his cookbook, *The Table* (1889), Filippini tells how hundreds of tons of Vermont and other turkeys were slaughtered each December (when the birds were fattest) and then "dressed, frozen hard in boxes, and preserved in that condition for use in the spring and summer." A chef of great integrity, he even approved of the birds being frozen: turkeys, he reminded his readers, are tough and unpalatable when freshly slaughtered.

Filippini's cookbook is a fascinating document, revealing a great shift in American eating habits in the last quarter of the 19th Century, and it is so good a cookbook it could be used today. But what makes it interesting, apart from its 1,500 recipes, are his comments on the bounty of his day and the uses to which it was put in the most elegant circles. "There is no place in the civilized world where the market for the supply of food is so well provided as in New York, both to variety and excellence, and even as to luxuries," he said. Thanks to gourmands, the country's abundance "and the encouragement given to the culinary art of the period, our American table has arrived at a stage of virtual perfection"—and this was 1889. Filippini raved over the quality of beef entering the New York market. Never in Europe did he see cuts so fine as these. But not only did New York have the world's finest beef to offer, but excellent mutton, which (and here *is* a surprise), "if not superior to, stands at least fully on a par with, the English rival." (One wonders what happened to American mutton, the most forgotten of our meats.)

Game practically throws Filippini into a frenzy, and one can see him kissing his fingertips in joy over a haunch of venison, a wild pigeon, a plump-breasted quail. "No game is more highly prized or more eagerly sought after in Europe," he writes, "than our American canvasback ducks,

Much Flavor
in a Small Package

The most flavorful tomato available when other varieties are out of season is the small, bright-red specimen usually called "cherry tomato." Unpeeled and unstemmed, these little tomatoes make an attractive and delicious garnish. Sliced, or cut into wedges or whole, they can be used in salads with lettuce, cucumber or onions. Moreover, they are available the year around in city markets, and can easily be grown in the backyard in almost any part of the United States.

grouse and wild turkeys." And he pulls no punches when he tells how to cook a canvasback: for roasting he recommends that the bird be kept in a "brisk oven" for 18 minutes; for broiling, he cuts down the cooking time by four minutes—seven minutes to a side. Giving the duck so brief an application of heat preserved the canvasback's delicate flavor, imparted to its meat by its diet of tape grass, a marsh plant. And when it comes to carving the canvasback, "The King of Birds," Filippini politely reminds us that it is only the breast that should be sliced away and eaten.

Filippini's book is complete with menus, one for every three meals of the day for a whole year. Oysters appear so often in them that the piles of shucked shells behind kitchens must have risen window-high, provided, that is, anyone actually ate the way Filippini urged them to do. Yet, recalling how jowly Americans of the Victorian era look in their photographs, it is possible to believe that some at least took him at his word. Here is the menu for a Sunday in July; it is typical. Breakfast calls for omelet with asparagus tips, broiled kingfish, hashed chicken *à la crème,* sweet potatoes, hollandaise and Milan cake. Mind you, that was breakfast. Lunch consists of frogs' legs, broiled turkey legs with mustard sauce, broiled potatoes, lobster salad and watermelon. How could dinner possibly top that? It could, providing it consisted (as this one did) of littleneck clams, chicken *à la créole,* radishes, olives, salmon *à la génoise,* broiled lamb chops with green peas, tenderloin of beef with sauce béarnaise, asparagus and hollandaise, punch *au kirsch,* roast woodcock, lettuce and mayonnaise salad, *plombière à la Hamilton* and coffee. Menus for the Fourth of July, Thanksgiving and Christmas day defy the imagination; tables must have cracked under the weight of the food, while cooks collapsed in the kitchen from exhaustion, and hosts, hostesses and guests tumbled from their chairs in anacondalike slumbers.

Unbelievable as all this may seem, we do have the record of Ward McAllister to confirm it. McAllister was a bon vivant and incorrigible snob who hobnobbed with the best of American society. He was the kind of man who, when giving a dinner party, would "telegraph to Baltimore for my canvasbacks." And when he put on one of his picnics at his farm, for which he was famous, he would invite over the neighbor's cows and sheep to give the place a genuine look and startle his guests into thinking that he was also a prosperous farmer.

McAllister lived at a time when American fortunes were growing; at first it was considered something to make a million; then, with incomes exploding into the millions, it was almost an embarrassment in his set to have made that little. McAllister tells how three rich young men competed to give the best dinner at Delmonico's. "Charge what you will, but make my dinner the best," each said. So Delmonico's came up with a Silver, a Gold and a Diamond dinner, with favors for the guests appropriate to the selected themes. At one, McAllister remembered eating canvasback duck (it was suggested to him once that this bird, not the eagle, be the national emblem), "cut up and made into an aspic . . . string beans, with truffles, cold, as a salad, and truffled ice cream; the last dish, strange to say, very good."

But these three dinners were as nothing compared to a $10,000 dinner

Continued on page 56

An Added Zest for Baked Apples

Baked apples are a fine American dessert that can be improved by adding a zesty stuffing. For best results use the Rome Beauty, York Imperial or Jonathan apples (next pages).

First core 6 large apples and arrange them in a buttered baking dish. Combine 1 cup of sugar, 2 cups of boiling water and a cinnamon stick in a saucepan, and cook for 8 minutes. Mix ½ cup of currants or raisins with ½ cup of chopped walnuts, and stuff the centers of the apples with the mixture. Pour the syrup over the apples and bake them in a 375° oven for 40 minutes. Transfer the apples to individual serving dishes and pour any remaining syrup over them.

The Big Apples of America

The 12 apples shown on these pages represent man's successful efforts to improve nature's bounty. The Cortland apple (7), for example, was created in 1898 by crossing the McIntosh and Ben Davis varieties. Since the Pilgrims brought the first apple seeds and cuttings to the Massachussetts Bay Colony, New World technology has transformed haphazard apple production into a highly developed science that produces 135 million bushels a year. Across the country new and old varieties are baked, fried, stewed, spiced, pickled, jellied, converted into juice, eaten raw as slices in salads, or munched whole. The ones shown here are the nation's best-selling apples.

1 STAYMAN: Moderately tart and juicy; popular as an eating apple. Available October through December mostly in Eastern United States.

2 GOLDEN DELICIOUS: Ranks third in sales in the United States; a firm, fine-grained, sweet eating apple whose flesh does not turn brown when cut. One of our most widely grown apples, available all over the United States.

3 YORK IMPERIAL: A moderately juicy, firm apple that is good for cooking, but also enjoyed raw. Grown mostly in Appalachian area. Bulk of crop is sold for canning, freezing and other commercial uses.

4 ROME BEAUTY: Firm and juicy; excellent for baking, which brings out its flavor. Available countrywide.

5 NORTHERN SPY: Tender and tangy; primarily for cooking. Makes excellent pies, but most of the crop is sold to processors for freezing and canning. Available in Northeast and Michigan.

6 MCINTOSH: Second in popularity; tender, juicy and aromatic; primarily an eating apple. Available mostly in East and Midwest.

7 CORTLAND: A delicately textured fruit; mainly an eating apple. Available in East and Midwest.

8 JONATHAN: A moderately tart, tender apple primarily for eating. Available generally.

9 RHODE ISLAND GREENING: A crisp, tart cooking apple, used for green apple pie. Grown mostly in the Northeast; limited availability in that region.

10 RED DELICIOUS: The world's leading apple. Crisp and tender; mainly an eating apple. Washington State is the largest grower. Available all over the country.

11 WINESAP: One of the oldest American varieties. The spicy, winelike flavor makes it a fine eating apple. Stores well. Generally available.

12 NEWTOWN PIPPIN: Moderately tart and aromatic; mainly for cooking. Found mainly on West Coast.

1

2

3

4

given at Delmonico's in 1884. Delmonico's seems to have been somewhat dumfounded by the prospect of having to use up all *that* money on food, and so it went overboard on decorations. An oval table for 72 guests filled nearly the entire room, "and every inch of it was covered with flowers, excepting a space in the centre, left for a lake, and a border around the table for plates." In the lake swam four swans borrowed from Prospect Park; in so distinguished a company they were unable to retain their composure, and two of them fought. But McAllister was not ruffled in the least, which is understandable—he had been moistening his throat with floods of Blue Seal Johannisberg, "incomparable '48 claret, superb Burgundies, and amber-colored Madeira." And then, just at the very moment when he could hardly bear the exquisite pleasure of it all any longer, "soft music stole over one's senses." So ravished was McAllister by the $10,000 dinner that he neglected to tell what he had to eat at it. One can safely assume, however, that canvasback duck in one form or another figured importantly on the table.

Those days are gone, killed off by two wars, Prohibition, the Depression and taxation, and they bear no repeating. Some of the luxuries of McAllister's day such as canvasback ducks and other game have disappeared or declined alarmingly. But many of the privileges of the table that belonged only to the American rich of the 1890s are now commonplace, and there is much that is new as well—who had ever heard of an avocado then? Fifty years ago the orange was a treasure to stuff down inside a Christmas stocking; now it begins the mornings of millions as a cool, sweet, eye-opening, mouth-refreshing trickle of juice. And not the least miraculous thing about this is that the juice most people use is bought frozen or canned, and costs less as a convenience product than it would if oranges were carried home from the store and then used; freezing has eliminated the expense of shipping the bulky fruit long distances to market, plus a host of other incidental costs. Now that the orange is ordinary, there are other native-grown citrus fruits to fill the place it once occupied as an exotic: tangelos (a cross between a tangerine and the pomelo, the "mother" of the grapefruit), exquisitely sweet honey tangerines, and bumpy-skinned king oranges. And the chances are good, such being the ways of America, that these fine fruits too will someday become cheaper to raise and cheaper to buy and will find their way in increasing numbers to American tables.

In the 20th Century our bounty has multiplied, not just in terms of quantity but in variety too—and that American phenomenon, the supermarket, is its most impressive showcase, admired the world over. Luther Burbank alone gave this country more than 800 new plants (how much Jefferson would have admired him for that). Just to show that all things were possible botanically, Burbank made artichokes that swelled to a diameter of a foot (imagine trying to boil them), walnuts with shells so thin the birds ate them like cherries, and a walnut tree that grew so vigorously, thrusting its branches up through the overhead wires, that the telephone company had to come out and do battle with it. But Burbank was essentially a practical man. If we enjoy improved varieties of apples, strawberries, cherries, nectarines, pears, plums, prunes, peas, peppers, rhubarb and

The Food of the Gods for a Christmas Treat

Ambrosia, an orange dessert, gets its name from the Greek word for "the food of the gods." Traditionally served on Christmas day in the South, it is made of oranges that are peeled and seeded, then thinly sliced and sprinkled with sugar and grated fresh coconut. Other fruits, such as diced pineapple, cherries or bananas, also may be added.

Fresh berries, melon balls and orange slices in a scooped-out pineapple form an attractive centerpiece, salad or dessert.

squashes, plus a host of other good things to eat, it is thanks largely to him. He was the founding father, the man who got American horticulture off to a booming start. He developed fruits that were not only delicious, but shippable over long distances, fresh on delivery.

Where Burbank left off, others—notably the U.S. Department of Agriculture—have taken over. Strawberries, for example, used to have their season, but new American varieties have been developed that make it possible for us to eat them fresh practically all year long. Today they are being flown to market in increasing quantities, fresher than ever, from California, which produces 43 per cent of the strawberries consumed in this country. By no means have all the man-made agricultural miracles been restricted to the realm of plants. Animal husbandry is a well-developed science in this country, and our poultry and livestock have long been receiving its scrutiny, with some startling results. The turkey has been bred up to a 75-pound size—a pure impracticality, however, as the bird that tipped the scales at this weight did not have the bone structure to carry it, and collapsed. More interesting, the turkey has been bred *down* to size, made smaller and smaller, and today it can be enjoyed not only seasonally with the family expanded by an inflow of relatives, but as a bird that a few people, at any time of the year, can eat at a sitting.

As our bounty grows—and our incomes increase with it—we are becoming more and more selective in what we buy. We search out convenience, and yet we are willing to make the effort whenever a recipe seems worth it. Supplied with the best of everything, we can cook almost anything we may choose—and by using a little more effort, be known not only as the world's most fortunate cooks, but the world's best cooks as well.

CHAPTER **II** RECIPES

The recipes for this chapter are a reflection of America's bounty. Not only are they based upon vegetables and fruits available in enormous quantities in this country, but, for the most part, on those found in markets the year round.

Cabbage in White Wine

To serve 6 to 8

8 tablespoons (1 quarter-pound stick) butter
3 pounds green cabbage, cored and coarsely chopped
1 cup dry white wine, such as a California Chablis
1 teaspoon fresh tarragon or ½ teaspoon dried
1 teaspoon salt
Freshly ground black pepper

In a heavy 10- or 12-inch skillet, melt the butter over moderate heat. When the foam subsides, add the cabbage and, with a fork, toss it in the melted butter until it is well coated. Cook uncovered, stirring occasionally, for 10 minutes, then add the wine, tarragon, salt and a few grindings of pepper.

Bring to a boil, cover tightly and reduce the heat to low. Simmer for 5 to 10 minutes, or until the cabbage is tender. With a slotted spoon, remove the cabbage from the pan to a heated vegetable dish or platter. Boil the liquid in the pan rapidly, uncovered, for a few minutes to concentrate its flavor before pouring it over the cabbage.

Wild Rice with Mushrooms

To serve 4 to 6

4 tablespoons butter
2 tablespoons finely diced scraped carrots
2 tablespoons finely diced celery
2 tablespoons finely chopped onion
1 cup wild rice
1 teaspoon salt
2 cups chicken stock, fresh or canned
½ pound mushrooms, coarsely chopped
2 tablespoons finely chopped fresh parsley
¼ cup finely chopped pecans

In a heavy enameled or stainless-steel 2-quart saucepan, melt 2 tablespoons of the butter over moderate heat, and, when the foam subsides, add the carrots, celery and onions, cover and cook for 10 to 15 minutes, stirring occasionally, until the vegetables are soft but not brown. Stir in the cup of rice and the salt and cook for 2 to 3 minutes uncovered, stirring to coat the rice thoroughly with the butter. In a small saucepan bring the stock to a boil and pour it over the rice. Bring to a boil again, cover tightly and reduce the heat to its lowest point. Cook undisturbed for 25 to 30 minutes, or until the rice is tender and has absorbed all the stock.

Meanwhile, over moderate heat melt the remaining 2 tablespoons of butter in an enameled or stainless-steel skillet. When the foam subsides, add the mushrooms and parsley; cook, stirring, for 5 minutes. Add the pecans and cook for 2 to 3 minutes more. With a fork, stir the contents of the skillet into the finished rice. Taste for seasoning and serve.

Buttermilk Fried Onions

To serve 4 to 6

3 egg yolks
1½ cups flour
½ teaspoon baking soda
1½ teaspoons salt
2 cups buttermilk
Vegetable oil or shortening for deep frying
4 large yellow onions, 3 to 4 inches in diameter, peeled and cut in ¼-inch-thick slices
Salt

In a mixing bowl, combine the egg yolks, flour, baking soda and salt, and beat them together with a large spoon. Pour in the buttermilk slowly, beating until the mixture forms a fairly smooth paste. Heat the shortening in a deep-fat fryer—the fat should be at least 3 inches deep—until it registers 375° on a deep-fat thermometer.

Separate the onion slices into rings, drop them in the batter and then, 7 or 8 rings at a time, fry them in the fat for 4 to 5 minutes until lightly browned. Transfer them to paper towels while you proceed with the next batch. When all the onion rings are done, fry them again in the hot fat for a minute or two to heat them through and crisp them. Drain on paper towels and serve sprinkled with salt.

Mushrooms and Onions in Sour Cream

In a heavy 10-inch skillet, melt the butter over medium heat. When the foam subsides, add the onions and cook for 6 to 8 minutes until they are lightly colored. Stir in the mushrooms, cover the pan and cook, still over moderate heat, for about 7 minutes. Add the sour cream, lemon juice, salt and a few grindings of pepper; simmer, stirring, until the cream is heated through. Don't let it boil. Taste for seasoning and sprinkle with chopped parsley. Serve as a first course over pieces of freshly made buttered toast, as a vegetable to accompany a main dish, or as a luncheon or supper dish in the center of or around a molded spinach ring (below).

To serve 4 to 6

4 tablespoons butter
2 medium onions, thinly sliced
1 pound fresh mushrooms, 1 to 1½ inches in diameter
1 cup sour cream
1 teaspoon lemon juice
1 teaspoon salt
Freshly ground black pepper
2 teaspoons finely chopped fresh parsley

Spinach Ring

Preheat the oven to 350°. Lightly butter and flour a 1½-quart ring mold. Melt the 2 tablespoons of butter in a heavy 3- or 4-quart saucepan, remove from heat and stir in the 2 tablespoons of flour. Then pour in the milk and stir with a whisk until the flour is partially dissolved. Return the pan to low heat, and cook, stirring constantly, until the sauce comes almost to a boil and is thick and smooth. Remove from heat and beat in the egg yolks, one at a time, whisking until each one is thoroughly blended in before adding the next. Stir in the spinach, grated onion, salt and pepper, and allow the mixture to cool slightly.

Beat the egg whites with a wire whisk or rotary beater—and in an unlined copper bowl if possible—until they are stiff enough to form unwavering peaks on the beater when it is lifted from the bowl. Stir a large spoonful of egg white into the spinach mixture and then gently fold in the remaining egg whites. Ladle the mixture into the mold. Place the mold in a baking pan and pour enough boiling water into the baking pan to reach ⅔ of the way up the sides of the mold. Bake on the middle shelf of the oven for 30 minutes, or until it is firm to the touch.

To turn out the spinach ring, wipe dry the outside of the mold and run a knife around its inside surfaces. Place a serving plate upside down over the top of the mold, and, firmly grasping plate and mold together, invert the two. Rap them sharply on a table, and the spinach ring should slide out easily onto the plate. Serve at once.

To serve 4 to 6

2 tablespoons butter
2 tablespoons flour
½ cup milk
3 egg yolks
2 ten-ounce packages chopped frozen spinach, thoroughly defrosted and squeezed dry, or 1¼ pounds fresh spinach, cooked, drained, squeezed dry and finely chopped
½ teaspoon grated onion
¾ teaspoon salt
⅛ teaspoon pepper
3 egg whites

Potato Salad

Place the potatoes in boiling salted water to cover, and cook until they are tender but do not fall apart when gently pierced with a knife. Drain them in a colander and when they are cool enough to handle, peel and cut them into ½- to ¾-inch cubes. Place the potatoes in a large bowl and gently stir in the salt, vinegar, celery, onion, green pepper and parsley.

To make the mayonnaise, beat the egg yolks with a whisk or rotary or electric beater for 2 to 3 minutes until they thicken and cling to the beater. Add the lemon juice, vinegar, mustard, salt and pepper. Beat in the oil ½ teaspoon at a time until ¼ cup is used, making sure each spoonful is absorbed. Still beating, slowly add the rest of the oil. Gently fold the mayonnaise into the potatoes. Taste for seasoning. Garnish with egg slices and chopped parsley.

To make 2 quarts

3 pounds new potatoes, unpeeled
1 teaspoon salt
2 tablespoons white-wine vinegar
¾ cup finely chopped celery
¾ cup finely chopped onion
1½ cups finely chopped green pepper
2 tablespoons finely chopped fresh parsley

MAYONNAISE
3 egg yolks, at room temperature
1 teaspoon lemon juice
1 tablespoon white-wine vinegar
¼ teaspoon dry mustard
1 teaspoon salt
¼ teaspoon white pepper
2 cups vegetable oil

3 hard-cooked eggs, sliced
2 tablespoons finely chopped fresh parsley

To serve 6 to 8

2 cups dry green split peas
2 quarts chicken stock, fresh or
  canned
1 cup coarsely chopped onion
1 stalk celery, coarsely chopped
⅛ teaspoon ground cloves
1 bay leaf
1 cup coarsely chopped fresh mint
1 teaspoon salt
Pinch white pepper
½ to 1 cup chilled heavy cream
Sprigs of fresh mint

Cold Split Pea Soup with Mint

Wash the split peas thoroughly under cold running water and continue to wash until the draining water runs clear. Pick over the peas and discard any discolored ones. In a heavy 4- to 5-quart saucepan or soup kettle, bring the chicken stock to a boil and drop in the peas slowly so that the stock does not stop boiling. Add the onions, celery, cloves, bay leaf and mint. Reduce the heat and simmer with the pan partially covered for 1½ hours or until the peas can be easily mashed with a spoon.

Purée the soup through a food mill or fine sieve into a large bowl, and then rub it through the sieve back into the saucepan or into another bowl. Add the salt and pepper, and chill the soup in the refrigerator. (If you wish to serve the soup immediately, place the soup in a bowl and set the bowl in a larger container filled with crushed ice or ice cubes. With a metal spoon, stir the soup until it is ice cold.) Before serving, stir in ½ to 1 cup of chilled heavy cream, thinning the soup as desired, and taste for seasoning. Garnish with sprigs of fresh mint.

Encased in an ice-filled container, chilled, mint-flavored split pea soup is unusual and refreshing for a summer buffet or picnic.

Pumpkin Soup

In a heavy 4-quart saucepan, melt the butter over moderate heat. When the foam subsides, add the onions and cook for 2 or 3 minutes, stirring, until they are transparent but not brown. Add the pumpkin, chicken stock, milk, the cloves, sugar, lemon juice, Tabasco and salt. Stir thoroughly to blend all the ingredients.

Bring to a boil, then reduce the heat to its lowest point and cook the soup, stirring occasionally, for 15 minutes. Then purée the soup by forcing it through a fine sieve or food mill into a large mixing bowl. Do not use a blender; it will result in too bland and smooth a texture. Stir in the cream. Return the soup to the saucepan and heat it through without letting it come to a boil. Taste for seasoning, garnish with croutons, if desired, and serve hot.

NOTE: This pumpkin soup may also be served chilled. If you serve the soup cold, omit the croutons and garnish each serving with a thin slice of peeled, chilled orange.

To serve 4 to 6

1 tablespoon butter
2 tablespoons finely chopped onion
2 cups cooked pumpkin, canned or fresh, thoroughly drained
2½ cups chicken stock, fresh or canned
2½ cups milk
⅛ teaspoon ground cloves
½ teaspoon sugar
1 teaspoon lemon juice
2 to 3 drops Tabasco
½ teaspoon salt
¼ cup heavy cream

Hearty pumpkin soup is brought to the table piping hot in an ironstone tureen.

Caesar Salad

No one really knows how Caesar Salad got its name, but it is believed to have originated in Southern California in the 1920s.

Separate the romaine lettuce and wash the leaves under cold running water. Dry each leaf thoroughly with paper towels. Then wrap the lettuce in a dry kitchen towel and chill while you assemble the other ingredients. Cut a loaf of bread into 1½-inch-thick slices. Trim the crusts and cut each slice into 1½-inch squares. In a heavy skillet, large enough to hold all the croutons in one layer, heat 4 tablespoons of the vegetable oil over high heat until a light haze forms above it. Add the croutons and brown them on all sides, turning them with tongs, and, if necessary, add up to another 4 tablespoons of oil. Remove the pan from the heat, then add the chopped garlic and toss the croutons about in the hot fat. Remove the croutons to paper towels to drain, cool and crisp.

Plunge the eggs into rapidly boiling water for 10 seconds, remove and set aside. Break the chilled romaine into serving-sized pieces and scatter them in the bottom of a large salad bowl, preferably glass or porcelain. Add the salt, pepper and olive oil, and toss the lettuce with two large spoons or, better still, with your hands. Then break the eggs on top of the salad, add the lemon juice and mix again until the lettuce is thoroughly coated with the dressing. Add the cheese and the anchovies, if you are using them, and mix once more. Scatter the croutons over the top and serve at once on chilled salad plates.

Celery Victor

Celery Victor was named after Victor Hirtzler, the San Francisco chef who created it at the St. Francis Hotel.

Remove the outer stalks of the celery, leaving a heart about 1 inch wide and 6 inches long. Cut each celery heart in half lengthwise. Cut away all but the small leaves and trim the root ends (do not cut too deep; the celery halves should hold together). Use the cut-away leaves for the herb bouquet. With a sharp knife, scrape the outer stalks if they seem coarse.

Arrange the celery halves side by side in a 10- or 12-inch skillet, preferably enameled or stainless steel, and pour in the stock, using more stock or water if the celery is not completely covered. Add the herb bouquet, with as much salt and pepper as suits your taste, and bring to a boil. Reduce the heat to its lowest point, cover tightly and simmer the celery for about 15 minutes, or until it shows no resistance when pierced with the tip of a sharp knife. With tongs or a slotted spoon, transfer the celery halves to a deep platter that will hold them in a single layer.

With a whisk, beat the vinegar and the oil together and pour over the celery while it is still warm. Refrigerate for at least an hour before serving. To serve, arrange the celery halves on individual chilled plates and crisscross 2 anchovy fillets and 2 strips of pimiento over each serving. Or instead, if you prefer, garnish the celery with a slice of tomato and a slice of hard-cooked egg. In either case, moisten the celery with a spoonful or so of the vinegar-olive oil sauce and sprinkle with chopped parsley.

To serve 4 to 6

2 medium-sized heads romaine lettuce
10 to 12 croutons, preferably made from French or Italian-style bread
4 to 8 tablespoons vegetable oil
1 teaspoon finely chopped garlic
2 eggs
⅛ teaspoon salt
⅛ teaspoon freshly ground black pepper
½ cup olive oil
4 tablespoons lemon juice
1 cup freshly grated Parmesan cheese
6 to 8 flat anchovies (optional)

To serve 6

3 bunches celery, about 2 inches in diameter
1½ cups chicken stock, fresh or canned
An herb bouquet of 4 sprigs parsley, 1 bay leaf and celery leaves tied together
Salt
Freshly ground black pepper
3 tablespoons white-wine vinegar
½ cup olive oil
12 flat anchovy fillets
12 strips pimiento
6 slices tomato (optional)
6 slices hard-cooked eggs (optional)
1½ teaspoons finely chopped fresh parsley

Rich, highly seasoned Caesar salad *(opposite)* is sometimes served as a meal in itself.

To serve 4

6 tablespoons butter
2 medium onions, finely chopped (1 cup)
2 large cucumbers, peeled and finely chopped (2 cups)
3 cups chicken stock, fresh or canned
2 tablespoons flour
2 egg yolks
½ cup heavy cream
Salt
White pepper
1 medium-sized cucumber, peeled and diced into ¼-inch pieces
2 tablespoons finely chopped fresh parsley or chives

Cucumber Bisque

In a heavy 2- to 3-quart saucepan, melt 4 tablespoons of the butter over moderate heat. When the foam subsides, stir in the chopped onions and the chopped cucumbers and, stirring occasionally, cook them for about 5 minutes until the onions are transparent but not brown.

Add the chicken stock and bring to a boil. Lower the heat and simmer, uncovered, for 20 to 30 minutes, or until the vegetables are tender. Pour the soup into a sieve set over a large bowl and force the vegetables through with the back of a wooden spoon.

Melt the remaining 2 tablespoons of butter in the saucepan. Remove the pan from the heat and stir in the flour. Pour in the puréed soup, beating vigorously with a wire whisk. Return to moderate heat and cook about 3 to 5 minutes, whisking constantly, until the soup has thickened slightly.

In a small bowl, combine the egg yolks and heavy cream. Beating constantly with a whisk, pour into it 1 cup of the hot soup, 2 tablespoons at a time.

Then reverse the process. Slowly pour this warmed mixture back into the remaining soup, still beating with the whisk. Simmer over very low heat for 5 minutes but do not let the soup come to a boil. Just before serving, stir in the diced raw cucumber, season with salt and white pepper, and sprinkle with the chopped parsley or chives.

To serve the soup cold, let it cool to room temperature, then cover and refrigerate for at least 3 hours. Add the diced raw cucumbers, seasonings and chopped herbs just before serving. If you like, you may serve the cold soup with a spoonful of slightly salted, stiffly whipped cream in each portion, or a spoonful of sour cream may be used.

To serve 4 to 6

2 envelopes unflavored gelatin
½ cup cold beef stock, fresh or canned
2 tablespoons butter
¼ cup finely chopped onions
3 tablespoons tomato paste
4½ cups canned tomatoes with juice (2 one-pound, 3-ounce cans)
¾ teaspoon salt
¾ teaspoon sugar
½ teaspoon Worcestershire sauce
1 teaspoon finely chopped fresh tarragon or ½ teaspoon dried tarragon
1 teaspoon vegetable oil
1 cup mayonnaise combined with 2 tablespoons finely cut chives, or 1 cup sour cream combined with 1 tablespoon red caviar

Tomato Aspic

Soften the gelatin in the cold beef stock for about 5 minutes. In a heavy 2- to 3-quart saucepan, melt the butter over moderate heat. When the foam subsides, add the onions and cook, stirring, for 4 or 5 minutes until they are transparent but not brown. Stir in the tomato paste, the canned tomatoes and the softened gelatin, and mix together until the ingredients are thoroughly combined.

Then add the salt, the sugar, Worcestershire sauce and the tarragon, and bring to a boil, stirring constantly. Reduce the heat to its lowest point and simmer the mixture with the pan partially covered for about 30 minutes. Rub the mixture through a fine sieve or food mill into a mixing bowl.

With a pastry brush or paper towel, lightly coat the inside of a 1-quart mold with the vegetable oil. Pour in the tomato mixture, let it cool slightly and then refrigerate for 2 to 3 hours, or until the aspic is firm. To unmold, run a knife around the inside surfaces of the mold and place a serving plate upside down on top of the mold. Grasping the plate and the mold together firmly, invert the two. Rap the plate firmly on a table, and the aspic should slide out onto the plate. Serve the tomato aspic as a salad course with mayonnaise mixed with finely cut chives, or with sour cream mixed with red caviar.

Spinach Salad

Wash the spinach under cold running water, drain and pat thoroughly dry with paper towels. Strip the leaves from the stems and discard the stems along with any tough or discolored leaves. Peel the cucumber and slice it in half lengthwise. Run the tip of a teaspoon down the center to scrape out the seeds. Cut the halves into strips ¼ inch wide and then crosswise into ¼-inch dice. To rid the cucumber of excess moisture, in a small bowl mix the diced cucumber with 1 teaspoon of salt. Let it rest for 15 minutes to ½ hour, then drain the liquid that will accumulate and pat the cucumber dice dry with paper towels.

Trim the leaves and stems of the celery; wash the stalks under cold water and dry them thoroughly with paper towels. Cut each stalk in ¼-inch strips and then cut into ¼-inch dice. Toss the spinach, cucumber and celery in a salad bowl, preferably of glass, add the olives and nuts and toss again. Chill until ready to serve.

For the dressing, with a whisk beat the vinegar, salt, pepper and mustard together in a small bowl. Still whisking, gradually pour in the oil and beat until the dressing is smooth and thick. Pour over the salad, toss until all the ingredients are thoroughly coated with the dressing and serve at once on chilled salad plates.

To serve 4 to 6

½ pound uncooked young spinach
1 large cucumber
1 teaspoon salt
4 medium-sized stalks celery
¼ cup coarsely chopped black olives
½ cup pine nuts

DRESSING
2 tablespoons red wine vinegar
½ teaspoon salt
Freshly ground black pepper
½ teaspoon dry mustard
6 tablespoons vegetable oil

Tender young spinach, usually thought of as a cooked vegetable, is the principal ingredient in this crisp, refreshing salad.

III

The Flavor
of the Regions

Some of America's most
distinctive regional foods
are served at an outdoor
buffet near Talkeetna,
Alaska, where Mount
McKinley looms in the
background. Included are
king-crab legs *(far end of
table)*, cranberry catsup,
(to right of crab legs),
reindeer salami, hot
fiddlehead ferns, and a king-
crab salad *(foreground)*.

American cooking, in many parts of the country, is still regional
cookery, full of the flavors and aromas of a certain place. Just as we all
speak differently—each with his own accent, twang or drawl—so we
often eat differently, savoring such diverse foods as the abalone of California, the catfish of the Midwest and the South, the jambalaya of New
Orleans and the pepper pot of Philadelphia.

True American regional cookery has been shaped by a variety of things—
history, climate, terrain, the availability of ingredients. New England
cooking, with which I, as a Northeasterner, am most familiar, is famous
for its seafood and especially for its abundant supply of lobsters and
other shellfish, all of which tells of the closeness of the Atlantic Ocean.
But it can be characterized still further by its sensibleness, reflecting,
among other things, the effect of the long, cold winters that often cur-
tailed the growing season and threatened the supply of food in larders.
One of the best-known New England dishes, the boiled dinner, originated
in the early days of settlement when an iron pot might be a family's only
cooking vessel, and the available meat and vegetables were thrown into it
together and later served on a large wooden platter. The juices passed
back and forth in a delicious blend of flavors, and so well liked was the
dish that the New England boiled dinner is cooked and served today
much as it was 230 years ago *(page 90)*. Even now, whatever meat remains on the platter may be saved and re-used the next day, transformed
into red-flannel hash, so named because the beets that go into this dish
give it a brilliant color *(page 90)*. *Continued on page 70*

A Gastronomic Guide to the United States

From New England to Hawaii, the traveler crossing the United States can enjoy an exciting variety of regional foods, if he knows what to look for. Such colorful specialties as red-flannel hash, she-crab soup, steelhead trout, reindeer steaks, wild brush honey, kukui nuts and mooseburger await the visitor. The map and text on these pages, keyed by letters and colors, provide a condensed guide to good eating; a comprehensive one would fill a bigger book than this.

ALASKA
A
Fairbanks

Anchorage

Juneau

A *Alaska*

Alaskans like mooseburger, barbecued reindeer steaks, caribou sausage, bear chops, pot roast of beaver, trapper's-game stew and ptarmigan pie. The sea is the source of such delicacies as baked king salmon, king-crab salad, butter-fried razor clams, broiled shee fish, whale steaks and Arctic char. Berries and vegetables of prodigious size come from the Matanuska Valley. Fiddlehead ferns, raw rosehips and cranberry catsup are also Alaskan favorites. Sourdough bread is traditional; sourdough batter is also used in pancakes and rolls.

B *Hawaii*

Visitors to Hawaii like to sample the islands' chief gastronomical delights at a single occasion—a traditional Hawaiian *luau*. Before the feast the guests are served a potent cocktail called *mai tai*. The main course features a pit-roasted pig and pit-roasted chickens. Served with the meal are macadamia and kukui nuts, marinated raw fish, steamed crabs, poi (a paste made from taro, a starchy vegetable), fresh coconuts, bananas, pineapples, guavas, papayas and fruit punch. Hawaii also offers Chinese, Japanese, Korean and Portuguese cooking.

C *Washington—Oregon*

Waterfront seafood restaurants are popular here, and with good reason. They feature fresh salmon steaks, kippered salmon—mild or strong—halibut, trout, Dungeness crabs, razor clams, large Pacific oysters and tiny Olympia oysters. Wild berries grow in profusion, and several areas are famous for particularly excellent fruits—the Wenatchee Valley for apples, Yakima for peaches, the Hood River Valley for Comice pears. Among the favored snacks of the region are Tillamook cheese, Frango ice cream, and apricot and apple candy.

D *California*

California produces fresh fruits and vegetables the year round in abundance *(pages 44-45)*. The state also provides 80 per cent of the wine consumed in the United States. The best vineyards are in the northern coastal counties around the San Francisco Bay area. Among the best red-wine grapes are Cabernet Sauvignon, Pinot Noir and Zinfandel. Among the whites, the best are Johannisberg Riesling and Pinot Chardonnay. Most of the major vineyards also produce good rosés. Rex and petrale sole and sand dabs are regional delicacies.

E *Mountain States*

The abundance of game lends a special zest to the cooking of this area. Delicious trout—rainbow, lake, steelhead and cutthroat—are abundant; so are black and white bass, grayling, crappie, char and perch. No visitor in hunting season should consider his stay complete until he has sampled the area's braised moose and venison steaks. Other popular game meats are whitetail deer and mule deer, while game birds include wild turkey, ruffed grouse, partridge and pheasant. Picnics where food is cooked over a campfire are popular.

F *Arizona, New Mexico, Texas*

Southwesterners barbecue everything from whole steers to quail. En route the grilled dishes include antelope, wild turkey, bear and *cabrito* (kid). Their most distinctive regional foods are the "Tex-Mex" dishes: enchiladas, tacos, wheat tortillas, tamale pie, chili con carne and *chiles rellenos*. Other favorite regional foods include wild brush honey, agarita jelly, pickled okra, mustang-grape pie, piñon nuts, mayhaw jelly and *garbanzo* salad. Southern dishes, such as black-eyed peas with okra, hominy bread and pecan pie, are popular too.

Kauai *Oahu* HAWAII
Honolulu *Molokai* B
Lanai *Maui*
Hawaii

G Plains States

Specialties in this region range from braised pheasant in the Dakotas to barbecued beef in southern Oklahoma. Nebraska is noted for its excellent beefsteaks; Dakota cooks turn out fine breads and pastries, many of them made from old Scandinavian recipes. Bohemian and Russian influences also are noticeable in the Dakotas, while Southern dishes are favored in parts of Oklahoma. Other foods popular in Oklahoma include fried rabbit and squirrel, navy beans cooked with ham hocks, and cornbread and hot biscuits.

H Midwest

Foreign cuisines have influenced cooking in many of the large cities of the Midwest. In Chicago, Milwaukee, St. Louis and Cincinnati the influence is mostly German. In Detroit and Cleveland, it's Polish. But in the southern parts of the region a more familiar influence—the cooking style of the South—prevails. Favored dishes in that area include persimmon pudding, poke greens and wilted lettuce. In the Great Lakes area, around the Ozark lake region and along the Mississippi River, freshwater fish—trout, bass and perch—are plentiful.

I New England

New England's lobsters, clams, scallops and salt-water fish are nationally acclaimed. This corner of the country is also famous for pure maple syrup, baked beans, brown bread and clam chowder. Less well known outside the region but also popular among New Englanders are sautéed cod cheeks and tongues, red-flannel hash, broiled tripe with mustard sauce, butternut fudge, beach-plum jelly, wild blueberries with cream and maple sugar, and a variety of dishes that were introduced to certain areas by the Portuguese.

J Mid-Atlantic

Almost every kind of cooking and imported food in the world can be found in New York City. The seafood throughout most of this region is outstanding—ranging from littleneck and cherrystone clams to striped bass and Chincoteague oysters. Epicures prize Maryland's terrapins, while nearly everyone likes New Jersey's beefsteak tomatoes. Strictly regional cooking prevails only among the Pennsylvania Dutch, who still make old-fashioned shoofly pie, *ponhaus* (scrapple) and memorably good chicken pot pie.

K The South

Southerners like grits for breakfast, served with eggs, bacon, fried apples and a host of other foods. They prefer hot bread—biscuits, rolls and cornbread—with every meal. Fried chicken and Smithfield or country ham are great regional specialties, and Southerners like to flavor their vegetables with salt pork, bacon or ham. The Deep South is the home of collard greens, cornbread and black-eyed peas. In New Orleans, the Creole cooking is a world unto itself, containing such unusual dishes as dirty rice, chicory coffee and Creole cream cheese.

L Florida

Florida's cooking owes its distinction to the state's wide variety of fruits and seafoods, and to the ingenuity of local cooks. Fruit dishes include Key lime pie and orange cake. Pineapples, fresh coconuts, kumquats, mangoes, avocados, papayas, guavas and tamarinds are also used in desserts, salads and relishes. Seafood specialties include shrimp prepared in a variety of ways, steamed stone crabs, broiled red snapper, sautéed pompano and coquina broth. Around Miami and Tampa, some of the best cooking is done in Cuban restaurants.

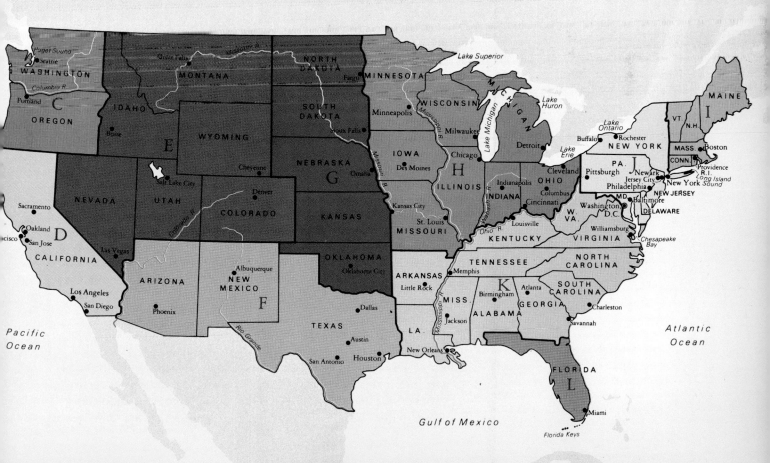

Another celebrated New England culinary invention, baked beans *(page 91)*, was also born of Yankee practicality. In the early days this nourishing combination of dried beans, salt pork, brown sugar and molasses or maple syrup—and a pinch of dry mustard—was often baked in the oven with the week's bread and kept there after the bread had been removed, thus making sure that every bit of remaining heat was utilized. As the beans cooked slowly in a glazed brown pot all day Saturday, the dish filled the house with its sugary aroma. That evening and the following day, the beans were eaten with hot slices of steamed brown bread. And even the brown bread had its practical side: one of its prime ingredients, rye flour, was milled from a grain that grew well in the cool climate.

The sensible nature of New England cooking set an example for much of the rest of the country, prompting pioneers to take many of the region's recipes and foodstuffs west with them. In fact, New England cooking may exist today in purer form in parts of the Dakotas, the Northwest or even Alaska than it does in those areas of the East vacated long ago by the original Yankees and inhabited now by people of Polish, Italian, Irish or Portuguese descent. Alaskans—some of them at least—may not know it, but they are following an old New England custom when they go out in the spring to cut the fuzzy, curled sprouts of fiddlehead fern just unwinding from the ground. In New England such a dish was

In an early American setting of pewterware and oil lamps, a New England boiled dinner *(page 90)* stands ready for serving at the Connecticut home of actress Bette Davis. The traditional dinner includes corned beef, cabbage, beets, carrots, onions and potatoes.

once an expedient, the first fresh vegetable of the new year, bringing relief from the monotony of a winter diet, but in Alaska (and elsewhere) today cooked fiddleheads, simmered gently and served in melted butter, are rightly considered a delicacy.

American regional cookery has been shaped also by nationalities and ethnic backgrounds. In some parts of the country Old World enclaves have survived almost intact with their own unique cooking styles. The Pennsylvania Dutch—who of course are not of Dutch descent at all, but German— preserve perhaps the purest ethnically derived, regional cookery in the United States. Not only does the rich farm land on which they live suggest in its appearance parts of Germany (especially the Palatinate, where most of the early settlers originated), but many of their dishes closely resemble those left behind in Germany by their ancestors almost 250 years ago. The Pennsylvania Dutch have always had the courage to be themselves, to be nothing but plain, and they cannot be budged from their principles. One of their most closely held beliefs is that food is God's reward for labor, God's gift to men. Reflecting the hard work they do, their food is solid fare, more practical than imaginative, but always good.

The Pennsylvania Dutch favor such hearty food as pork cooked in all manner of ways, including scrapple, bits of meat mixed with cornmeal and buckwheat and simmered for an hour, then put in cake tins to set be-

A variety of homemade Pennsylvania Dutch foods is displayed at the Green Dragon Market near Ephrata, Pennsylvania. Among the preserves included are watermelon-rind pickle, pickled peppers, jellies and fruit butters. Customers from a 100-mile radius patronize this market.

fore being sliced and fried. They like hams that are black on the outside with carbon from the pungent smoke of sassafras or hickory-wood fires, and their sausages are spiced with sage and coriander. Chicken, too, is another Pennsylvania Dutch favorite, simmered in well-seasoned broth between layers of homemade egg noodles and sliced raw potatoes. Corn is another of their staples. They cook dried corn with cream, butter, sugar, salt and pepper. Fresh corn is used in fritters, baked in pies, or eaten plain dripping with butter. Dried apple slices, simmered in water with ham and tiny yellow dumplings, are used to make a delicious main course called *schnitz un knepp*. And dandelion greens, over which a hot cider vinegar, egg and sugar dressing containing crisp tidbits of bacon is poured, make as sharp and refreshing a salad as can be eaten anywhere in the United States in the spring.

With the main stuff of dinner, the Pennsylvania Dutch are likely to take their sweets and sours, appetizing relishes and preserves that are made with home-grown produce. These may consist of jellies and jams, like blackberry and strawberry, bread-and-butter pickles, spiced peaches, pickled green peppers stuffed with chopped cabbage, pickled Jerusalem artichokes (crisp to the bite), pickled beets, gooseberry catsup—almost anything the homemaker can put up in jars and store in her cellar. Besides being made into relishes and even jams, tomatoes are sliced while still green, and baked in a pie shell. Or they may be fried and served in a cream sauce *(page 91)*, a dish so individual in character that it recommends itself for inclusion on a brunch table. Similarly, apples—including crab apples—are put to a variety of uses besides *schnitz un knepp* by the Pennsylvania Dutch, and the most savory of these is surely butter—apple butter, the essence of red, ripe fruit, reduced through slow boiling to a velvety and well-spiced spread *(page 77)*.

Ethnic backgrounds and nationalities have had their most widespread effect where immigration was most recent and where peoples of similar origins came to live in well-defined communities, as in the Midwest. All too often the Midwest is thought of solely in terms of its culinary classics, specialties such as Kansas corn chowder, Omaha's steaks, Chicago's planked whitefish, St. Louis' angel food cake, and Ohio's and Idaho's fried chicken (better, insist those who have tasted it, than the Southern variety). But what people who have not been to the Midwest so often fail to realize about this great region is that some of the finest foreign cooking in the United States is done there. Among the Poles of Chicago, the Czechs of Iowa, the Germans of Wisconsin, the Scandinavians of Minnesota, the Dutch of Michigan survive many of the most delicious of Old World favorites. *Kielbasa*—sausage made with pork, caraway and garlic—belongs as much to Chicago today as it does to Poland, and *kolaches*—pastries stuffed with poppy seeds, prunes or apricots—are such a normal part of coffeetime in Nebraska that one scarcely stops to think of them any longer as Bohemian. Not the least impressive point about the European flavor of so much Midwestern cookery is that the best of the old dishes show no signs of dying out here. Guaranteeing their survival are not only the love and nostalgia that go into their preparation, but the superiority of the American ingredients with which they are made.

I recall a weekend spent with friends in Galesburg, Illinois—as typically American a town as I could imagine, with its lawns, white clapboard houses with spacious front porches, and tall elms (many, alas, now gone), surrounded by rolling cornfields with pink and black hogs rooting among broken cornstalks. Yet this was a town filled with Americans of Swedish descent, very much in touch with the foods of their ancestors—and catering to their needs were stores with such Old World foods as *limpa*, lingonberries and *lutfisk*.

Eating in my friends' home was instructive. We had for dinner what one might have expected—and hoped to find—in the Midwest: individual steaks from a corn-fattened steer, baked potatoes and sautéed mushrooms (I was urged to come back when the wild morels were in season), and for dessert, a large wedge of apple pie, its flaky crust thrusting out over the tart apple slices lying shoulder to shoulder inside. But what interested me, and in retrospect pleased me more, was the food we ate at other intervals during the day. The morning had begun with coffeecake, warm and alive from the oven, smelling of cinnamon and butter, baked from a Galesburg recipe that puts crunchy crumbs and nutmeats in between layers of the batter as well as on top. Did I taste the faintest trace of Sweden in it? And with our afternoon coffee there were cookies, called by my hostess by their old Norwegian names, *goro, fattigmann, berliner-*

A Glossary of Odd Names for American Dishes

APPLE PANDOWDY *Deep-dish apple pie with a biscuit-dough top instead of pie crust*

BAREFOOT BREAD, also called CHURCH OF GOD CORNBREAD *Corn pone*

BOAT STEERS *Clam fritters*

CAPE COD TURKEY *Codfish balls*

CHITTERLINGS *Small intestines of a pig, dipped in batter and fried*

CORN PONE *Cornbread made without milk or eggs, and baked or fried*

CORN DODGERS *Hard sticks or cakes made from corn-pone batter*

DIRTY RICE *Rice mixed with ground chicken giblets*

FANNYDADDIES *Fried clams*

GRUNT *Stewed berries with a dumpling topping*

HANGTOWN FRY *Oysters and beaten eggs fried in butter*

HOE CAKES *Biscuit dough baked on the blade of a hoe in an open fire*

HOPPIN' JOHN *Black-eyed peas and rice*

HUSH PUPPIES *Spoonfuls of cornbread batter fried in deep fat*

JERKY *Dried strips of beef, buffalo or venison*

JOLLY BOYS *The fried center of the doughnut, cut out when the doughnut is made*

LIMPING SUSAN *Braised rice and okra*

RED-EYE GRAVY *Gravy made from the pan juices of fried country ham*

SHOOFLY PIE *Crumb-crust pie with filling of molasses, brown sugar and spices*

SNICKERDOODLES *Cookies rolled in sugar and cinnamon*

STACK OF WHEATS *Pancakes*

STREAK OF LEAN *Salt pork*

STRICKLE SHEETS *Pennsylvania Dutch coffeecake*

kranser, krumkaker—spoken, I should add, with a Midwestern accent, yet pronouncedly Scandinavian in taste.

The charming woman who was my hostess may be a third-generation American (descended on her father's side from Danes, and on her mother's side from Norwegians), but she has by no means lost touch with her cultural roots. Her cookie recipes, handed down to her by her mother, are her only heirlooms, and she has committed them to memory and will pass them on to her daughters. Whatever other Norwegian specialties she may want to summon up out of the past, she can find by consulting a gift from her mother, a collection of Scandinavian recipes put out by the Nordic Arts Club of Northfield, Minnesota.

The Old World influence can be felt almost everywhere you go in the United States. Even the oldest of American cooking styles, the New England and the Southern, can be shown to have slightly foreign accents. How else can we explain the presence in the regional cookbooks of these areas of grunts and fools, English desserts that continue to be enjoyed by some people in England today—to say nothing of dozens of other basically English dishes. Southern cooking, despite its Anglo-Saxon origins (which were modified, somewhat, by African cooks), has a strong dash of French in it as well—and I am not thinking simply of New Orleans cooking. Many of the Huguenots who came to the Colonies in the late 17th Century settled in the Carolinas to lend a lasting flavor to Southern food, as did the French planters of Santo Domingo who fled to America after the revolt of the Negro slaves and mulattoes in the early 1790s and established themselves in Baltimore and other Southern cities.

Yet nowhere in the United States, perhaps, is the culinary effect of ethnic and national backgrounds more evident than in New York City. Here Hungarians, Italians, Germans, Puerto Ricans, Chinese and others have transplanted their cooking and their culture, settling often in enclaves where Old Country languages are spoken and familiar foodstuffs are sold in stores. And the varied ethnic and national groups, rubbing shoulders together, have given New York a distinctive cosmopolitan flavor that makes it a region unto itself. Among New York's many pleasures are the foods contributed by different ethnic groups, including, for example, the city's Jewish population. To paraphrase a familiar New York advertisement, "You don't have to be Jewish to like Jewish food." Chopped chicken livers, a Jewish specialty, has acquired a fame far beyond New York's five boroughs. New York's cheesecake—which is creamier and smoother and richer than the cheesecake in any other American city—is known the country wide. Also special—and also a part of New York's Jewish inheritance—are hot pastrami, a spicy, cured beef, speckled with cracked kernels of coriander and black pepper; and tender lox, a delicately salted and smoked slab of pinkest salmon, sliced thin and "noshed" with cream cheese and bagels (those shiny, doughnutlike rolls that are boiled *and* baked).

All of these areas already mentioned—New York, New England, the Middle Atlantic states and the Midwest—have long been familiar to me. But until quite recently I had not had an opportunity to acquaint myself with the food in other parts of the country and to study the influences that have affected it. And so my wife and I, with our two-year-old daughter, embarked on an extended gastronomic tour of the country. Before our journey was over, we would have tasted everything from Florida's Key lime pie *(page 94)* and South Carolina's wild orange marmalade (a real rarity) to Louisiana's mirliton, or vegetable pear, stuffed with Gulf shrimp, and Oregon's kippered salmon. I welcomed so unique an opportunity to show my Dutch wife this beautiful country and to introduce her to its regional cooking—but I was also, to tell the truth, a little worried. I felt that mass communications and mass travel might have succeeded in throwing a net of conformity over many formerly colorful areas. How wrong I was, only the trip could tell.

We decided to make our first stop Williamsburg, Virginia, thinking that here we might taste many of the old Southern specialties. We knew of the town's proximity to Smithfield, home of Smithfield hams, and to Chesapeake Bay, which from the first days of this country's history has been sending to the tables of Easterners and others a providential hoard of crabs, oysters and fish. But we had another reason for going there: throughout an especially hectic autumn, New York had been all too much with us, and we looked forward to spending a few days immersed in another century, an illusion that can seem almost real in Williamsburg off-season, when the streets are all but empty of tourists.

We left on the worst of disagreeable days, with the wind throwing fistfuls of snow into our faces as we dashed for our plane. And what was to have been a short flight was drawn out into a long one by the storm, which eventually put us down four hours late at Norfolk, instead of Newport News, where we were supposed to land. We were in no mood to think happy thoughts when we crossed the bridge over Hampton Roads in a bus. The water on either side, pounded by the wind, looked like beaten lead. But by the time we had arrived at Williamsburg, with darkness all around us and little lights in the windows, our mood had begun to change, and we realized suddenly that we were hungry. And so we ate.

I remember the supper well. It was our introduction to that Southern institution, the pannier of hot breads; only in this instance, it was not a basket that came to the table, with the breads done up in a napkin, but a stainless-steel box, with rolltop front. From its maw the waitress brought forth with tongs biscuits (hot and powdery, soaking up melting butter), rolls (yeasty and as soft outside as our baby daughter's cheek), tiny, crumbly corn muffins and miniature Graham gems, crisp all around the edges. I spotted fried chicken on the menu, and recommended it to my wife, who had never had it before. For myself, I chose a Chesapeake Bay rockfish, broiled and flaky. And together we drank to the trip—and to the first of our many American meals on it—with a tart, white German wine.

Liet loved the chicken, and its crisp, succulent goodness had her nibbling at the bones. I explained to her how she had just eaten one of America's most controversial foods, which surprised her. How could anything so downright simple be controversial, she wondered. I explained that every Southern cook had her own way of preparing it, some dipping the chicken pieces in batter, some in buttermilk, some in nothing at all; some frying them in deep fat, some in only a little fat, some in oil.

One of the things Liet admired about the meal was the genteel way it was served. There was a Southern grace about our waitress and waiter, a delightful unhurriedness, that showed that they too knew that good food can't be rushed. But Liet was even more charmed by the presence of finger bowls on the table and half a lemon done up in cheesecloth for my fish, which enabled me to squeeze out the juice without getting any seeds. Bred to expect such touches, Europeans are more than thankful when they find them in America, where all too often these are displaced by casualness—which Liet would agree has its own definite advantages.

The Southern breakfast was, we knew, a large one; but we had not expected to encounter a meal quite so large as the Plantation Breakfast we wakened to the next morning. Dutch breakfasts are enormous, but even Liet could do no more than make a few selections here and there from the dining-room table that bore squarely on its broad, mahogany shoulders this staggering array of food. Up at one end stood great bowls of grits, which a waiter served to us in big spoonfuls—and into which we were urged to put several pats of butter. A little way down the line was a large panful of creamed chipped beef, surrounded by dishes bearing, among other things, spiced apples, crinkled, fried bacon and glistening pork sausages. Eggs, sunny-side-up or once-over-lightly, were ours for the asking. Beyond the eggs reared a large Virginia ham, from which several slices had already been carved, and a pile of golden fried chicken. And down at the farthest end of the table were stacks of toast and various breads—and plates of griddle-hot buckwheat pancakes, ready to be glazed with maple syrup or honey and melted butter.

How right we had been to start our trip in Williamsburg. Our daughter could run through the formal gardens chasing peacocks, and we could wander from one old kitchen to another, which had been given an added note of authenticity by the log fires kept burning in the fireplaces to take away the chill. At the bakery behind the Raleigh Tavern, which I visited alone, they were making gingerbread, and its warm, spicy odor forced me to buy a cookie and then a large gingerbread man for my girls. That night we attended a candlelight concert in the Governor's Palace, the path lit with lanterns, the entry hall black and yellow from the light of a crackling fire, and the ballroom aglitter with honey-colored sparkles refracted from the crystal chandeliers in which tall candles burned.

We came away from Williamsburg rested and in a mood for travel, exhilarated by the prospect of the delicious food we would find waiting for us along the way. Our next stop was Charleston, South Carolina. We had chosen it because we knew that it was a city proud of its traditions and culinary reputation. And yet at first we had our doubts. We arrived in Charleston on a Sunday night; the city seemed half dead, and when we searched out a suitable restaurant, I had to rap more than once before a woman in red appeared and indifferently opened the door.

Having come so far (and having had this place recommended to us highly by the people at our hotel), we were in no mood for a bad meal. When we were seated at a table, my eyes lit on roast oysters, printed in bold type on the menu, and I convinced Liet that we should try them. This, after all, was a Southern coastal specialty. I had read about oyster roasts held under the live oaks, with the Spanish moss hanging down in festoons over the tables, and I told Liet how it was the custom for the cook to shovel the scrubbed oysters onto a piece of sheet iron over a fire and cook them under wet burlap.

Our oysters arrived in a big steel box, a couple of dozen or more. Onto each of our plates was dropped a rolled napkin, containing a small, daggerlike knife with a blunt blade and a rounded tip, and a laborer's cotton glove—puzzlingly, with two thumbs. The gauntlet had been tossed, so to speak; and after our reception we were in a fighting mood. The oysters had better be good!

We put on the gloves and, all thumbs, clasped an oyster in our hands, worked the blade between the shell and pried it open. Inside, steaming hot, but only just cooked, lay a little pocket of oyster flesh. I ate mine at once. It was filled with the buttery ocean flavor that is an oyster's alone, and we pounced on another and another—dipping them sometimes in hot sauce but preferring more often to eat them plain. Eating roast oysters is a delightfully sloppy business, properly done outdoors, and we were thankful for the absorbent glove and the big napkin. The point of the two thumbs, we were told, is to provide a glove that left-handers or right-handers can use in the contest to see who can eat the most oysters. We managed to find a use for the extra thumb, however—as soon as the first was wet through, we switched to the second. And for the first time that evening, we laughed.

"Try my flounder, stuffed with crab," said the woman in red. And to erase any doubts that we might have had about its being fresh, she pointed to the picture window and to the fishing boats moored at the dock outside. "The fish were caught this morning." We had heard *that* before, but to my amazement, this time it proved to be true. The creamy crab was good enough in itself, but the fresh flounder was firm and tender, as good a fish as we had had in a long while.

We found out the next day that Charleston was not the dead city we had imagined it to be; in fact, we would call it one of the most charming, the most visually exciting, of American cities. We had the morning to ourselves, and the three of us went out to explore the town, and to build an appetite, which Liet and I found necessary after a breakfast of pecan waffles and honey. We were in downtown Charleston, and we decided to head toward the Battery, or harbor area; at once the city began to assert itself. The houses were mostly white, with long, double-story piazzas running from the street front through to the gardens; here and there palms poked up, and we brushed past palmettos fanning out over walls.

We had been directed to a restaurant beyond the old Charleston market. We had been warned that the restaurant would not be fancy, and it certainly wasn't, with plastic-topped tables and a screen door that slapped shut; but it had a scrubbed neatness that we found promising. We ordered as plain a Southern meal as we could find on the menu—pork, collard greens, black-eyed peas and candied sweet potatoes. Now I think I can understand why many Southerners in the North become nostalgic at mention of these. There is a heartiness to such food, and the collard greens and beans have a meaty quality about them that is satisfying. Whatever bitterness the greens may possess I like. Accustomed as we are to

Old-fashioned Apple Butter

To make about 3 pints

4 pounds tart apples
2 cups cider
4 to 5 cups sugar
2 teaspoons cinnamon
1 teaspoon ground cloves
½ teaspoon ground allspice

Cut the apples into quarters but do not peel or seed them. Combine them with the cider in an enameled or stainless-steel pot. Bring the cider to a boil, then reduce the heat to its lowest point and cover the pot. Simmer the apples, stirring them occasionally, for about 25 minutes, or until they are soft. Remove from the heat and, with the back of a wooden spoon, mash the apples through a sieve. Measure the pulp and transfer it to a 6- to 8-quart casserole or heavy saucepan. Add ½ cup of sugar for every cup of pulp, and add the cinnamon, cloves and allspice. Stirring occasionally, cook over medium heat about 4 hours, or until a tablespoon of the apple butter will stick to a saucer when the saucer is turned upside down. Ladle the apple butter that is to be stored into sterilized jars. Let it cool to room temperature, then seal it with paraffin and cover it tightly.

Charleston Okra Soup

1 large beef bone (plenty of meat)
2 medium onions (chopped)
3 pounds fresh okra, chopped fine
Salt and pepper, bay leaf
3 quarts water
1 piece breakfast bacon
8 large fresh tomatoes, or 2 (No. 2½)
    cans tomatoes

Cook meat in water slowly for 2 hours.
Add okra, bacon and peeled tomatoes,
bay leaf, onions, and salt and pepper
to taste. Let cook another two hours;
add more water if needed. Hot rice
and buttered corn sticks are a tasty
accompaniment. Serves 8-10.
    —From Charleston Receipts,
    compiled by the Junior League
    of Charleston, S.C., Inc.

inflated New York prices, we found it hard to believe that such a lunch could cost only $1.25 a person.

Our dinner date that evening was for 7:30. We were the guests of the William Chapmans, who live in one of Charleston's big, old houses. We had drinks first in the spacious living room, the walls of which rise higher and higher and disappear in shadows. Dinner was served in a long dining room, at a table set with family china and silver. The meal began with okra soup, another first for me; Liet knew okra from Indonesia, where this conical green pod, filled with small, plump seeds, is as much appreciated and used as it is in the South—but certainly she had never had okra cooked this way before. Mrs. Chapman—a talented cook who runs her own restaurant at Middleton Place outside Charleston—had followed an old recipe, cutting the okra into quarter-inch slices, and simmering it with tomatoes, onions, salt, pepper and bay leaf, and shin beef; but she had given it a modern touch by whirling it in the blender. Out had come a kind of a purée, which lay thick on the spoon, and tasted so good that Liet and I both had seconds.

The course that followed involved another Charleston specialty, shrimp, which here can range from the tiny variety found in the creeks to the larger river specimens and the biggest of all, those from the ocean. The ones we ate were of the middling kind, sweet and crisp, without a trace of the iodine flavor sometimes found in shrimp. They had been bathed in a delicious curry-flavored cream sauce and were served on a bed of rice. With these we ate a cheese-flavored casserole of small, sliced summer squash, highly peppered.

We were curious to know more about Charleston eating habits, and while we were dining the Chapmans sketched in some of the details. They told us of summer breakfasts of grits (or hominy, as grits are called here) with a lake of butter in the middle, boiled shrimp and ice-cold slices of garden-ripe tomatoes. They also explained to us the Charleston custom of 2 o'clock weekday dinners—keeping the old English hour—with perhaps a siesta afterward, and of long Sunday afternoons following church, with glasses of bourbon preceding a large, leisurely, family-style meal. Such a meal might include okra or she-crab soup (rich and creamy with tiny beads of red crab roe floating in it), roast beef, rice and gravy, sweet potatoes, two vegetables—perhaps turnip greens, string beans or baked squash —hot breads and relishes, and for dessert, Lady Baltimore cake or a crunchy pecan pie (page 94).

Charleston was so impressive it would make much of what we were subsequently to see in the South seem anticlimactic—with the exception of New Orleans. We approached that city with apprehension, if not prejudice —at least I did. I was all too aware of its advertised image as *la belle* Nouvelle Orléans: somehow I expected to find it about as real as a Mardi Gras float. But behind the all too familiar wrought-iron look of the Vieux Carré, the old French quarter, we soon found cool courtyards, with moss-dotted walls of damp, crumbling brick, where quietness descended. And in the Garden District, closest to our hotel, we discovered a whole other city of stately homes conveying Greek Revival elegance through columned porches and handsome doorways. But I suppose all we would have actually needed to convince us of New Orleans' individuality was one taste of its food—and that came soon enough.

Creole cookery still flourishes here, and of the many cooking styles practiced in the United States, it is the most fully developed, the one most deserving to be called a cuisine. Truly it is a superb melange, a beautiful blend of French, Spanish, Anglo-Saxon and Indian influences, as interpreted and modified by Negro cooks using local ingredients—crabs, oysters, crawfish, hot pepper sauce, filé powder (made from the finely crushed leaves of sassafras). Creole cooking is extremely subtle, such a carefully contrived balance of seasonings that no one spice or herb ever asserts itself over another in a recipe—neither the thyme, nor the bay leaf, nor the garlic that are Creole favorites.

But in spite of its complexity and richness, Creole food reflects the greatest of household economies. Creole cooks have always been hardheaded. They learned that leftover rice and meat made a perfectly acceptable jambalaya *(page 97)*, a beautiful and savory dish derived from the Spanish *paella* (New Orleans was ruled by Spain between 1762 and 1803), and they knew how to turn other odds and ends into delicious croquettes, *rissoles* and soufflés. And such were their skills that they could take a poor cut of beef, splash it with wine, then sprinkle it with herbs and spices, slowly simmer it and have it emerge new-born again as *daube*—or when cooked with pig's or calf's feet, as *daube glacé*, which they served cold (and still do) in shimmering, spicy slices.

I talked about Creole cooking with Jim Plauché, owner of Corinne Dunbar's, a restaurant specializing in Creole food. Jim is himself a Creole (in New Orleans this is the designation for a descendant of the original French and Spanish inhabitants, not a person of mixed blood). We sat by the indoor Roman pool of his house in the Vieux Carré, drinking sazeracs, a New Orleans cocktail consisting of rye, a touch of Pernod, a few drops of bitters, a little sugar and a twist of lemon. Jim outlined for me the five steps to perfect Creole cooking. These are, in the order he gave them, the iron pot, preferably a well-used one; the brown *roux* (made from flour and butter); the stock (often made from bits and parts of an animal that less-wise cooks might throw away); the herbs and spices; and finally, the spirits.

While Jim Plauché was growing up, it was the custom in his parents' home to have gumbo on Fridays and red beans and rice on Mondays. The last is a standardized dish; it always contains, in addition to rice and beans, either ham or salt pork, and it is good in its plainness and its pleasing combination of textures. Gumbo, by contrast, is a variably seasoned dish of many possibilities; half soup, half stew, it is known throughout the South, but nowhere has it come to such perfection as in New Orleans *(Recipe Booklet)*. Although the word for it is derived from the Congolese for okra, Creole versions often omit the okra. Gumbo may be made from a wide assortment of meats and shellfish—turkey, rabbit, squirrel, wild duck, crab, oysters, shrimp. There is even a *gumbo z'herbes,* which may contain upwards of a dozen fresh greens and herbs.

Only a short while before going on our trip, Liet and I had studied an elaborate recipe for a Creole gumbo made from oysters, crabs, shrimp

---

She-Crab Soup

"She-crab" is much more of a delicacy than "he-crab," as the eggs add a special flavor to the soup. The street vendors in Charleston make a point of calling "she-crab," and of charging extra for them.

1 tablespoon butter
1 quart milk
¼ pint cream (whipped)
Few drops onion juice
⅛ teaspoon mace
⅛ teaspoon pepper
½ teaspoon Worcestershire
1 teaspoon flour
2 cups white crab meat and crab eggs
½ teaspoon salt
4 tablespoons dry sherry

Melt butter in top of double boiler and blend with flour until smooth. Add the milk gradually, stirring constantly. To this add crab meat and eggs, and all seasoning except sherry. Cook slowly over hot water for 20 minutes. To serve place one tablespoon of warmed sherry in individual soup bowls, then add soup and top with whipped cream. Sprinkle with paprika or finely chopped parsley. Secret: if unable to obtain "she-crabs," crumble yolk of hard-boiled eggs in bottom of soup plates. Serves 4-6.
—From *Charleston Receipts,*
compiled by the Junior League
of Charleston, S.C., Inc.

and okra; veal, chicken wings and ham bone; onions, garlic, bay leaf, thyme, green pepper, black pepper, parsley and tomatoes; Tabasco, Worcestershire and lemon juice. The recipe had left us terribly hungry, but we had despaired of ever assembling all the ingredients for it, much less of finding the time to cook it. Now here was that very dish, delivered to our room as the kind offering of Lysle Aschaffenburg, owner-manager of the Pontchartrain Hotel. It had been made especially for us by Mr. and Mrs. Aschaffenburg's personal cook, whose trick is to sauté the okra before adding it to the pot to rid this vegetable of its mucilaginous juice (a trick the recipe, though crediting Mr. Aschaffenburg as the source, neglected to include). One taste of this seafood gumbo had us crying out in delight; the more we ate of it, the hungrier we became. It was as delicious a dish as we were to encounter on the entire trip. And how secretly relieved we were to eat the gumbo in the privacy of our room, and not in the Caribbean Room downstairs, which, though probably New Orleans' finest restaurant, would have been too formal a setting for our way of attacking the gumbo. We picked up the red pieces of cracked crab and sucked all the meat and goodness out of their shells; and then we scraped right down to the bottom of the bowl with the serving spoon and licked it and our forks clean.

Pursuing a respected New Orleans custom, we breakfasted the next day, a Sunday, at Brennan's. Ella Brennan, a moving spirit behind the restaurant, sat down at the table with us. She was in a mood to show us her best. To awaken our appetites and prime them, Ella ordered a milk punch for Liet, *Suissesse*, which tasted of Pernod, for me—and for Elisabeth, a plain milk with two straws. With our appetites now wide awake, we were ready to cope with a large tureen of oyster soup, and even the two poached-egg dishes that followed; but we began to falter with the third breakfast course, roast quail, dressed in a red-wine sauce and sitting in a nest of wild rice and diced artichoke hearts. "I wanted you to taste a little of our Louisiana game," explained Ella, toasting us with tart Moselle that made dessert just seem possible. I had Crêpes Fitzgerald, a famous Brennan's dish, filled with cream cheese and sour cream, over which crushed strawberries flamed in kirsch had been dribbled. Liet tried another Brennan's specialty, Bananas Foster, coated with a rum sauce. The effect of so much food and drink, so early in the morning, was soporific, and Ella must have seen the laziness creeping over Liet and me, for she invited us out into the lush courtyard behind the dining room for *café brûlot*, a stimulating New Orleans decoction of strong black coffee, flavored with cloves, cinnamon and orange and lemon peel, and set afire with curaçao and cognac. After such a breakfast, we had but one alternative —to taxi back to the Pontchartrain and join Elisabeth for her nap. It was a great, fat bourgeois kind of nap; I'm sure that I must have snored, but Liet, who looked over at me in my slumber, said that I made not a sound, that I looked as relaxed as she had ever seen me.

Our visit to New Orleans would not have been well rounded if we had failed to eat crawfish, those tiny fresh-water crustaceans that are caught by the thousands in the swamps and bayous around the city and cooked by the Creoles and Cajuns in multiple ways—and, as far as we are con-

The pecan pie's rich, nutty flavor has made it a classic in the Old South and the Southwest, where pecan trees abound.

cerned, always deliciously. I undertook what amounted to a cram course in the crawfish at the Bon Ton, a small restaurant with a Cajun owner (Cajuns are descendants of the Acadians, the displaced French settlers of Nova Scotia). There I had a thick crawfish bisque, with the bright red heads —stuffed with the meat, garlic and bread crumbs—bobbing on top. This was followed in succession by crawfish *étouffée*, a sautéed mixture of crawfish, onions, garlic, green pepper, celery and parsley, among other things; crawfish Newburg; crawfish omelet; and crawfish jambalaya. I had found it hard not to eat all of everything presented to me, so extraordinarily new and delicious did I find the flavors; but I held back. Deciding that I would be hurting the owner's feelings if I refused his dessert, which he seemed anxious for me to try, I sampled some: it was bread pudding, not the plain pudding I had known in childhood and later forgotten, but a New Orleans version, made with chunks of French bread, over which a warm and sugary bourbon-and-butter sauce was poured. I ate it all.

The owner of the Bon Ton assured me that in Cajun country, where he came from, "people eats like this every day." They may well do that, but after all, he did say that "you will not make a good bisque in less than two days." He was certainly speaking from pride; this is a dish not to be trifled with, but with care it can be cooked outside Louisiana and it should be: it is too good to be restricted to one region alone *(page 96)*.

The next day we found ourselves blinking in Texas sunshine, under a silver-blue sky, waiting to be met at the Austin airport by Wick Fowler, the celebrated chili expert. We had come to Texas not only to taste chili on its home ground, but to see regional cookery in the process of growing. While both New Orleans' and Charleston's cooking styles are deeply rooted in the past, Texas'—as such things go—is relatively young, in a state of flux, very much a product of the New World. It is being shaped increasingly by the sophistication that money brings, but is proud still of its honesty. (One Texan told me of serving Danish pastries at a party, and of the winning comment of a guest, "The best dang fried pies I ever set tooth to.")

Like the cooking of New Mexico and Arizona, Texas cooking today exhibits the strong influence of northern Mexico, with its chili pepper and cumin base. *Cabrito*, baked kid, one favorite delicacy of that area, is also much appreciated in parts of this enormous state. But the Texans are doing more than turning out facsimiles of Indian-inspired Mexican dishes; they are using these foods as departures for a Tex-Mex cookery of their own, either giving their recipes less spice than the originals, or—and this is often the case—a great deal more. The enchiladas of German-descended Texans are richer and blander than their Mexican prototypes, but *chiles rellenos*, Texas style, can raise the hair *(page 98)*. It is perhaps still too early to say what Texas cookery will be like in another dozen years, but I hope that here and elsewhere in the great culinary leap forward, all recipes for congealed salad, that inland jellyfish of many hues and ingredients (known also as the gelatin salad), will have been forgotten and replaced by something more intrinsically edible.

Wick Fowler—who came up to us on the sidewalk outside the airport waiting room with a warm apology for being late—struck us at once as a

Café Brûlot

1 cinnamon stick, 4 inches long
12 whole cloves
Peel of 2 oranges, cut into thin slivers
Peel of 2 lemons, cut into thin slivers
6 sugar lumps
8 ounces brandy, warmed
2 ounces curaçao
1 quart strong black coffee

In a brûlot bowl or chafing dish set over an alcohol flame, mash the cinnamon, cloves, orange peel, lemon peel and sugar lumps with a ladle. Add the brandy and curaçao, and stir together. Carefully ignite the brandy and mix until the sugar is dissolved. Gradually add the black coffee and continue mixing until the flame flickers out. Serves 10-12.
—From Brennan's Restaurant, New Orleans

The ceremonious creation of *café brûlot (opposite)*, with a spiral of orange peel and flaming brandy, is the traditional conclusion to breakfast at Brennan's, a famed restaurant in an old New Orleans townhouse.

man who enjoys his own chili (he weighs 225 pounds), and my daughter took to him in a way that she had not, a few days earlier, to Santa Claus. In a very short while she was calling him "Uncle Week."

"You know that chili is not Mexican?" said Wick, steering the car with one hand while he reached for a package of his own product, Two-Alarm Chili, which he handed to Liet. Thus began our education in chili. Driving through flat country with an occasional pecan tree poised like a many-armed candelabra in the landscape, we heard of chili's beginnings in San Antonio—and its popularization there in the last decades of the 19th Century. It was made then from such purely local ingredients as *chile ancho*—a coarse red pepper looked down upon by the Mexicans to the south—wild marjoram and tough beef, so tough it had to be chopped to make it chewable. When a German in New Braunfels, Texas, found a way to extract the pulp from the chili pods and mix this with the right combination of spices, chili powder was born, and only six years later, in 1908, he was successfully canning chili con carne in San Antonio. Thus began the chili brush fire that has never been put out, not even with beer, searing its happy victims wherever it may strike and turning them into lifetime fans of "the brimstone bowl" *(page 99)*.

We were presented with a kettle of Wick's chili that night at dinner. It had the bite of hot lava and was made from coarsely ground beef, not chopped meat, and the traditional sparking spices. A little *masa*, stone-ground cornmeal, had been used to tighten up the juices, and that was all: beans were conspicuous by their absence. (To purists, namely Texans, beans are an intrusion.) A rare steak soothed our tongues, and vanilla ice cream at the end of the meal snuffed out the last of the flames. With the dessert, Wick demonstrated how an accident can be a discovery: he poured a little tequila onto our ice cream and asked us to taste it. The combination was a good one, as good certainly as kirsch and ice cream, and he confessed that he had hit upon it when a waiter reached one night for the Cointreau bottle and picked up the tequila instead.

From Austin we went to San Antonio, to meet Maury Maverick Jr., yet another chili expert. He and his wife threw a party at their house, at which the drink was Border Buttermilk, a stiff brew concocted from frozen lime juice and tequila. The weather had turned suddenly cold during the day, with steam rising off the swimming pools, and the banana trees drooping in people's yards. The Mavericks had lit a fire in their fireplace by turning on their logs—which concealed gas jets—"a sign," said Maury, "of pure laziness." The combination of Border Buttermilk and the fire was a relaxing one, and soon we were out in the back pantry with Mrs. Maverick examining her pie safe, a cupboard with meshed doors that used to be a standard feature in Texas homes; under each leg a cup of water would be placed, into which any pie-hungry ants would fall. Mrs. Maverick demonstrated to Liet how simple it was to prepare some of the Mexican-style snacks she had been serving with the drinks. She took a crisp wedge of fried tortilla, cut a triangular piece of sharp, orange cheese to put on top, broiled it for a moment with a slice of jade-green *jalapeño chile* and then spooned a little sour cream on the pointed edge. Thus a *nacho* was born before our eyes.

While Liet and I moved around the living room talking to various guests, Maury Maverick was at his typewriter recording for our benefit his own favorite chili recipe, with its admonition to "add meat and sear over high heat—stirring constantly until meat is grey, not brown." A very masculine observation. And when it was time for us to go, Maury, as though to imprint once and for all in our mind the idea that chili is an American invention, took out a Mexican dictionary and proudly translated: "*Chile con carne:* detestable food with the false Mexican title which is sold in the United States from Texas to New York."

Texas cookery—as these things go—may be at a somewhat early stage of evolution (the barbecue became popular only a couple of decades ago), but I, for one, find it all the more interesting for being so demonstrably young. West Coast cookery, though also young, by contrast seems already to express a fully developed style. It is American in the best sense of the word, as Liet and I discovered, which means that it is imaginative, colorful, wonderfully free, open and responsive to outside influences, whether these be Mexican, Russian, Japanese or Mediterranean.

But it is also regional cookery, in a most up-to-date way, reflecting a whole new, easygoing way of life. Here, more than in any other area of the country, climate and geography have determined how people live and eat. For example, in the Pacific Northwest the coastal waters, warmed by currents from Japan, take the curse off winter and make cooking outdoors feasible through much of the year. Furthermore, the ocean teems with oysters, clams and fish, and Northwesterners have developed their own ways of preparing them *(page 142),* sometimes by adapting old Indian procedures

Opposite: New Orleans diners enjoy a "crab boil," one of their famous city's oldest culinary delights. The popular shirtsleeve feast includes boiled crabs, crawfish and shrimp, highly seasoned and washed down with beer.

to new recipes. Near the coast, where the rainfall is abundant, Japanese truck farms produce some of the most luscious vegetables in the nation *(pages 46-47)*, and these are brought directly to the markets of the Northwest, fresh from the dark, rich soil. To the east of the Cascade Range, the drier terrain is ideal for wheat and fruit orchards, and pears and apples come round and ripe to tables at harvesttime.

West Coast cookery—whether practiced in Washington, Oregon or California (the world's *new* fertile crescent)—is a cookery founded on freshness and variety. The range of foods available to cooks, coupled with the creative viewpoint of the people, impressed Liet and me deeply, and we ranged as far afield as possible to check out our impressions. We wandered wide-eyed through Seattle's Pike Place Market and found ourselves just as excited by Los Angeles' Farmers' Market. We ate salmon, kippered, pickled and broiled, in Oregon, and we discovered the pleasures of Olympia oysters in Washington. We dined one night in San Francisco on cioppino *(page 102)* and then picnicked in St. Mary's Park the next day on hot snacks from a Chinese delicatessen. And that evening, we sat down in the honey-colored light of the Palace Court and waited hungrily for the hotel's famous seafood salad *(page 105)*. Actually—when I think back on it now—we need not have roamed so widely. We could have deduced almost as much about West Coast living and cooking by staying in one place, Cambria Pines, a small settlement directly on the coast, just south of San Simeon. Here during winter live our friends George and Helen Papashvily, authors of the best-selling book *Anything Can Happen*.

From the beginning, it was a relaxing experience. Driving through grass-covered, wrinkled hills toward home, George stopped the car beside a glen to get out and knife from a leaf-laden tree a sprig of California's laurel or bay; at once the car filled up with its odor, and Liet and I crushed the tough leaves with our fingers and soaked up their tingling perfume. A little later, he stopped again, and Helen got out this time and came back from a bakery with a great, crusty loaf of sourdough French bread for us to taste. We pulled the loaf apart with bay-scented fingers and ate hungrily from it. The bread was slightly acidulous and gummy, but not sour or chewy enough for Helen, who remembers what it was like when she was a girl growing up in California. But for me, it put in mind a perfect New Year's Eve supper I had once had in San Francisco, where the food consisted of cracked Dungeness crab, this bread and champagne.

We arrived at the Papashvilys' house, to be met by their golden retriever, whose personality is indisputably happy, and he pranced alongside us with swinging tongue into sun-filled rooms, from every window of which there was a gleaming view of the Pacific. After a drink we had lunch, and it was an appropriate meal, putting first things first by consisting of tamales and enchiladas, twin dishes that descend directly from the oldest cooking style of this immensely colorful region. Helen was quick to point out the differences between a California tamale and a Mexican one. The California version is about four times as big, and is beautiful not only to eat but to see. As its corn-husk wrappings are peeled away, they leave their ladderlike imprint on the *masa*, or cornmeal casing inside—and this, forked open, reveals a gorgeous stuffing of meat.

In Pojoaque, New Mexico, red chilis are hung out to dry. Picked in autumn, they will season the region's hot dishes.

On the table sat a small bouquet of orange-red nasturtiums, fresh from the garden, each flower like a little paw print; and the light surrounding us was silver, cast into the room by the mirror of the Pacific. A Vermeer-like calm drifted down on us as we spooned up our dessert, California apricots, preserved without any sugar at all by a friend of Helen's, and yet marvelously sweet—and so incredibly soft that we could burst them, like Keats's grape, against our palates fine.

Our handful of days in Cambria moved on casually; one day we picnicked on the beach, driving through a pasture to get there past a flock of wild turkeys strutting up a hill, then through a herd of brown and white cattle with the spotted calves dancing away to Elisabeth's delight. We parked the car and descended a cliff, in a human chain, and sat upon the pebbles before a surrealistic seascape while seals flopping around on a rock in the distance barked at us. We cut off great slices of creamy-colored Monterey, a mild California cheese, and arranged these on a bed of sour bread and sweet butter, and then washed everything down with a deep-red Napa Valley Burgundy.

That afternoon we went shopping for dinner at a fish market on a spit of land jutting out into the sea. The air had the damp, cool, exciting freshness I associate with so much of the West Coast, and mingling in it were puffs of crab-scented steam billowing from a red-brick cooker just outside the entrance. Helen bought some cracked Dungeness crab legs, and several slices of abalone (in an adjacent room I could see the large mallet with which the white meat of this California shellfish had been pounded to soften it). When I pointed out to Helen some large Morro Bay oysters, she bought those too, and we went home to cook this trove of Pacific seafood. Helen broiled the oysters until the edges began to curl slightly, and we started the meal with these. Then we had the cracked Dungeness crab, and what a pleasure that was. We picked the sweet morsels of meat from the legs and dipped them in lemon-and-mayonnaise sauce; not the least exciting thing about eating the crab was that we could have as much as we wanted. Helen went back into the kitchen to fry the abalone steaks, and we watched her from the table. She stood there at her stove, at stiff attention, ticking away like a human time bomb: "One, two, three, four, five. . . ." Abalone must not be cooked a second too long, or it will toughen and lose its subtlety.

"If you ever liked sucking on a copper penny and chewing on a gum eraser," Helen told Liet facetiously as she placed the golden steaks on the table, "you'll love abalone." And though both experiences had been denied Liet as a child, she did like it, but perhaps as much for my reason as anything else—the idea of its rarity, the fact that to taste it fresh you must have it in California, since it is usually frozen for shipment to other parts of the country.

Now, as I recall that easy meal, I grow hungry again; and under my hunger, alas, lurks a feeling of envy. Squeezed into our little Manhattan apartment, my education in American regional cookery well rounded, if not yet complete, I am reminded by my hunger of all the foods and dishes people living elsewhere can call their own, and I yearn for them—and for a bigger table as well.

The tough but subtle-flavored abalone is strictly a Pacific shellfish, found mostly in California and Mexico waters. Here Aimé Michaud, a Pebble Beach, California, real estate executive, prepares abalone in his modern kitchen while his wife, Carla, selects greens for a salad. Abalone is filleted and must be pounded until it is tender; Michaud marinates the fillets and then browns them in hot butter.

The recipes in this chapter follow the general outline of the text. While culinary differences among the regions of the United States have tended to become less distinct in recent years, each of these recipes is derived from or closely associated with a specific section of the country.

New England Boiled Dinner

To serve 6

4 pounds corned beef
2 pounds green cabbage, cored and
 quartered
12 to 16 new potatoes, about 1½
 inches in diameter, peeled
6 small carrots, scraped
12 small white onions, about 1 inch
 in diameter, peeled and trimmed
6 medium-sized beets
2 tablespoons finely chopped parsley

Before cooking the corned beef, ask your butcher whether it should be soaked in water to remove some of the salt. If it has been mildly cured, soaking will not be necessary.

Place the corned beef in a 5- or 6-quart pot and cover it with enough cold water to rise at least 2 inches above the top of the meat. Bring to a boil, skimming off any scum that rises to the surface. Half cover the pot, turn the heat to its lowest point (the liquid should barely simmer) and cook the beef from 4 to 6 hours, or until tender. If necessary, add more hot water to the pot from time to time to keep the meat constantly covered.

Cook the cabbage separately in boiling salted water for about 15 minutes. The potatoes, carrots and onions may be cooked together in a pot of salted boiling water of their own. The beets, however, require different treatment. Scrub them thoroughly, then cut off their tops, leaving 1 inch of stem. Cover them with boiling water and bring to a boil. Simmer the beets from ½ to 1½ hours, or until they are tender. Let them cool a bit, then slip off their skins.

To serve the dinner in the traditional way, slice the corned beef and arrange it along the center of a large heated platter. Surround the meat with the vegetables and sprinkle the vegetables with chopped parsley. Horseradish, mustard and a variety of pickles make excellent accompaniments to this hearty meal.

NOTE: In New England the vegetables, other than the beets, are often added to the simmering corned beef during the last half hour or so of cooking. For some tastes, however, the briny flavor imparted to the vegetables by the corned beef detracts from their natural flavors.

Red-Flannel Hash

To serve 4 to 6

¼ pound bacon, cut in ¼-inch pieces
½ cup finely chopped onion
2 cups (about 1 pound) finely
 chopped, cooked corn beef *(above)*
1 cup diced cooked beets, fresh or
 canned
3 cups coarsely chopped cooked
 potatoes
4 tablespoons finely chopped fresh
 parsley
¼ cup heavy cream
Salt
Freshly ground black pepper

In a 10- or 12-inch skillet, preferably of the nonstick variety, fry the bacon until brown but not too crisp. Then set it aside to drain on paper towels. Pour off all but 2 tablespoons of fat from the pan and reserve. Add the onions and cook them over moderate heat for 3 to 5 minutes, but don't let them brown. Scrape them into a large mixing bowl. Add the corned beef, beets, the reserved bacon, potatoes, 2 tablespoons of chopped parsley and the cream. Mix together gently but thoroughly, taste for seasoning, and add salt and freshly ground pepper to taste.

Heat the bacon fat reserved in the skillet. Add the hash, and, with a spatula, spread it evenly in the pan and pat it down. Cook uncovered over moderate heat for 35 to 40 minutes, shaking the pan occasionally to prevent the hash from sticking. As it cooks, remove any excess fat from the top or sides of the pan with a spoon or bulb baster. When the hash is done (it should be crusty brown on the bottom) slide a metal spatula around the inside edge of the skillet and as far under the hash as you can without crumbling it. Then place a large, round platter over the skillet, and, gripping platter and skillet firmly together, invert the hash onto the platter.

If any of the hash has stuck to the pan, lift it out with a spatula and patch it in place. Sprinkle with the remaining chopped parsley and serve with poached eggs if desired.

Boston Baked Beans

To serve 6 to 8

4 cups dried pea or Great Northern
  beans
2 teaspoons salt
2 medium-sized whole onions,
  peeled
4 cloves
½ cup molasses
1 cup brown sugar
2 teaspoons dry mustard
1 teaspoon black pepper
2 cups water
½ pound salt pork, scored

Put the beans in a large saucepan and pour in enough cold water to cover them by at least 2 inches. Bring to a boil over high heat, cook briskly for 2 minutes, then remove the pan from the heat and let the beans soak for about 1 hour. Bring them to a boil again, add 1 teaspoon of the salt, half cover the pan and simmer the beans as slowly as possible for about 30 minutes, or until they are partially done. Drain the beans and discard the bean water.

Preheat the oven to 250°. To bake the beans, choose a traditional 4-quart bean pot or a heavy casserole with a tight-fitting cover. Place 2 onions, each stuck with 2 cloves, in the bottom of the bean pot or casserole and cover with the beans. In a small mixing bowl, combine the molasses, ¾ cup of the brown sugar, mustard, and 1 teaspoon each of salt and black pepper. Slowly stirring with a large spoon, pour in the 2 cups of water.

Pour this mixture over the beans and push the salt pork slightly beneath the surface. Cover tightly and bake in the center of the oven for 4½ to 5 hours. Then remove the cover and sprinkle with the remaining ¼ cup of brown sugar. Bake the beans uncovered for another ½ hour and serve.

Pennsylvania Dutch Fried Tomatoes

To serve 4 to 6

4 to 5 large firm ripe tomatoes, 3 to
  4 inches in diameter, thickly sliced
2 teaspoons salt
Freshly ground black pepper
½ cup flour
4 to 6 tablespoons butter
2 tablespoons sieved brown sugar
1 cup heavy cream
1 tablespoon finely chopped fresh
  parsley

Sprinkle the tomatoes on both sides with salt and a few grindings of black pepper. Then dip the tomato slices in the flour, coating each side thoroughly and very gently shaking off any excess. In a 12-inch heavy skillet, preferably of the nonstick variety, melt the butter over moderate heat.

When the foam subsides, add the tomato slices and cook them for about 5 minutes, or until they are lightly browned. Sprinkle the tops with half the brown sugar, carefully turn the tomatoes over with a spatula and sprinkle with the rest of the brown sugar. Cook for 3 to 4 minutes, then transfer the slices to a heated serving platter.

Pour the cream into the pan, raise the heat to high and bring the cream to a boil, stirring constantly. Boil briskly for 2 to 3 minutes, or until the cream thickens. Taste for seasoning, then pour over the tomatoes. Sprinkle with the finely chopped parsley.

NOTE: Traditionally, this recipe is made with green tomatoes; however, they are not easily available. If you can find them, cook them somewhat more slowly and for a few minutes longer on each side.

A Good, Old-fashioned Clambake

There are few eating experiences to match an old-fashioned New England clambake. It draws a small army of hungry people to the edge of the sea, hones their appetites with marvelous cooking smells, and lets them eat their fill. But the old-fashioned clambake is a big production, requiring the services of an expert. The clambake shown here in Barrington, Rhode Island, was prepared by Elton Pierce, 71, a bake-master all his life, and his 28-year-old son. They brought with them bushels of soft-shelled steamer clams, white and sweet potatoes, onions, haddock, sweet corn, chicken and dozens of lobsters. They dug a pit and lined it with smooth, dry stones. Then they built a great pyre, let it burn down and cooked the food in trays over the red-hot stones.

Preparing the "bake," bake-masters layer dry stones and maple logs in a pile about 4 feet square.

The logs burn an hour and a half, or until the stones are properly hot. Then all embers are raked away.

Over hot stones go heaps of wet rockweed; pods in weed will pop open, "seasoning" the steam.

Trays of onions and potatoes cover the clams. Food trays will ultimately stack up over 3 feet high.

The clambake steams under canvas and several layers of tarpaulin while "clambakers" explore the beach.

A DO-IT-YOURSELF CLAMBAKE

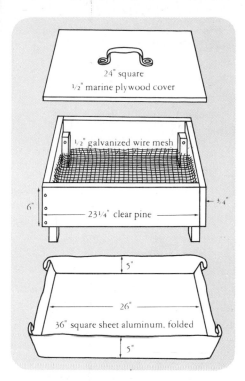

Anyone can prepare a clambake with a pit fire and the "bake" diagramed here. The "bake" can be built with lumberyard materials to specifications at the left. The first step is to nail together four square frames. Then nail a 1-by-1-by-6-inch block inside each corner, protruding 1 inch below the bottom of the box, to keep the box from slipping. Staple ½-inch galvanized wire mesh in the bottom of each box, high enough so that the wire does not sag. Now fold a 36-inch-square piece of sheet aluminum upward 5 inches along each side, and crimp the corners together tightly so it will hold water. Finally, cut out a 24-inch-square marine plywood lid, attaching a handle to the top and nailing cleats along the undersides to keep the lid from slipping. For cooking, layer the bottom of each box with rockweed. Then fill the boxes with food and pour 2 inches of water in the pan. Build a fire in a pit lined with stones; stack the boxes in the pan over the fire and cover with canvas. Keep the water at a boil so there will be plenty of steam to cook the food. We suggest arranging the food as shown at right, with the clams on top—in contrast with the old-fashioned clambake. When the clams pop open, you can eat them as the first course and give the slower food a few more minutes.

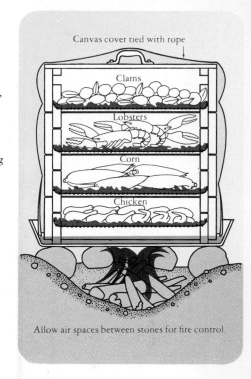

The cooking completed, the Rhode Island "clambakers" enjoy their feast. The food cooked for one hour, and nearly 100 people were served.

To make one 9-inch pie

1¼ cups all-purpose flour
4 tablespoons chilled vegetable
    shortening or lard
2 tablespoons chilled butter, cut in
    ¼-inch pieces
⅛ teaspoon salt
3 tablespoons ice water

FILLING
4 eggs
2 cups dark corn syrup
2 tablespoons melted butter
1 teaspoon vanilla
1½ cups pecans

Pecan Pie
THE SOUTH AND SOUTHWEST

Preheat the oven to 400°. In a large mixing bowl, combine the flour, vegetable shortening or lard, butter and salt. Use your fingertips to rub the flour and fat together until they look like flakes of coarse meal. Pour the ice water over the mixture, toss together, and press and knead gently with your hands only until the dough can be gathered into a compact ball. Dust very lightly with flour, wrap in wax paper and chill for at least ½ hour. Lightly butter a 9-inch pie plate. On a floured surface, roll the dough out into a circle about ⅛ inch thick and 13 to 14 inches in diameter. Lift it up on the rolling pin and unroll it over the pie plate, leaving enough slack in the middle of the pastry to enable you to line the plate without pulling or stretching the dough. Trim the excess pastry to within ½ inch of the rim of the pie plate and fold the extra ½ inch under to make a double thickness all around the rim. With the tines of a fork or with your fingers, press the pastry down around the rim.

To prevent the unfilled pastry from buckling as it bakes, either set another pie plate lightly buttered on the underside into the pastry shell or line it with a sheet of lightly buttered foil. In either case do not prick the pastry, or the filling will run out when it is added later. Bake the shell in the middle of the oven for 8 minutes, then remove the pan or foil and let the shell cool while you make the filling.

With a wire whisk or rotary beater, beat the eggs in a mixing bowl for about 30 seconds. Then slowly pour in the syrup and continue to beat until they are well combined. Beat in the melted butter and vanilla, and stir in the pecans. Carefully pour the filling into the pie shell. Bake in the middle of the oven for 35 to 40 minutes, or until the filling is firm. Serve the pie warm or cooled to room temperature.

To make one 9-inch pie

Pastry for pie shell *(above)*
5 egg yolks
One 14-ounce can sweetened
    condensed milk
¾ cup fresh lime juice, preferably
    from Key limes
3 egg whites
1 cup heavy cream, whipped
    (optional)

Key Lime Pie
FLORIDA

Make the pie shell as described for the pecan pie above, but prebake the shell at 400° for 10 minutes, remove the pie plate or foil and then turn the oven down to 350° for 10 minutes more so the shell will be fully cooked. Let the shell cool while you make the filling.

Preheat the oven to 325°. With a wire whisk or rotary beater or electric mixer, beat the yolks of 5 eggs for 3 to 5 minutes until they are thick. Slowly beat in the condensed milk and then the lime juice. In another bowl, beat the egg whites until they form soft peaks and waver gently on the beater when it is lifted out of the bowl. Be careful not to overbeat; the whites should not be stiff. With a rubber spatula, fold them gently but thoroughly into the egg yolk mixture. Spoon the mixture at once into the cooled pie shell. Bake in the middle of the oven for 20 minutes, or until the filling is firm. Serve at room temperature or, as is often preferred, first chill the pie in the refrigerator. The whipped cream may be piped decoratively over the top of the pie or passed separately in a bowl.

NOTE: The tiny limes of the Florida Keys are seldom sold in stores. However, they are widely grown in the yards of Florida homes. Key limes are preferred for their flavor in this pie, but other limes may be used.

Grits and Cheddar Cheese Casserole
THE SOUTH

In a small skillet, melt 2 tablespoons of butter over moderate heat. When the foam subsides add the ¼ cup of onion and cook for 4 or 5 minutes until translucent but not brown. Meanwhile, bring the 2 cups of water to a bubbling boil in a 1-quart saucepan. Add the salt and pour in the grits slowly without allowing the water to stop boiling. Boil for about a minute, stirring constantly, then reduce the heat to medium and cook for another 2 minutes. With a rubber spatula, scrape into the saucepan the onions and add the Tabasco, a few grindings of black pepper and 1½ cups of the grated Cheddar cheese combined with the 3 tablespoons of soft butter.

Preheat the oven to 400°. Lightly butter a 1-quart casserole or soufflé dish. With a wire whisk or rotary beater, beat the egg whites until they form stiff peaks on the beater when it is lifted from the bowl. With a rubber spatula, thoroughly fold the egg whites into the grits mixture. Pour into the casserole and sprinkle the top with the remaining grated Cheddar cheese. Bake in the middle of the oven for about 30 minutes, or until the mixture has puffed and browned. Serve at once as an accompaniment for any meat or poultry dish.

To serve 4 to 6

2 tablespoons butter
¼ cup finely chopped onion
2 cups water
½ teaspoon salt
½ cup quick grits
1 teaspoon Tabasco
Freshly ground black pepper
1¾ cups grated Cheddar cheese
3 tablespoons soft butter
2 egg whites

Southern Fried Chicken with Cream Gravy

Wash the chicken pieces under cold running water and pat them thoroughly dry with paper towels. Sprinkle the pieces with salt on all sides. Put the cup of flour in a sturdy paper bag. Drop the chicken into the bag a few pieces at a time and shake the bag until each piece is thoroughly coated with flour. Remove the chicken pieces from the bag and vigorously shake them free of all excess flour. Lay them side by side on a sheet of wax paper. Preheat the oven to 200° and in the middle of the oven place a shallow baking dish.

Over high heat melt the lard or combined lard and shortening in a 10- or 12-inch heavy skillet. The fat should be ¼ inch deep. If it is not, add a little more. When a light haze forms above it, add the chicken pieces, starting them skin side down. It is preferable to begin frying the legs and thighs first, since they will take longer to cook than the breasts and wings. Cover the pan and fry the chicken over moderate heat for about 6 to 8 minutes, checking every now and then to make sure the chicken does not burn. When the pieces are deep brown on one side, turn them over and cover the pan again. Transfer the finished chicken to the baking dish in the oven and continue frying until all the pieces are cooked. Keep the chicken warm in the oven while you make the gravy.

Pour off all but 2 tablespoons of fat in the frying pan. Add 2 tablespoons of flour, and stir until the fat and flour are well combined. Pour in the chicken stock and ½ cup of the light cream, and cook over moderate heat, beating with a whisk until the gravy is smooth and thick. If it is too thick for your taste, stir in the remaining cream to thin it. Strain it through a fine sieve if you wish. Taste for seasoning, then pour into a heated gravy boat and serve with the fried chicken arranged attractively on a heated serving platter.

To serve 4

A 2½-pound frying chicken, cut into
   serving pieces
Salt
1 cup flour
1 cup lard, or ½ cup vegetable
   shortening combined with
   ½ cup lard

CREAM GRAVY
2 tablespoons flour
¾ cup chicken stock, fresh or canned
½ to ¾ cup light cream
Salt
White pepper

Stuffed crawfish heads embellish a New Orleans specialty, crawfish bisque.

To serve 8 to 10

5 pounds live crawfish
4 quarts water
2 cups coarsely chopped onion
Herb bouquet of 3 sprigs parsley, 1
    bay leaf, ¼ teaspoon thyme, 6
    peppercorns tied together in
    cheesecloth
8 tablespoons butter
1 cup finely chopped onion
½ cup finely diced carrot
½ cup finely diced celery
1 teaspoon finely chopped garlic
2 tablespoons finely chopped parsley
¾ teaspoon thyme
8 tablespoons flour
2 teaspoons salt
2 tablespoons paprika

STUFFING (for about 40 heads)
2 tablespoons butter
3 tablespoons minced onion
½ teaspoon finely chopped garlic
1½ cups fresh bread crumbs
1 egg yolk, lightly beaten
3 tablespoons chopped parsley
2 tablespoons sherry
½ teaspoon salt
Pinch of cayenne

Crawfish Bisque with Stuffed Heads

Wash the crawfish under cold running water, then soak in water for at least 10 minutes. In a heavy 8- to 10-quart pot, bring 4 quarts of water to a rapid boil. Add the chopped onion and the herb bouquet. Then drop in all the crawfish a handful at a time and boil uncovered for about 5 minutes. Remove the crawfish and set aside. Strain the cooking liquid through cheesecloth, then return it to the thoroughly washed pot.

In a heavy skillet, melt the butter over moderate heat. When the foam subsides, add the onion, carrot, celery, garlic, parsley and thyme. Cook for about 5 minutes, until the vegetables are limp but not brown, then stir in the flour. Stir this mixture over low heat for about 10 minutes. With a rubber spatula, scrape it into the crawfish stock. Bring to a boil, mixing with a whisk until the stock thickens slightly. Turn the heat to low and simmer gently while you shell the crawfish.

Break the heads from the crawfish and pick the meat from the tails, adding the tail shells to the simmering stock as you proceed. Discard the vein in the tail meat, chop the meat fine and reserve in a bowl. In another bowl, shake the yellow fat from the crawfish heads by gently tapping them against the sides of the bowl. With a small knife, scrape the heads clean of any black matter and set aside 35 to 40 of them to be stuffed. Add the remaining heads to the stock, and stir in the 2 teaspoons of salt and the paprika. Simmer partially covered for 45 minutes.

While the bisque is simmering, make the stuffing. In a small skillet, melt 2 tablespoons of butter over moderate heat. When the foam subsides, add the minced onion and garlic and cook for about 4 minutes, or until they are transparent but not brown. Scrape them into a mixing bowl. Add half the reserved crawfish meat, the bread crumbs, egg yolk,

The Creole-Cajun dish, jambalaya, a mosaic of highly flavored rice, ham, shrimp and tomatoes, is another New Orleans favorite.

parsley, sherry, salt and cayenne, mix and taste for seasoning. Pack each head with stuffing, then place in one layer in a shallow baking dish. Dot with soft butter and bake for about 10 minutes in a preheated 350° oven.

Before serving, strain the bisque through a fine sieve and discard the crawfish shells. Bring the bisque to a simmer once more, and add the remaining crawfish meat. Divide the stuffed heads among individual soup plates, pour the hot bisque over them and serve.

Jambalaya

Preheat the oven to 350°. In a heavy 3- or 4-quart casserole, fry the bacon over moderate heat until it has rendered its fat and is brown but not crisp. Drain on paper towels and reserve. Add the onions to the fat in the pan and cook them for 8 to 10 minutes, stirring occasionally until they are transparent but not brown. Mix in the green peppers. They will wilt slightly in about 3 minutes, at which point the rice should be stirred in. Turn the rice about in the hot fat and vegetables over moderate heat until the grains become somewhat opaque and milky. Then add the garlic, tomatoes, the bacon, thyme, salt and a few grindings of black pepper, stirring them together thoroughly. Pour in 1½ cups of chicken stock and bring it to a boil. Add the ham and stir again. Cover the casserole tightly and place it in the lower third of the oven. After 10 minutes add the shrimp, pushing them down beneath the rice, and continue to cook tightly covered for about 10 minutes longer, or until all of the stock is absorbed and the rice is tender. If at any point during this time the rice appears dry, add a few tablespoons more of hot stock to it. Serve directly from the casserole if you wish, or mound the jambalaya on a large, heated platter. Garnish with fresh chopped parsley.

To serve 4 to 6

¼ pound sliced bacon, cut in 1-inch pieces
½ cup finely chopped onion
2 medium-sized green peppers, seeded and cut in 1-inch strips
1 cup raw rice
1 teaspoon finely chopped garlic
A 1-pound 3-ounce can whole-pack tomatoes, drained and coarsely chopped
½ teaspoon thyme
1 teaspoon salt
Freshly ground black pepper
1½ to 2 cups chicken stock, fresh or canned
½-pound cooked smoked ham, cut in 2-inch by ½-inch strips
1 pound medium-sized raw shrimp, shelled and deveined
1 tablespoon finely chopped fresh parsley

Pacific Oyster Stew

NORTHWEST

To serve 4

4 tablespoons soft butter
1½ pints light or heavy cream
1½ pints Pacific oysters, or other
    oysters, and their liquor
Salt
Freshly ground black pepper
Paprika (optional)

Warm 4 deep soup bowls in a shallow baking pan that is half filled with boiling water. Add 1 tablespoon of soft butter to each bowl. In a small saucepan, bring the cream almost but not quite to a boil over moderate heat. When small bubbles appear around the edge of the pan, reduce the heat to its lowest point and keep the cream barely simmering.

Pour the oysters and all their liquor into a 12-inch enameled or stainless-steel skillet. Set it over moderate heat and poach the oysters, turning them gently about in their liquor with a wooden spoon for 2 or 3 minutes, or until the oysters plump up and their edges begin to curl. Immediately pour the simmering cream into the skillet, add salt and pepper to taste, and simmer a moment longer. Ladle the stew into heated soup bowls, sprinkle with a little paprika if you like and serve at once accompanied by crackers or, less traditionally, hot French or Italian bread.

Barbecued Spareribs

SOUTHWEST

To serve 4 to 6

¼ cup vegetable oil
1 teaspoon garlic, minced
2 medium onions, finely chopped
1 six-ounce can tomato paste
¼ cup white vinegar
1 teaspoon salt
1 teaspoon basil or thyme
¼ cup strained honey
½ cup beef stock
½ cup Worcestershire sauce
1 teaspoon dry mustard
4 pounds spareribs

Heat the vegetable oil over high heat in a 10- or 12-inch skillet. When a light haze forms above it, add the garlic and onions, and cook, stirring frequently, for 3 to 4 minutes without letting the onions brown. Combine the tomato paste and the vinegar, and then add it to the skillet. Stir in the salt, basil or thyme, the honey, beef stock, Worcestershire sauce and mustard. Mix thoroughly and simmer uncovered over low heat for 10 to 15 minutes. Remove from heat. Preheat the oven to 400°. Place the spareribs fat side up on a rack set in a shallow roasting pan and with a pastry brush thoroughly coat the surface of the meat with the barbecue sauce. Bake in the middle of the oven for 45 minutes to 1 hour, basting thoroughly with the barbecue sauce every 10 minutes or so. When the spareribs are brown and crisp, cut into individual portions and serve at once.

Chiles Rellenos

SOUTHWEST

To serve 4

8 fresh green chili peppers, peeled
    and seeded, or 2 four-ounce cans
    of roasted and peeled chilis
1 pound Monterey Jack cheese, cut
    into 1-inch cubes
4 egg whites
4 egg yolks
½ teaspoon salt
¼ cup flour
Vegetable shortening for deep frying

To prepare the fresh chilis, preheat the oven to 475°. Place the chilis side by side on a rack in a shallow roasting pan and bake them for 8 to 10 minutes until their skins scorch and blacken slightly. Remove from the oven and wrap them in a damp, clean towel. Let them rest in the towel a few minutes, then gently rub with the towel until the skins slip off. Cut the chilis in half lengthwise and remove the seeds. Canned chilis need only be drained of their canning liquid and any seeds discarded. Handle them gently; they disintegrate easily. Carefully wrap a strip of chili around each cube of cheese, enclosing it completely. Skewer with toothpicks.

For the batter, first beat the egg whites in a mixing bowl with a whisk or rotary beater until they form firm, unwavering peaks when the beater is lifted out of the bowl. Without washing the beater, in a separate bowl beat the egg yolks for 2 or 3 minutes until they are thick and lemon colored. Then beat in the salt and the flour. With a rubber spatula, gently fold the beaten egg whites into this mixture. Heat the vegetable shortening in a deep fryer (the fat should be at least 3 inches deep) until it reaches a temperature of 375° on a deep-fat-frying thermometer. (The chilis may also be fried in a skillet containing 2 inches of hot oil, lard or vegetable shortening. If you choose this method, turn them over with a large spoon to brown them on all sides.) Dip the chilis in the batter and when they are well coated drop them into the hot fat. Turn them gently in the fat with a large spoon, and cook them until they puff and turn a golden brown on all sides. Drain on paper towels and serve.

Three-Bean Salad
SOUTHWEST

If you plan to use canned cooked beans and chick peas, drain them of all their canning liquid, wash them thoroughly under cold running water, drain again and pat dry with paper towels. If you plan to cook the beans yourself, follow the initial soaking directions for beans in the recipe for baked beans on page 91, and then cook them until tender. One half cup of dry uncooked beans yields approximately 1¼ cups cooked.

In a large bowl, combine the chick peas, red kidney beans and white kidney beans, the chopped onion or scallions, garlic, parsley and the chopped green pepper if you plan to use it.

Add the salt, a few grindings of pepper and the wine vinegar. Toss gently with a large spoon. Pour in the olive oil and toss again. This salad will be greatly improved if it is allowed to rest for at least an hour before serving it.

To serve 6 to 8

1 cup red kidney beans, freshly cooked or canned
1 cup white kidney beans, freshly cooked or canned
1 cup chick peas, freshly cooked or canned
¾ cup finely chopped onion or scallions
½ teaspoon finely chopped garlic
2 tablespoons finely chopped parsley
1 small green pepper, seeded and coarsely chopped (optional)
1 teaspoon salt
Freshly ground black pepper
3 tablespoons wine vinegar
½ cup olive oil

Chili con Carne
SOUTHWEST

Pat the meat dry with paper towels. Then, in a 12-inch heavy skillet, heat 4 tablespoons of the oil until a light haze forms above it. Add the meat and cook over high heat for 2 to 3 minutes, stirring, until the meat is lightly browned. With a slotted spoon transfer it to a 4-quart heavy flameproof casserole. Add the remaining 2 tablespoons of oil to the skillet and in it cook the onion and garlic for 4 to 5 minutes, stirring frequently.

Remove the skillet from the heat, add the 4 tablespoons chili powder, or to taste, oregano, cumin and pepper flakes, and stir until the onions are well coated with the mixture. Then add the tomato paste, pour in the beef stock and with a large spoon mix the ingredients together thoroughly before adding them to the meat in the casserole. Add the salt and a few grindings of black pepper. Bring to a boil, stirring once or twice, then half cover the pot, turn the heat to low and simmer for 1 to 1½ hours, or until the meat is tender.

If you plan to use the beans, add them to the casserole 15 minutes or so before the meat is done or, if you prefer, serve the chili with the three-bean salad above. In either case, before serving the chili, skim it of as much of the surface fat as you can. If the chili is refrigerated overnight, the fat will rise to the surface and can be easily skimmed off before reheating.

NOTE: Chile con carne is often made with coarsely ground chuck in place of the cubed round steak. Follow the above recipe, but be sure to break up the ground chuck with a fork as you brown it.

To serve 6 to 8

3 pounds top round, cut into ½-inch cubes
6 tablespoons vegetable oil
2 cups coarsely chopped onion
2 tablespoons finely chopped garlic
4 tablespoons chili powder
1 teaspoon oregano
1 teaspoon ground cumin
1 teaspoon red-pepper flakes
1 six-ounce can tomato paste
4 cups beef stock, fresh or canned
1 teaspoon salt
Freshly ground black pepper
1½ cups freshly cooked red kidney beans or drained canned kidney beans (optional)

Overleaf: for many citizens of the Southwest, pure joy is a pot of chili, a three-bean salad, and beer. The region's great humorist, Oklahoma-born Will Rogers, once said he judged a town by its chili.

To serve 4

4 doves or pigeons, approximately 1
    pound each
4 tablespoons soft butter, unsalted
½ teaspoon thyme
2 teaspoons finely chopped fresh
    tarragon or ½ teaspoon dried
    tarragon
2 tablespoons finely chopped fresh
    parsley
½ teaspoon salt
Freshly ground black pepper
2 small onions, peeled and halved
2 tablespoons butter
2 tablespoons oil
2 strips of bacon, cut in half
4 tablespoons finely chopped onion
2 cups chicken stock, fresh or canned
6 green olives, blanched and sliced

To serve 6

½ cup vegetable oil
1 cup finely chopped onion
1 medium green pepper, seeded and
    coarsely chopped
2 teaspoons finely chopped garlic
4 medium-sized tomatoes, peeled,
    seeded and coarsely chopped, or
    an equivalent amount of canned
    tomatoes, thoroughly drained
2 tablespoons tomato paste
2 cups dry white wine
½ cup finely chopped fresh parsley,
    Italian flat-leaf if possible
1 teaspoon salt
Freshly ground black pepper
2 live lobsters, about 1¼ pounds
    each, cut into serving pieces, or 1
    large Dungeness crab, or 4 small
    blue crabs
2½ to 3 pounds firm white-fleshed
    fish, cut into serving pieces
1 pound raw, medium-sized shrimp,
    shelled and deveined
1½ dozen small hard-shelled clams
    in their shells, well washed and
    scrubbed
1½ dozen small mussels in their
    shells, well washed, scrubbed and
    bearded

Roast Dove or Pigeon
WEST COAST

Wash the birds under cold running water and dry them thoroughly with paper towels inside and out. In a mixing bowl, cream the butter by beating it against the side of the bowl with a wooden spoon until it is light and fluffy. Then beat in the thyme, tarragon, parsley, ½ teaspoon salt and pepper. Rub the cavities of the birds with salt and then with the butter mixture, dividing it equally among them. Place ½ onion inside each bird and truss them securely.

Preheat the oven to 425°. In a heavy 12-inch skillet, heat the butter and oil over moderate heat. When the foam subsides add the birds to the skillet and brown them on all sides for about 10 minutes, turning them with tongs. Be careful not to let them burn. Then transfer them to a rack set in a shallow roasting pan that is just large enough to hold all of them comfortably.

Tie ½ strip of bacon on the breast of each bird and roast in the middle of the oven for 20 minutes. Reduce the heat to 350° and roast for 20 minutes more, basting the birds every 5 minutes or so with the drippings in the pan.

When they are done, remove the trussing strings, transfer the birds to a heated platter and sprinkle them lightly with salt. Cover the platter loosely with a piece of foil to keep the birds warm while you make the sauce. Add the chopped onions to the drippings remaining in the roasting pan and cook them over moderate heat on top of the stove for 2 to 3 minutes.

Then pour in the chicken stock and bring it to a boil, stirring in any brown bits clinging to the bottom and sides of the pan. Boil briskly until the sauce is reduced to about half its volume. Strain it into a saucepan. Skim the surface of as much fat as you can and stir in the sliced green olives. Cook for a minute or so until they are heated through, and serve in a gravy boat.

NOTE: To blanch the olives, cover them with cold water in a small saucepan and bring to a boil. Cook briskly for 2 minutes, or a few minutes longer if the olives seem excessively briny, then drain and run cold water over them.

Cioppino
CALIFORNIA

In a heavy 6- to 8-quart casserole, heat the oil over high heat until a light haze forms above it. Then add the chopped onions, green pepper and garlic, and cook, stirring occasionally, for 4 to 6 minutes, or until the vegetables are wilted but not brown. Add the tomatoes, tomato paste, wine, ¼ cup of the chopped parsley, salt and a few grindings of pepper, and bring to a boil. Lower the heat, half cover the casserole and simmer the sauce for about 15 minutes.

Add the lobster or crab, baste thoroughly with the sauce and cook over low heat, tightly covered, for about 10 minutes before adding the cut-up fish. Cover the casserole again and cook the fish for about 8 minutes, or until it is firm to the touch. Add the shrimp, pushing them beneath

One of California's famous dishes, a casserole of cioppino, is served in an elegant apartment in San Francisco. The main ingredients for the dish—mussels, shrimp, crab, fish and clams—came from the sea close by.

the sauce and cook for 3 to 4 minutes, or until they turn pink and are firm.

Meanwhile, steam open the clams and mussels by dropping them into a large skillet or casserole filled with about 1 inch of boiling water. Cover the pan tightly and cook the shellfish over moderate heat for 5 to 10 minutes, or until their shells open. Steam those that do not open a little longer, finally discarding any that remain closed. Add the opened mussels and clams (shells and all) to the casserole and baste thoroughly with the sauce. If you like, strain the broth from the steamed shellfish through cheesecloth and add it to the cioppino. However, be careful not to thin the sauce too much.

Cover the pan and cook the cioppino about 2 to 3 minutes longer, then taste for seasoning. Serve either directly from the casserole or from a large tureen. In either case, sprinkle with the remaining ¼ cup of chopped parsley and accompany the cioppino with hot garlic bread.

103

The Palace Court salad *(recipe opposite)* is served in the famous San Francisco hotel restaurant where it was created in the 1920s.

Avocado-Tomato Cocktail

CALIFORNIA

To serve 4 to 6

1 ripe avocado, peeled and cut in ¼-inch dice
1 teaspoon lemon juice
2 medium-sized tomatoes, peeled, seeded and cut in ¼-inch dice
2 tablespoons minced onion
2 tablespoons finely chopped fresh parsley
1 teaspoon salt
Freshly ground black pepper
2 tablespoons red-wine vinegar
¼ cup vegetable oil

Cut the avocado in half, and, with a teaspoon, remove the seed and any brown tissuelike fibers clinging to the flesh. Remove the skin by stripping it off with your fingers, starting at the narrow, or stem, end (the dark-skinned variety does not peel as easily; use a small, sharp knife to pull away the skin if necessary). Dice the avocado and moisten it with the lemon juice to prevent discoloration. In a mixing bowl, combine the avocado, diced tomato and the minced onion. Add the parsley, salt and a few grindings of pepper, and gently mix the ingredients together.

With a whisk or fork, beat the vinegar and oil together, then pour it over the avocado-tomato mixture. Stir thoroughly again, then chill for at least an hour. Serve as a first course in chilled cocktail glasses or as a luncheon salad, arranged on a bed of crisp lettuce.

Palace Court Salad

CALIFORNIA

Bring 1 quart of lightly salted water to a boil in an enameled or stainless-steel saucepan. Drop in the shrimp and boil them briskly for about 5 minutes, or until they turn pink and are firm to the touch. Do not overcook. Drain them at once and plunge them into cold water to stop their cooking. Drain again on paper towels and chill.

To make the dressing, in a small bowl combine the mayonnaise and the strained chili sauce, the chives, parsley and tarragon. Mix together thoroughly and taste. Season with salt and white pepper if necessary.

For the shrimp mixture, toss all but 6 of the shrimp (reserve them for the garnish) with the lemon juice and ½ teaspoon salt. Then add 3 tablespoons of mayonnaise to the shrimp and stir gently until they are well coated.

Construct the salad on individual chilled salad plates. Place a thin bed of shredded lettuce about 3 to 4 inches in diameter in the center of each plate. Put a tomato slice in the center of the lettuce, arrange an artichoke bottom on top of it and spoon equal amounts of the shrimp mixture into the slight hollow of each artichoke bottom. Sprinkle the chopped egg around the exposed circle of lettuce and garnish each mound of shrimp with the reserved shrimp. Top with a strip of pimiento if desired. Serve chilled and pass the dressing separately.

NOTE: This salad is often made with Dungeness crab and decorated with crab legs. Any crab meat may be substituted for the shrimp.

To serve 6

1 pound medium-sized raw shrimp, shelled and deveined

DRESSING

1¼ cups mayonnaise, freshly made, or a good, unsweetened commercial variety
¼ cup chili sauce, strained
1 tablespoon chopped fresh chives
2 tablespoons finely chopped fresh parsley
1 teaspoon fresh tarragon, finely chopped, or ½ teaspoon dried tarragon
Salt
White pepper

SALAD

1 teaspoon lemon juice
½ teaspoon salt
3 tablespoons mayonnaise
2 cups shredded iceberg lettuce
6 half-inch slices tomato, about 2½ inches in diameter
6 artichoke bottoms, canned or freshly cooked
3 hard-cooked eggs, finely chopped
6 strips pimiento (optional)

Fried Rabbit with Sour Cream Gravy

WEST COAST

Wash the rabbit pieces under cold running water and dry them thoroughly with paper towels. Sprinkle each piece generously with salt and a few gringrinds of pepper. Place the flour in a sturdy paper bag and drop the rabbit pieces into it, a few at a time. Shake the bag vigorously until each piece is thoroughly coated with flour, then remove the rabbit from the bag and shake the pieces free of excess flour. Set aside on wax paper.

In a heavy skillet large enough to hold all the pieces comfortably, heat the butter and oil over moderate heat. When the foam subsides, add the pieces of rabbit and cook them for 6 to 7 minutes on each side, turning them with tongs. When all the rabbit pieces are brown, cover the skillet and turn the heat to its lowest point. Cook the rabbit for 35 to 40 minutes, or until the flesh shows no resistance when pierced with the tip of a small, sharp knife. Arrange the pieces of rabbit attractively on a large heated platter and cover loosely with foil to keep them warm.

Pour off all but a thin film of fat from the skillet, add the chopped onion and garlic, and cook for 4 to 5 minutes over medium heat until the onions are lightly colored. Pour in the chicken stock, stirring in any brown bits that cling to the pan, and bring to a rapid boil.

Boil briskly until the stock reduces by about ⅓, then turn the heat down and, with a whisk, slowly beat in the sour cream. Simmer only long enough to heat the gravy through. Taste for seasoning and pour over the rabbit. Or, if you like, serve the gravy separately in a sauceboat.

To serve 4

A 2½- to 3-pound fresh rabbit or defrosted frozen rabbit, cut in serving pieces
Salt
Freshly ground black pepper
1 cup flour
4 tablespoons butter
4 tablespoons vegetable oil
¼ cup finely chopped onion
1 teaspoon finely chopped garlic
1 cup chicken stock, fresh or canned
1 cup sour cream

IV

U.S. Choice:
Meat and Poultry

A crown roast of lamb, gaily
decorated with paper frills,
is a dish fit for a king. Whole
new potatoes and sprigs of
mint embellish this regal
dish, whose hollow is filled
with fresh peas. The size of
the roast is determined by
the number of guests—two
chops each. The recipe is
on page 120.

Of all the foods cooked in America, none can arouse the appetite faster—or provide more complete satisfaction—than meat. The husky odor
of a roast cooking in the oven and the spattering sound of its juices in
the pan, the rich, gorgeous smell of a steak sizzling on the charcoal grill
or of chops browning and crisping under the broiler flame can make hunger pangs seem sweet torture indeed. Not surprisingly, in a land where
meat is good and plentiful, the taste for it continues to grow. Over the
past three and a half decades we have regularly added 16 ounces of red
meat to our diet every year. The average American now annually consumes
more than 176 pounds of beef, pork, veal and lamb (in descending order
of their popularity), to say nothing of 46 pounds of poultry and an un-
estimated amount of game. As a nation we may make up less than one
fifteenth of the world's population and occupy a sixteenth of its land,
but we eat fully 30 per cent of its meat—and pay less for it, in terms of
our earnings, than people anywhere else.

Not only do we eat a lot of meat, but we choose it from a bewildering variety. There are literally enough different cuts and kinds of meat in the
markets and butcher shops, from rib roasts and chops to precooked hams
and chicken parts, for the housewife to make a new selection for her family's dinner table every day of the year. But as wide as this choice may be
for her, she has demonstrated, by buying beef four out of seven times,
that her preference is for this most robust and available of meats. Moreover, as a sign of growing affluence, she has taken of late to buying the
more expensive cuts; apparently she finds broiling a sirloin or porterhouse

steak a lot less bothersome than braising or stewing chuck or other tougher cuts to tenderize them.

Beef has long been America's most sought-after meat. *Harper's Weekly* reported as early as 1854 (the year the first Texas Longhorns reached New York City) that "From Portland to St. Louis, and from the Green Mountains to Florida, the most usual repast, the surest accompaniment to table, is steak." And by the 1880s American beef was being enjoyed abroad—and in Britain it was even beginning to usurp the place of English beef. Crowed a Chicago newspaper of the day, mixing its metaphors and puns, "American beef . . . is now actually ruling the roast there."

How tender such American meat may have been—at least by today's standards—is open to question. In the early days the principal source of beef was not cattle raised to be eaten, but rather oxen—cattle used as beasts of burden. They uprooted trees, drew ploughs through stony fields and dragged loaded wagons behind them. When they were too old or too weak to pull their weight, they were slaughtered and the flesh was eaten. Just how tough and stringy it must have been is suggested by several old New England recipes. One urges the housewife to make holes with an awl or screwdriver in a chunk of beef four to five inches thick, fill them with strips of salt pork, and steam the meat for three hours. A second—to obviate the necessity of aging the beef to tenderize it, an impossibility certainly in hot weather—recommends that a steak be soaked first in a half pint of red wine, then boiled and finally simmered until it can easily be cut with a blunt knife.

In those days even beef cattle—those raised specifically for meat—could not have been much more tender than oxen. Before there was a West, America's most important source of beef was the South—the Carolinas and Georgia. But in the absence of railroads and refrigerator cars, the only way to get Southern beef to market was on the hoof—live. Thus cattle were walked from their grazing lands to Charleston, Norfolk and Baltimore, and even as far north as Philadelphia—and the exertion could have done the animals little good as far as tenderness was concerned. After Ohio and Illinois became beef centers, cattle were driven from the Midwest to New York; making seven miles a day, the lowing beasts required 40 to 50 days to complete the journey, and lost as much as 150 pounds en route.

The most famous of America's cattle, the Texas Longhorns, could hardly have been very tender either. Yet for their times they were nearly perfect animals. Descended from Spanish stock that had been bred to withstand the heat and drought of Andalusia, the lean but sturdy Longhorns thrived under the similar conditions of Texas and proved their adaptability many times over on the range. They were resistant to diseases that killed other cattle; they could get along on little water (a blessing in an area where wells had not yet been drilled), and, most important of all, they were capable of making the long trek to the rail centers. At the peak of the great drives, as many as 2,000 at a time might be pointed northward and herded 1,000 or more miles—a three-month journey over a trail that wandered from the Mexican border through Texas and Indian territory to Kansas. Some even went as far as Illinois and were wintered there, before being driven the rest of the way to New York City. In the 30 years after the Civil War, an estimated 10 million head of cattle walked from Texas to Kansas for shipment, or to more northerly locations for final fattening.

Texas Longhorns have long since been displaced by meatier breeds imported from Scotland and England—the Black Angus; the Shorthorn, or Durham; and the Hereford, today America's most common beef animal. Yet during their reign, the Longhorns did more than feed the country; they helped give America one of its most colorful periods, and because of them beef has been associated ever since in the American consciousness with the romance of the Wild West. Had there been no cattle to round up and drive north, there would have been no cowboys—and had there been no cowboys, American folklore would have been a far poorer thing. But historians, alas, in taking a closer look at the two crucial decades, 1866 to 1887, when cattle country was not yet fenced in and lawlessness seemed to abound, have pared away some of the wildness. (The cowboy's trusted Colt revolver, until redesigned in 1871, had an effective range of no more than 25 to 30 yards, and those scalp-peeling Indians actually may have been more interested in rustling cattle than killing cowboys.) But one aspect of this period remains unchallenged: the everyday life of the range and the foods the cowboys ate. Theirs was a cookery founded on beef, and no matter how tough the meat they consumed week after week may in fact have been, their evening meal, in all its dusty plainness, is still one of the most romantic ever devised, and it can still, in the retelling, set a man's appetite on fire.

Imagine the setting, somewhere out in the grasslands, with the huge, pale-blue sky stretching to the distant rim of the horizon. There is a chuck wagon drawn up in the breeze, and a cook is cutting off steaks from the carcass of a young animal killed only yesterday. He pounds the steaks with a hammer or hacks them with a cleaver, then dusts them with flour and salt and lowers them into his Dutch ovens, suspended over the fire. At the bottom of each oven glistens an inch of melted beef suet, and the meat pops and snaps as it glides into its searing bath. The cook fixes the covers in place and turns back to the wagon; the steaks must be allowed to simmer in their own juices. Over to one side, a bucket of red beans—Mexican or prairie strawberries, as cowboys sometimes called them—hump up in the steady heat of a pit filled with ashes. They have been cooking slowly all day long, and have reached mealy perfection, and yet not one of their skins has burst. Now the cook mixes up a batch of sourdough biscuits on the tail gate of the chuck wagon, puts them in another Dutch oven to puff and bake, and places the coffeepot on the fire.

"Come and get it!"—the cry of the chuck-wagon cook—rings in the crystal air of evening, and the boys come in a hurry. Their chairs are the earth; their legs, forked under them, their table; and long experience has taught them how to cut their steaks without knocking the plates off their knees. There is enough meat here to satisfy every man, more than enough gravy—and the biscuits break into warm, moist crumbs in the mouth to be washed down with gulps of scalding black coffee.

Though it could hardly be credited with imagination, cowboy cooking at least could claim consistency as its virtue: beef, a little salt pork, per-

A Hearty Meal in One Pot

The pot roast, which gets its name from the vessel in which it is prepared, can be cooked on top of the stove, but it is better when cooked in the oven, where the heat surrounds it and cooks it more evenly. The best beef roast is rump or chuck that is first browned on all sides in hot fat in an uncovered pot on top of the stove, then covered tightly and cooked at low heat. A little liquid—water, stock or tomato juice—should be added to make the meat moist and tender, but the less liquid the better. Flavor with garlic, onion, bay leaf, celery, thyme, carrots, or a combination of these ingredients. The roast should be cooked until it can be easily pierced with a fork. A few small whole onions and such root vegetables as potatoes, carrots, parsnips and turnips are usually added in time for them to be done when the roast is cooked. You may reheat the leftover beef again and again, adding fresh vegetables each time if you desire.

109

Fans at a Harvard-Yale football game at New Haven, Connecticut, cook steaks on a portable grill before kickoff time. The combination of portable grill and handy charcoal briquets has made possible the easy outdoor cooking of choice meats.

haps some game—that was it. (The cowboy's contempt for the sheep is summed up in his description of a lamb chop as wool with a handle.) Occasionally the chuck-wagon cook would vary the diet of steak with a pot roast, cooked as long as four or five hours, or with a stew. Among the most famous of American dishes—although probably the one the fewest living Americans have tasted—is the cowboy's very own son-of-a-bitch stew, sometimes called son-of-a-gun stew (whenever it is, you can be sure a woman is talking, or has written the cookbook). It was made almost entirely of what are known today as variety meats—the tongue, liver, heart, sweetbreads and marrow gut—of a calf, and though some of these ingredients could be omitted and the proportions might vary from cook to cook, no son-of-a-bitch stew worthy of the name ever failed to include the marrow gut. This is a tube connecting two of the stomach's four sections in cud-chewing animals, and in the calf it is filled with a marrowlike substance that helps digest the mother cow's milk. It has a flavor all its own. Although an onion (a "skunk egg," as the cowboys often called it) on occasion might go into the pot, along with salt and pepper and perhaps a little chili powder, the prime seasoning, the most important flavoring agent, was the marrow gut. "A sonofabitch might not have any brains and no heart," said one well-meaning cowboy, "but if he don't have guts, he's not a sonofabitch."

So great is the legend of the West that cowboy cooking—or rather, the romance associated with it—may well be at the root of our national mania for the meal prepared and eaten out of doors. The chuck-wagon tail gate certainly has its modern counterpart in the station wagon tail gate. And the cowboy cook has his counterpart in the suburban father building a good fire, manipulating the charcoal, adjusting the grate—and often calling, when the meat is done just right, "Come and get it!"

The barbecue (with beef the meat most often barbecued) is the one American meal pioneered by men—and I am not thinking in terms of its present backyard incarnation. (Tips for barbecuing may be found on page 203.) The tradition behind the barbecue is much more venerable than most people suppose, and goes as far back as the Indians. The word itself would seem to come from the French phrase, *barbe à queue*, a reference to the way a barbecued animal is spitted from the *barbe* to the *queue* —from the whiskers to the tail. But some etymologists argue that the word's origin is Spanish, from *barbacoa*, the name, in parts of Central and South America, for a wood grid on which meat is roasted or dried. Whatever its origins, this much is certain: the barbecue emerged as a popular feast as early as the 17th Century in Virginia, where a sturgeon or hog would be roasted whole over the coals. The custom spread, and in New York City a favorite diversion of the 18th and early 19th Centuries was the turtle barbecue—with the poor animal brought live to the sacrifice all the way from the West Indies.

Later, the barbecue began to acquire political significance. Candidates for office were soon throwing barbecues to win votes—and these events could be gargantuan. The one given at Zanesville, Ohio, in 1840 by William Henry Harrison, while campaigning for President, was a good example. Before it had run its course, no less than 18 tons of meat, venison, pies and hard cider had been consumed.

Where the barbecue still exists as an elaborate institution, complete with pit over which the meat is roasted, as in the South and Southwest, it continues to be a feast of gigantic proportions. When the meat is chunky beef, it can make the beans and the corn on the cob served with it seem superfluous—and dessert of fruit pie or cherry cobbler seem beside the point, to say the least. It is total satisfaction, as I discovered while traveling through Texas; and if now I were not so far from San Antonio, where I experienced it first, I would be tempted to go down and get some beef right away. In San Antonio I was taken to a barbecue restaurant called Koehler's by Sam Zisman, one of the country's leading architects and city planners. Before ordering, Sam led me out behind the kitchen to see the pit itself. A lackadaisical cook, surrounded by the tools of his trade (long-handled pitchforks for turning the meat and a mop to swab it with peppery sauce) lifted the great metal lid over the pit so I could peer down into the smoky darkness to see the lacquered beef cooking slowly over the embers. "How do you know when to turn it?" I asked the cook. Ask a silly question and sometimes you get a good answer: "I turn it when it's ready," he said.

Re-entering Koehler's, Sam urged me to help myself to a tray, which I carried hungrily to a woman in white who stood carving off great wedges

Broiling Hamburgers the Easy Way

Hamburgers should be made from ground chuck or top round that has not been trimmed of all its fat before grinding. Most people handle the meat too much while forming it into patties; this makes it too tough. To make sure the hamburgers are moist and juicy, put a small piece of ice in with each patty. Searing the hamburgers also helps keep them from becoming hard and dry. Outdoors, sear them by grilling over a very hot fire. Indoors, pan-broil them in a heavy skillet. First, heat enough fat or vegetable oil in the skillet to coat the bottom thinly; then, on high heat, brown the hamburgers quickly on both sides to give them a light, tasty crust. Reduce the heat to medium and cook, uncovered, to the desired degree of doneness. (Well-done hamburgers must be turned two or three times during cooking.) Hamburgers may be sprinkled with salt and pepper at any point after they have been browned. If you prefer cheeseburgers, try grating the cheese of your choice and mixing it with the meat instead of placing a slice of cheese on top of the hamburgers.

111

of barbecued beef. "A pound of lean," said Sam, surprising me with the size of the order, "and give us some brown ends." The meat was passed over to me on a sheet of pink butcher's paper, which was to serve as my placemat. Onto my tray, in rapid succession, the woman plunked a couple of green and white scallions, a slice of onion half an inch thick, a hot *jalapeño chile,* some sweet peppers, and, at Sam's direction, a can of beer, fresh off the ice. The sight of the meat—tender even to the eye—with its dark, crusty edge and quarter-inch border of red indicating the depth to which the sauce had penetrated, had me famished, and I practically galloped to the table.

The only utensils in sight were small red plastic forks and yellow plastic knives, more fitted for child's play than adult use; and so we ate the tender meat the way it should be eaten, with our hands. It crumbled at the bite, and its wonderful, dark flavor had me picking at the last little shreds left on my tray. Best of all, from my viewpoint, were the brown ends, hardened crusts of beef and sauce, which in their taste of flame and smoke seemed to satisfy some atavistic need in me.

Beef as tender as that would seem to be the acme of perfection—and it is. But still the American beef industry is not entirely satisfied with its product, as I was to find out later the same day on a tour of a meat-packing plant. The industry feels that beef could be more uniformly tender—and, surprisingly, more uniformly lean. As much as 20 per cent of the edible portion of a prime steer must be discarded as fat. When Americans worked hard at physical labor, the fat on their meat provided them with fuel. Fat had its commercial value too, for use as tallow and as a lubricant. The chuck-wagon cook used to say, "The wheel that creaks gets the grease," and he would slop it on the axle. But tastes and needs have long since changed, and in most homes today fat is abhorred. Even so, I would have thought that the plump carcass being pointed out to me by a meat inspector—displaying a red, marbled loin with a great, cream colored crescent of fat wrapped halfway round the meat—would be considered nothing but delicious. But the man I was talking to thumped it in frustration. "Too gobby," he said, pointing to the excess fat and using a cattleman's word. "This animal was fattened too long, and no matter how good it may look to you—no matter how good it may in fact be—nobody wants to have, much less pay for, *that* much fat."

The beef industry and the government are both at work on a solution to the problem. A scientifically controlled diet, administered to cattle after they have been taken from their grass diet on the range to be fattened in the feed lot, has shown that good meat can be developed without excessive fat. Selective breeding has also been an enormous help in moving toward the industry's ideal—an animal that grows rapidly, comes to maturity early, utilizes its feed efficiently, reproduces regularly and yields a perfect carcass. Researchers have developed a test that can be made on a living animal to determine the proportion of fat to muscle, and even how tender and flavorsome the meat will be. And the government has begun work on a 35,000-acre breeding station in Nebraska on the site of a former ammunition dump, where by 1970 more than 200 veterinarians, agricultural engineers and market specialists will be going about the task

of producing new, streamlined cattle. Their goal is to achieve a standardized animal, cutting the unwanted fat from 20 per cent to 5 per cent without doing damage to the flavor or character of the beef. This saving will be passed along to the consumer in lower prices, and yet I cannot help but wonder how the housewife will react to what will then be more uniform beef—perhaps even providing cuts more or less of the same size. Not the least of our national differences is reflected in the weight of the beef cattle preferred by consumers in the various regions: the biggest go to the Boston and New York areas, heifers find a ready market in the Mississippi River Valley, and lighter animals are favored in the South and Southeast. In California, where more beef is eaten than in any other state, the preference is for cattle almost as large as those that are shipped regularly to the Northeast.

After beef, the meat that ranks next in popularity in the United States is pork. Each of us annually consumes some 63 pounds of it. Pork is, of course, traditional fare, our oldest meat, barring game; pigs came with the first settlers and were set loose to fatten in the woods—and an 18th Century writer noted that they swarmed like vermin upon the earth. In the Colonies, Virginia pork soon acquired a reputation for being "the best and the most delicate," and Virginia hams were much sought after in England. What gives Virginia or Smithfield ham its character is the hog's

Cowboys on a dude ranch in Wyoming grill steaks and hashed brown potatoes for guests. In an earlier time of more ample eating, enormous pits were dug in which whole steers could be roasted.

113

diet. Ideally, through almost all of the pig's first nine months it should be allowed to feed on nuts in the forest. Fleshed out by this wild food, it is then set loose in harvested peanut fields, there to root about and grow big on the protein-rich peanuts left behind by the reapers. In the final stages of its development, the hog is rounded to plump perfection with corn and dispatched; then the curing of the meat begins.

After the hams are salted and peppered, they are hung in a warm haze of oak, apple and hickory smoke. Once the smoking process has come to an end, they are aged upwards of a year (they can be aged even longer than that, and an old Virginia recipe is very specific in its instructions for cooking a ham that is five years old). They gradually shrink, gathering their spices and flavors unto themselves. The dry meat has no peer, and it is still—as it has been for more than 300 years—sliced wafer-thin and served as a very special treat.

Virginia ham has its fierce partisans, but there are other country-style hams from other areas, and *their* partisans would say that these are every bit as good or better. To someone living in Nashville or Louisville, for example, a Tennessee or Kentucky-cured ham "is richer, more nutlike and delicate." For those who are used to ordinary ham (which today is cured by injecting brine into the blood vessels and smoking it over sawdust, a process that can take as little as four days' time), the strong taste of country ham may be a welcome surprise. Anyone lucky enough to come by the genuine article should soak it first, then cook it slowly, bearing in mind this little bit of 17th Century Virginia wisdom, penned, of all places, on the flyleaf of a Bible: "Let it simmer, not boil—for simmering brings ye Salt out and boiling drives it in."

Where country hams are at their briniest, as in the Deep South, they are often sliced and fried and served for breakfast with red-eye gravy and grits. The gravy gets its name from the little eye of grease that forms at the center of it during the cooking. Some people make the gravy with cof-

Young turkeys, the fowl that the New World gave to world cooking, forage for seeds and insects on an Oregon ranch *(below)*. An American favorite, turkeys are hatched in incubators, let outdoors after 6 to 12 weeks where the weather is mild, and fattened for two to seven months before being slaughtered. On the opposite page ducklings strut about a Long Island, New York, farm. Brought to the United States from Peking in 1873, ducklings have multiplied enormously and become an American delicacy.

fee instead of water, and this is said to give it an even more bracing flavor.

Other Southern rural favorites founded squarely on cured hog's meat are fat back, streak of lean and sowbelly, all variations of salt pork that, when cooked with greens, yield yet another old Southern speciality—pot-likker. The last qualifies almost as an elixir, containing not only juices from the pork, but vitamins from the vegetables; in the past it was drunk by the sickly, and often had a restorative effect. Salt pork has had its adherents in the North as well (my grandfather's favorite dish on the farm was cold, boiled salt pork and dandelion greens), and today there are still cooks in New England and the Midwest who know how to fry it so that it comes out of the pan brown, yet free of grease, and who serve it with fried-apple slices, baked potatoes and a cream gravy, edged with the briny taste of the salt-cured meat.

Surely one of pork's greatest appeals to Americans of other centuries was the ease with which it could be preserved—not just by salting or smoking it, but in sausage form. A sausage stuffer was once an essential item of household equipment, and with each new wave of immigration came new recipes and ways of turning out this ancient food. Even today in the United States, more than 200 different kinds of sausages are sold, and many have retained their Old World names. In some urban areas, such as Milwaukee, sausage is a link to the past, with *Bratwurst, Knackwurst* or *Mettwurst* revealing the German origins of the family that serves them. The hot dog—so much a part of the American scene today—might still be called only a frankfurter had not a cartoonist in 1900, poking fun at its dachshundlike shape, rechristened it after its debut in a ballpark. But while we may owe a large debt to other countries for many of the sausages we now claim as our own, we have produced some that are truly American. In fact, what could be more American—excepting the flapjacks and maple syrup that go with it—than fresh pork sausage, smelling of thyme and sage? When sliced from a loaf and fried, it is still one of the fin-

est ways to greet a cold winter morning. American pork sausage has also taken some purely local forms, and these are often worth seeking out. *Andouilles*, the sausage of the Cajun country of Louisiana, is made from cubed rather than ground pork, and its peppery fire is tempered with sweetness during the smoking by basting the meat with sugar-cane syrup. Another excellent Louisiana sausage is chaurice, from the Spanish *chorizo;* a recipe for it, however, reads a little like a formula for a stick of gastronomic dynamite—cayenne, hot chili powder, red pepper, garlic, onions, thyme, parsley, bay and allspice.

Perhaps because pork was for so long the meat most Americans ate, it acquired the reputation of being ordinary, indigestible, even dangerous to the health. Properly prepared, however, it is none of these things. Most pork comes from animals under one year old, which means that it usually is tender. Moreover, it is a great deal leaner today than it was only 15 years ago, reflecting the results of new breeding and feeding programs. Tests have shown that pork is every bit as digestible as any other meat, although perhaps it could be viewed as a bit "heavy" for summer dining. And as for the dangers of trichinosis, scientists have recently shown that pork need not be cooked as long as most people think to make it safe. The parasites, when present (and the chances are slender indeed that they will be), are destroyed at the relatively low internal temperature of 137° F. (the recommended final internal roasting temperature for a pork loin, however, is 170° F.). If word were to get around about this, pork might soon be emerging from ovens well cooked, rather than overcooked—juicy instead of dry, and much more flavorful. In fact, pork's new lean look is a good enough recommendation in itself for cooking it less. For those who have not had pork to eat in a long while or who hesitate to serve it to guests, the recipe for a crown roast in the Recipe Booklet—a favorite dish with our grandparents—will be a reminder of how really fine this meat can be.

In contrast to the national taste for pork and beef, the American appetite for lamb and veal remains amazingly underdeveloped; each of us now eats about four pounds of these meats apiece, and this amount is down from what it was a few years ago. Lamb and veal deserve to be better known. Entire foreign cuisines are founded on their use, and the taste for both in the United States is kept alive, in part, by immigrants and second-generation Americans. French and Italians love veal and know how to use it well, and Greeks and Middle Easterners cook lamb to perfection. Much of the lamb raised in the United States has traditionally been shipped to Eastern markets; some also goes to urban areas on the West Coast and in the Great Lakes region. But even where lamb has long been a favorite, as in the East, many people fail to cook it properly, treating it much as though it were mutton and therefore needed to have the flavor, juices and fat cooked out of it. To understand how good lamb can be, try roast lamb with a pink center, the way the French like it *(Recipe Booklet);* it will be a different meat altogether, in looks, texture and flavor. The failure of lamb to enjoy wider popularity may have to do with the fact that much of the lamb reaching the markets today comes from animals a bit beyond the age at which many experts feel they make the best eating. In New York City at least, it is now possible to get baby lamb.

This lamb comes primarily from Pennsylvania and New Jersey, and it is never more than two months old. But for its tenderness and flavor there is a price to be paid—as much as $3.75 a pound.

A great deal of colorful lore attaches itself to the raising of lambs. Many shepherds today are Basques, brought over from the Pyrenees region of Spain and France for three-year stays. Tending their sheep, they lead a lonely life in mountain fastnesses, except when they come together for gregarious summer festivals. Then they take swigs from their *botas,* or leather wine bags, eat barbecued lamb and dance the energetic *jota.*

Veal consumption, like that of lamb, tends to reflect regional and ethnic preferences. Veal has long been a great favorite in New Orleans, for example. But how many people in the adjacent states of Texas and Mississippi

Three of America's most popular meats—sirloin strip steaks, hamburgers and hot dogs—form an ideal barbecue for the whole family, grownups and children alike. Tender and juicy, these meats are easily cooked to suit everyone's taste, whether for rare, medium or well done. Some hints for outdoor cooking are given on page 203.

eat it? And some of the best veal in the country, raised in the dairy states of Wisconsin and Minnesota, is shipped to the East Coast. Were there a real demand for veal in the United States, farmers undoubtedly would begin to supply it in quantity; but for it to be fine veal—milk-fed, whitish in color, no more than three months old—it would probably have to be quite expensive. In Italy, where pasturage is limited and veal is excellent, the farmer is doing the only sensible thing economically when he slaughters his calves; in America, as long as the market holds up, the land-rich farmer is wise to let his calves grow to full size. The yield from the mature animal in meat or milk is much higher than from a young one, and so is the profit. In spite of these problems, an Eastern supplier does market a fine veal labeled Plume de Veau. But it is meat produced under special conditions—the calf is kept in a stall and fed a special formula—and as might be expected, it fetches a fat two dollars-plus per pound.

Next to beef and pork, poultry is the third most popular main course of American meals. Chicken is, of course, the most popular poultry, but it was not always so cheap as it is today, nor so plentiful. In a relatively short time, beginning with the end of World War II, the broiler industry has not only managed to put a chicken in every pot at least once a week, but to breed an entirely new chicken—one that grows larger than its predecessors, in less time and on less feed. This success has been emulated around the world. I can remember how, on my first visit to Europe in 1953, I was offered chicken by friends who wanted to honor me; accustomed to chicken at home, I would have preferred their duck or goose. But chicken was then a costly bird; now, thanks to the adoption of American methods, it is almost as common in Europe as in the United States.

Today a broiler requires only two and a quarter pounds of feed to produce one pound of chicken meat (in contrast to the four and a half pounds it took in 1941), and it comes to market at a tender nine weeks of age, weighing about two and a half pounds. There are many of the older generation who look back wistfully on the June frier or broiler, an American specialty that is now available the year round, and say that the incubated, computer-fed breed does not compare to the earlier one in flavor. But then, what doesn't taste better in memory?

In 1934 broiler production stood at 34 million birds; today it is well over two and a half billion. Each of us now eats 37 pounds of chicken every year, which explains why, in recent years, chicken recipes have proliferated. In looking over recent winning entries in the annual National Chicken Cooking Contest (yes, there is such a contest, and it has been going on for 21 years), I was startled to find one that called for pecan halves, three Graham crackers, five gingersnaps, one half cup of quick-cooking oatmeal and one half teaspoon of pumpkin-pie spice. I was relieved and amused to see that this entry—"Hansel 'n' Gretel Chicken"—was the contribution of an 11-year-old boy.

Chicken, of course, is not the only poultry consumed in great quantities by Americans today. Turkey *(page 32)* remains the traditional holiday feast, and Americans ate eight pounds of turkey annually in the late 1960s. Long Island ducklings, first brought to New York from China by a Yankee clipper captain in 1873, are increasingly popular, and the com-

Tips for Cooking Crisper Bacon

Served with eggs for breakfast, with lettuce and tomato in a sandwich, or with calf's liver, bacon is best when it is crisp. An easy way to ensure crispness is to cook it in a moderate oven on a rack set in a baking pan. If the bacon is cooked on top of the stove, it should be started in a cold skillet on moderate heat and arranged in one layer with the slices barely touching each other. Pour off the fat occasionally and turn the bacon frequently as it cooks. When the slices reach the desired crispness, lay them on paper towels to drain for a minute or two before serving.

pact Rock Cornish hens grown in Connecticut and New York are sold in stores across the country.

While poultry, beef and pork are American staples, the availability of game in many parts of this country adds an extra zest and flavor to our eating. Some 20 million hunters take to the American woods and fields each year. In Colorado alone, in one recent year, 114,529 deer were killed by 128,000 registered hunters. What the annual national take in venison may be is not known, but deer are more numerous today in many states than they were in Indian days. Having their numbers thinned regularly by hunters has actually been to their advantage, man doing what nature once did when predators abounded.

In such a big country, the range and habitats of many wild animals vary. This has given many game dishes a distinctive regional character. The javelina, or peccary, of the Southwest, the antelope of the Mountain States and Oregon, the band-tailed pigeon of the West and Southwest are to be tasted only in those areas. Opossum—as ugly a little beast as I could ever hope to stumble across in the American wilderness—makes good local eating in the South. But as one West Virginia storekeeper has said, "You got to feed 'em first—pen 'em up and feed 'em on persimmons, or milk an' corn, t'edge up the flavor." Opossum thus fattened is roasted like suckling pig, minus the apple, but wreathed with sweet potatoes. I am sure that squirrel must also make good eating, but I have yet to taste it, and I wonder whether I would ever want to, conditioned as I have been by the squirrels' friendliness in Central Park. Perhaps someday I will meet in the South one of those purists who still use squirrel instead of chicken for Brunswick stew. So too, I may meet the man who put it in Kentucky burgoo, that great favorite of Derby week, still prepared and served in enormous quantities, but minus the ingredient that was once considered an essential part of it.

One of the game meats I would like to taste is buffalo. In the Western states, where sizable herds survive, the animals are annually cropped to protect their pasturage. Unfortunately for some of us, the greater part of the buffalo meat so obtained is consumed in the West, where it has become a seasonal speciality. A Texas cattleman I talked to likened buffalo to an "old bull steak," and he knew whereof he spoke; and yet the desire to try the meat that fed a nation moving westward lingers on.

Although game is hunted with enthusiasm in this country, it is all too often cooked with indifference, and on many occasions, way overcooked. William Levitt, of Alta, Utah, has been experimenting the past few years with new methods of preparing it, and he now serves his venison, antelope, elk, goose and duck rare. He says that game not only tastes a great deal better this way, but is more tender. And he has already won converts among local hunters.

But just as the cooking of game remains misunderstood by many, so too in an alarming number of homes does the cooking of ordinary meat. Of course, whether a roast or a steak is rare, medium or well done will always be a matter of personal preference, but is there any need for so much cooked meat to be overdone? In a country like this, where meat is basically so good, that seems like blaspheming our American heritage.

Taking the Gamble out of Cooking Eggs

Almost anybody can cook eggs. Cooking them well is another matter. Here are some tips, long known to experts, that can result in excellent eggs every time. Always use medium heat when frying eggs; high heat frizzles the whites around the edges. For scrambled eggs, beat the eggs together with some salt and pepper only long enough to blend the yolks and the whites. Stir them slowly and continuously in a buttered skillet over low heat until they begin to thicken, then stir them fast until they have almost reached the desired consistency. Take them off the heat and stir in some soft butter or heavy cream and fresh herbs. To soft-boil eggs, place them in a pan of boiling water, remove the pan from the heat, cover it tightly and let the eggs stand for 5 to 8 minutes. (Large eggs and refrigerated eggs take longer than small or room-temperature eggs.) For hard-cooked eggs, drop the eggs into cold water, bring to a boil and remove from heat. Cover the pan tightly and let stand for 20 minutes. At high altitudes such cooking takes longer; your county home-demonstration agent can advise you on specific cooking times.

CHAPTER IV RECIPES

To serve 6 to 8

A crown roast of lamb, consisting of
16 to 18 chops and weighing about
4½ pounds
1 clove garlic, cut into tiny slivers
(optional)
2 teaspoons salt
1 teaspoon freshly ground black
pepper
1 teaspoon crushed dried rosemary
16 to 18 peeled new potatoes, all
about 1½ inches in diameter
3 cups cooked fresh or frozen peas
2 tablespoons melted butter
6 to 8 sprigs of fresh mint

Crown Roast of Lamb with Peas and New Potatoes

Preheat the oven to 475°. With the point of a small, sharp knife make small incisions a few inches apart in the meaty portions of the lamb, and insert in them the slivers of garlic, if you are using it. Combine the salt, pepper and rosemary, and with your fingers pat the mixture all over the bottom and sides of the crown. To help keep its shape, stuff the crown with a crumpled sheet of foil and wrap the ends of the chop bones in strips of foil to prevent them from charring and snapping off. Place the crown of lamb on a small rack set in a shallow roasting pan just large enough to hold it comfortably and roast it in the center of the oven for about 20 minutes. Then turn down the heat to 400° and surround the crown with the new potatoes, basting them with the pan drippings and sprinkling them lightly with salt. Continue to roast the lamb (basting the lamb is unnecessary, but baste the potatoes every 15 minutes or so) for about an hour to an hour and 15 minutes, depending upon how well done you prefer your lamb. Ideally, it should be served when it is still somewhat pink, and should register 140° to 150° on a meat thermometer.

When the crown is done, carefully transfer it to a large circular platter, remove the foil and let the lamb rest about 10 minutes to make carving easier. Meanwhile, combine the peas with the melted butter and season them with as much salt as is necessary. Fill the hollow of the crown with as many of the peas as it will hold and serve any remaining peas separately. Put a paper frill on the end of each chop bone and surround the crown with the roasted potatoes. Garnish with mint and serve at once.

To carve the lamb, insert a large fork in the side of the crown to steady it and with a large, sharp knife cut down through each rib to detach the chops. Two rib chops per person is a customary portion.

To serve 4

One 5- to 6-pound Long Island
duckling, cut into quarters

MARINADE
¾ cup vegetable oil
½ cup red-wine vinegar
1 teaspoon salt
Freshly ground black pepper
1 cup thinly sliced onion
3 large garlic cloves, thinly sliced
2 large bay leaves, coarsely crumbled
Salt, preferably the coarse (kosher)
variety

Broiled Long Island Duckling

Wash the duck under cold running water and pat thoroughly dry. With poultry shears or a sharp knife, trim the quarters, cutting away all exposed fat. In a shallow glass, porcelain or stainless-steel pan large enough to hold the duck quarters in one layer, mix the oil, vinegar, salt and a few grindings of pepper. Add the onion, garlic and bay leaves. Lay the duck in this marinade, baste thoroughly and marinate at room temperature at least 3 hours, turning the pieces every half hour.

When you are ready to broil the duck, remove it from the marinade. Strain the marinade through a fine sieve and discard the vegetables. Preheat the broiler to its highest point. Arrange the duck, skin side down, on the broiler rack, sprinkle lightly with salt and broil 4 inches from the heat for about 35 minutes, regulating the heat or lowering the rack so the duck browns slowly without burning. Baste every 10 minutes or so with the marinade. Turn the pieces over with tongs, sprinkle with salt and broil 10 to 15 minutes longer, basting 2 or 3 times with the marinade. When the duck is tender and a deep golden brown, arrange it on a heated serving platter. Serve at once.

Baked Bourbon-glazed Ham

Preheat the oven to 325°. Place the ham fat side up on a rack set in a shallow roasting pan large enough to hold the ham comfortably. Bake in the middle of the oven, without basting, for two hours, or until the meat can be easily pierced with a fork. For greater cooking certainty, insert a meat thermometer in the fleshiest part of the ham before baking it. It should register between 130° and 140° when the ham is done.

When the ham is cool enough to handle comfortably, cut away the rind with a large, sharp knife. Then score the ham by cutting deeply through the fat until you reach the meat, making the incisions ½ inch apart lengthwise and crosswise. Return the ham to the rack in the pan and raise the oven heat to 450°. With a pastry brush, paint the ham on all sides with ½ cup of the whiskey. Then combine the sugar and mustard and ¼ cup of whiskey, and pat the mixture firmly into the scored fat. Stud the fat at the intersections or in the center of each diamond with a whole clove, and arrange the orange sections as decoratively as you can on the top of the ham with toothpicks or small skewers to secure them. Baste lightly with the drippings on the bottom of the pan and bake the ham undisturbed in the hot oven for 15 to 20 minutes, or until the sugar has melted and formed a brilliant glaze.

To serve 12 to 14

A 12- to 14-pound smoked ham, processed, precooked variety
¾ cup bourbon whiskey
2 cups dark brown sugar
1 tablespoon dry mustard
¾ cup whole cloves
2 navel oranges, peeled and sectioned

Stuffed Pork Chops

To make the stuffing, combine the bread crumbs and cream in a small mixing bowl, and stir together to saturate the crumbs thoroughly. Over moderate heat, melt the 2 tablespoons of butter in an 8-inch skillet. When the foam subsides, add the onions, garlic and crumbled sausage meat. Stirring constantly, cook until the sausage has rendered most of its fat and has lightly browned. Scrape the contents of the pan into a sieve and let the excess fat drain through. Then combine the sausage meat mixture with the bread crumbs in the mixing bowl. Add the thyme and chopped parsley and mix together gently. Taste for seasoning. Add as much salt as you think it needs, and a little freshly ground pepper.

Preheat the oven to 325°. With a small spoon, pack as much of the stuffing as you can into the pork chop pockets and seal the openings with small skewers. Sprinkle the chops generously on both sides with salt and a few grindings of black pepper. Heat 4 tablespoons of oil over high heat in a 10- or 12-inch heavy skillet until a light haze forms over it. Add the chops and cook them on each side for about 3 minutes, regulating the heat so that they brown easily and quickly without burning. Remove them to a platter. Pour off all but a thin film of fat from the skillet and add the ½ cup of chopped onion, carrot and thyme. Cook over moderate heat for 5 to 8 minutes until the vegetables color lightly. Then mix in the tablespoon of flour, add the stock and bring it to a boil. Stirring constantly, cook until the stock thickens lightly. Place the browned chops, and any liquid which has accumulated around them, in this mixture. Cover tightly, and bake in the middle of the oven, basting occasionally with the pan juices, for 30 to 40 minutes, or until tender.

To serve, arrange the chops on a heated platter and pour the sauce, strained or not, as you prefer, over them.

To serve 6

STUFFING
1½ cups fine, dry bread crumbs
¼ cup heavy cream
2 tablespoons butter
¼ cup finely chopped onion
¼ teaspoon finely chopped garlic
½ pound well-seasoned sausage meat
⅛ teaspoon thyme
3 tablespoons finely chopped parsley
Salt
Freshly ground black pepper

6 well-trimmed, center-cut loin pork chops, 1 inch thick, each chop slit on the side to create a pocket about 3 inches deep
Salt
Freshly ground black pepper
4 tablespoons vegetable oil
½ cup finely chopped onion
½ cup finely chopped, scraped carrot
¼ teaspoon thyme
1 tablespoon flour
1 cup chicken stock, fresh or canned

121

An Elegant But Easy Ham

Garnished with oranges and parsley and glazed with brown sugar, mustard and bourbon, this delicious 14-pound ham represents a triumph of American technology. In the old days hams were soaked and boiled for days, but this precooked cured ham needed to be baked *(page 121)* for only two hours.

6 pairs sweetbreads, about 3 pounds
2 tablespoons lemon juice
2 teaspoons salt
2 cups water
²/₃ cup sherry
6 tablespoons butter
12 unpeeled mushroom caps, 1½ to
 2 inches in diameter, rubbed lightly
 with a damp paper towel

Sweetbreads and Ham under Glass

To prepare the sweetbreads for poaching, soak them for about 2 hours in enough cold water to cover them, changing the water every 45 minutes or so. Then soak again, for another hour, in 2 quarts of cold water mixed with 2 tablespoons of lemon juice and 2 teaspoons salt. Drain. Separate the sweetbread lobes, and cut away and discard the soft, white connecting tubes. With a small, sharp knife, pull off as much of the thin outside membrane of the sweetbreads as you can without tearing the delicate flesh.

Place the sweetbreads in a 2-quart enameled or stainless-steel saucepan, and add 2 cups of water and ²/₃ cup of sherry. If the liquid doesn't quite cover the sweetbreads, add more water. Bring to a simmer over moderate heat, then lower the heat and cook as slowly as possible, uncovered, for about 15 minutes. Drain, plunge into cold water for 5 minutes, then drain again. Pat dry with paper towels.

Sweetbreads and ham provide a *grande cuisine* touch when served under a glass bell, which keeps them moist and warm.

Over moderate heat, melt 4 tablespoons of the butter in a 10-inch enameled or stainless-steel skillet, and when the foam subsides add the sweetbreads. Cook them on each side for about 3 minutes, or until they are a delicate brown. Remove to a platter. Melt the remaining butter in the skillet and cook the mushrooms briskly for a minute or two on each side to brown them lightly, then put them aside with the sweetbreads. Pour off all but a thin film of the butter from the pan and pour in the ½ cup of sherry. Over high heat, boil briskly for 2 minutes, then add the cream and boil rapidly for about 5 minutes, or until it thickens enough to coat a spoon. Add the lemon juice and season with as much salt and white pepper as you think it needs. Put it aside. Preheat the oven to 375°.

Arrange the toast rounds in individual 4- to 5-inch shallow ramekins. Top each round with a slice of ham, then a pair of sweetbreads and, finally, the mushroom caps. Pour equal amounts of the sauce over each cap and cover with individual glass bells. Heat in the middle of the oven for 12 to 15 minutes and serve at once.

Roast Pheasant with Applejack Cream Sauce

To make the stuffing, melt 2 tablespoons of the butter over moderate heat in an 8-inch skillet. When the foam subsides, add the chopped onion and the pheasant livers. Stirring frequently, cook the mixture for 3 to 4 minutes until the livers have stiffened slightly. Scrape the mixture into a bowl. Add the remaining 2 tablespoons of butter to the same skillet and, over high heat, brown the diced bread in it for 3 to 4 minutes. Add it to the livers in the mixing bowl. Mix in the apples and parsley, taste for seasoning, and add salt and pepper to taste.

Preheat the oven to 375°. Wash the pheasants quickly under cold water and dry them thoroughly inside and out with paper towels. Rub the soft butter into the skins of each of them and fill their cavities with the stuffing. Do not pack it in too firmly. Secure the openings with skewers or sew with strong white thread. Truss the birds by tying their legs together with cord. Drape the bacon strips over their legs and breasts, and place them, breast side up, on a rack set in a shallow baking pan just large enough to hold the birds comfortably. Roast undisturbed in the center of the oven for about 30 minutes. Remove the pan from the oven and sprinkle the birds lightly with salt and pepper. Heat ¼ cup of the applejack in a small pan until lukewarm. Set it alight with a match and pour it flaming, little by little, over the birds, shaking the pan gently until the flames die out. Baste thoroughly with the accumulated pan juices and return the pheasants to the oven. Roast for 10 to 12 minutes, or until the birds are brown, crisp and tender. Remove to a heated platter and make the sauce.

Pour the chicken stock and the remaining applejack into the roasting pan and bring it to a boil on the top of the stove, scraping into it any brown bits clinging to the bottom and sides of the pan. Boil briskly for 2 to 3 minutes, then stir in the cream. Bring to a boil once more, taste for seasoning, and either pour the sauce over the pheasants or serve it separately in a gravy boat.

Carve the pheasants by splitting them along their length into halves with a sharp carving knife or shears, allowing ½ bird per person.

SAUCE
½ cup sherry
1 cup heavy cream
2 teaspoons lemon juice
Salt
White pepper

6 circles of white bread, 3½ inches in diameter, lightly browned on both sides in 4 tablespoons of hot butter
6 slices cooked ham, ¼ inch thick, cut into circles 3½ inches in diameter

To serve 4

STUFFING
4 tablespoons butter
¼ cup finely chopped onion
2 pheasant livers, coarsely chopped
1½ cups ½-inch-diced day-old bread
½ cup peeled, cored and diced apple, cut into ½-inch cubes
1 tablespoon parsley
Salt
Freshly ground black pepper

2 drawn pheasants, approximately 1 pound each
2 tablespoons soft butter
4 strips bacon, cut in half
½ cup applejack
½ cup chicken stock, fresh or canned
¼ cup heavy cream

Duck in aspic forms a jewellike salad ringed by orange slices and filled with well-seasoned onion rings and orange sections.

To serve 6

A 5- to 6-pound duck, cut into
   quarters
Duck giblets
4 cups orange juice, fresh or frozen
4 cups chicken stock, fresh or canned
1 cup thinly sliced onion
½ cup thinly sliced carrot
¾ cup celery, cut into 2-inch pieces
Herb bouquet of 6 sprigs parsley and
   1 bay leaf, tied together
½ teaspoon thyme

Duck in Orange Aspic with Orange and Onion Salad

In a 4- or 5-quart casserole combine the duck, giblets, orange juice and chicken stock. Bring to a boil, skim off all the surface scum and froth, then add the onion, carrot, celery, herb bouquet and thyme. Season with salt if you think it necessary. Half cover the casserole, reduce the heat to its lowest point and simmer the duck for about 1½ hours, or until tender. Then cut the skin and duck meat away from the bones and return the skin and bones to the casserole. Simmer the broth about ½ hour longer. Cut the duck meat into ½- by ¾-inch pieces and refrigerate.

THE ASPIC: Strain the entire contents of the casserole broth through a fine sieve, pressing down on the vegetables and duck parts to extract all their liquid before throwing them away. Measure the broth. You should have 4 cups. If less, add chicken stock; if more, boil down rapidly to 4

126

cups. Skim the surface of the broth of every bit of fat you can (this is easier if you chill the broth first until the fat rises and congeals on the surface), then return the broth to a 3- or 4-quart saucepan. Soften the gelatin in the ½ cup of cold stock or water for 5 minutes, then stir it into the broth. To clarify the aspic, add the peppercorns, the coarsely chopped orange peel and the lemon juice, then beat the egg whites to a froth with a wire whisk and whisk them into the broth. Bring to a boil over moderate heat, whisking constantly. When the aspic begins to froth and rise, remove the pan from the heat. Let it rest 5 minutes, then strain it into a deep bowl through a fine sieve lined with a dampened kitchen towel. Allow all the aspic to drain through without disturbing it at any point. The aspic should now be brilliantly clear. Taste for seasoning and add salt if necessary. Pour the aspic into a 1½-quart ring mold and set the mold in a bowl in crushed ice. Stir with a metal spoon until it becomes thick and syrupy (don't allow it to set), then mix into it the duck meat and slivers of orange peel. Refrigerate at least 2 hours, or until firmly set.

When you are ready to serve it, run a thin, sharp knife around the insides of the mold (including the cone), and dip the bottom in hot water for a few seconds. Then wipe the outside of the mold dry, place a large, chilled, circular serving plate upside down over the mold and, grasping both firmly, quickly turn plate and mold over. Rap them sharply on the table and the aspic should slide out. If it doesn't, repeat the process.

Fill the center of the aspic ring with the orange and onion salad, and arrange extra orange slices around the ring if you wish.

ORANGE AND ONION SALAD: In a large mixing bowl beat the wine vinegar, salt, a few grindings of black pepper, the olive oil and lemon juice with a wire whisk or fork until they are all well combined. Add the oranges and onions, and toss them together gently. Taste for seasoning.

Braised Short Ribs of Beef

Preheat the oven to 500°. Season the short ribs generously with salt and a few grindings of black pepper. Dip them in flour, vigorously shaking off any excess, then arrange them side by side on a rack in a shallow roasting pan. Brown them in the middle of the oven for 20 to 25 minutes, checking periodically to make sure they do not burn.

Meanwhile, melt the 2 tablespoons of butter over moderate heat in a heavy, 6-quart, flameproof casserole. When the foam subsides, add the onion, carrot, garlic and thyme, and, stirring frequently, cook for 6 to 8 minutes until the vegetables are lightly colored. Place the browned ribs, preferably in one layer, on top of the vegetables, add the stock to the roasting pan and stir into it any brown bits clinging to the pan. Then pour it over the ribs in the casserole. Bring to a boil on top of the stove, add the bay leaves and cover the casserole tightly. Reduce the oven heat to 325°. Braise the short ribs in the middle of the oven for about an hour until the meat shows no resistance when pierced with a fork.

To serve, arrange the short ribs on a heated platter. Strain the braising juices through a fine sieve into a saucepan, pressing down on the vegetables to extract all their juices before discarding them. Skim the fat from the surface, taste the sauce for seasoning and pour over the meat.

ASPIC

2 envelopes unflavored gelatin
½ cup cold chicken stock or water
10 whole peppercorns
Peel of 2 oranges, coarsely chopped
2 teaspoons lemon juice
2 egg whites
Peel of 2 navel oranges cut into tiny slivers and blanched

ORANGE AND ONION SALAD

2 tablespoons wine vinegar
½ teaspoon salt
Freshly ground black pepper
6 tablespoons olive oil
½ teaspoon lemon juice
4 navel oranges, peeled, and either thinly sliced or sectioned
2 red onions, peeled, thinly sliced and separated into rings

To serve 6 to 8

5 to 6 pounds lean short ribs of beef, cut into 3- to 4-inch pieces
Salt
Freshly ground black pepper
½ cup flour
2 tablespoons butter
1 cup coarsely chopped onion
1 cup coarsely chopped, scraped carrot
½ teaspoon finely chopped garlic
⅛ teaspoon thyme
1 cup beef stock, fresh or canned
2 small bay leaves

The Most Tempting Game in America

The prevalence of easily available meat in the form of wild animals made the settlement of America possible, and this food has been an American favorite ever since. As the pioneers pushed westward, they survived by killing deer, birds and other game. Since then, some species have disappeared, but many fine varieties exist today in sufficient quantities to be hunted and enjoyed at the table. The drawings on these pages show a selection of the country's best-tasting and available wild game. The tips given here indicate how they may be enjoyed to the fullest. For a collection of wild-game recipes, see *Going Wild in the Kitchen*, by Gertrude Parke, published by David McKay Co. Inc. (1965).

MOURNING DOVE

Found in all of the "old" 48 states. Its flavor is heightened by braising with olives or sautéing with bacon.

BOBWHITE

Nests in almost all states. May be roasted in grape leaves or sautéed with white grapes.

PRONGHORN ANTELOPE

Inhabits the western half of the U.S. Excellent when marinated, braised and served with puréed chestnuts.

MALLARD DUCK

Ranges from Alaska to the Rio Grande. Roast it and serve the giblets, chopped and sautéed, on toast.

RING-NECKED PHEASANT

Abounds in northern states as far west as the Rockies. Try braising it with cabbage or sauerkraut.

CHUKAR PARTRIDGE

Lives west of the Mississippi. Roast it and serve with shoestring potatoes or homemade potato chips.

WOODCOCK

Found in the eastern United States. Can be roasted or spitted, and its meat makes an excellent pâté.

RUFFED GROUSE

Lives everywhere but in West and Southwest. Serve grilled with buttered bread crumbs and currant jelly.

WHITETAIL DEER
Roams most of the country except the Southwest. Excellent roasted. Its liver is highly prized for its flavor.

BLACK BEAR
Native to most of United States. The meat is sweetish. The paws are a delicacy roasted, sautéed or braised.

WILD TURKEY
Inhabits eastern two thirds of nation. Stuff and roast it *(page 32)*; more flavor than the domestic bird.

ELK
Lives in the Rockies and the Pacific states. Makes good hamburgers or, chopped into mincemeat, pies.

WILD BOAR
Range is North Carolina, Tennessee, California and Texas. Can be roasted or braised after marinating.

COTTONTAIL RABBIT
Found in every state. Young rabbits are fried with cream gravy or grilled; older ones, stewed.

To serve 4

2 cloves garlic cut into paper-thin
   slivers
4 meaty lamb shanks (about 1 pound
   each)
Salt
Freshly ground black pepper
3 tablespoons vegetable oil
2 tablespoons butter
½ cup finely chopped onion
2½ cups beef stock, fresh or canned
2½ cups lentils, thoroughly washed
   and drained
1 bay leaf
½ cup chopped scallions
¼ cup chopped fresh parsley

Roast Lamb Shanks and Lentils

Preheat the oven to 350°. With the point of a small, sharp knife, insert 2 or 3 garlic slivers into the meaty portion of each lamb shank. Then sprinkle the shanks generously with salt and a few grindings of black pepper. In a 12-inch heavy skillet, heat the oil over high heat until a light haze forms over it. Add the shanks, and then, over moderate heat, cook them on all sides for about 10 minutes, turning them with tongs. When the shanks are a deep golden brown, transfer them to a rack set in a shallow roasting pan. Roast them in the middle of the oven for about an hour, or until the shanks are tender. Basting is unnecessary.

While the shanks are roasting, melt 2 tablespoons of butter over moderate heat in a 2- to 4-quart saucepan. When the foam subsides add the onions and cook them for about 6 minutes, stirring frequently until they are transparent but not brown. Pour in the stock and add the lentils, bay leaf, salt and a few grindings of black pepper. Bring to a boil. Cover the pot and reduce the heat to its lowest point. Simmer the lentils, stirring occasionally, for about 30 minutes, or until they have absorbed all the stock and are very tender.

To serve, stir into the lentils 2 tablespoons of drippings from the roasting pan and ½ cup of chopped scallions. Taste for seasoning. Arrange the lamb shanks and the lentils on a large, heated platter and sprinkle with parsley.

To serve 6 to 8

4 tablespoons black peppercorns
A 5-pound saddle of venison
2 teaspoons salt
6 tablespoons melted butter
4 to 6 cups beef stock, fresh or canned

SAUCE
2 tablespoons butter
2 tablespoons flour
2 tablespoons currant jelly
½ cup heavy cream

Roast Saddle of Venison with Cream Sauce

Preheat the oven to 475°. Crush the peppercorns in a mortar with a pestle or wrap them in a kitchen towel and press a rolling pin back and forth over them. The peppercorns should be quite coarse, not reduced to a powder. Sprinkle the meat with the salt, then with the heel of your hand press as much of the crushed pepper as you can into the meat. Place the meat on a rack in a shallow roasting pan large enough to hold it comfortably and pour 4 tablespoons of the melted butter over it. Pour 4 cups of the beef stock into the bottom of the pan. Roast the venison, uncovered, in the middle of the oven for 15 minutes, then pour 2 more tablespoons of butter over the meat and reduce the oven heat to 425°. Continue roasting, basting occasionally with the rest of the butter, for 1½ hours longer. (If the saddle is young and tender, and you prefer game rare, roast only 1 hour longer.) Add the remaining stock to the pan, ½ cup at a time, if at any point the pan drippings have evaporated.

When the venison is done, transfer it to a heated platter and let it rest while you make the sauce. In a 1- to 2-quart enameled or stainless-steel saucepan, melt 2 tablespoons of butter over moderate heat. When the foam subsides, stir in the flour. Cook over low heat, stirring constantly for a minute or so or until the mixture bubbles up and froths. Pour in 2 cups of the roasting pan juices (if there isn't enough, add to it as much stock or water as necessary). Bring to a boil, stirring constantly with a whisk until the sauce is smooth and slightly thickened. Reduce the heat to moderate and beat in the currant jelly and heavy cream. Simmer 2 or 3 minutes longer until the jelly is thoroughly dissolved. Taste for seasoning. Pour into a heated gravy boat and serve with the venison.

Piping-hot lamb shanks and lentils make a simple but sustaining winter meal.

V

A Delectable
Kettle of Fish

Against a dramatic backdrop of the Grand Teton mountains and a darkening sky, Wyoming fishermen cook a pair of cutthroat trout, which abound in the nearby Snake River. Rolled in cornmeal and fried in bacon drippings, the cutthroat is one of the country's most savory game fish.

I love fish. In my view, it is the quintessential nourishment, the one wild thing we all still eat. Millennia ago corn lost the ability to sow itself; now the domestic turkey, bred to plumpness, also needs man's help to reproduce. The broiler embryo develops in a rocking incubator that simulates the movements of the mother hen on the egg, and the chick pecks its way out of the shell into a controlled environment. Our fruits and vegetables are teased into higher and higher yields through genetics and fertilizers. Although berries and mushrooms still grow wild in the meadows and forests, they are beyond the reach of most of us who live in the cities. But we can still buy fresh seafood, brought up dripping and alive from a realm science has yet to conquer—and tasting of the deep.

Each year with a group of friends I go to an island in Long Island Sound for a clambake. It has become a ritual for us, a way to refresh ourselves. The island is a small one, with a stone lighthouse at one end and a ruined mansion at the other, and a tangle of trees, vines and goldenrod in between. The first year we felt a little like Columbus stepping ashore in a new world as we set out to explore the place, hopping from boulder to boulder, picking up shells and driftwood, and growing deeply and wonderfully hungry in the salt-stained air and blazing sunshine. But it was a long while before we ate: first we had to gather wood for the fire, and collect seaweed with which to bed down the lobster, clams, corn and chicken. Then we had to wait patiently for our feast to cook, and by the time it was ready, an hour or two later, we were ready. The afternoon had turned to evening, and the rippling water lay purple under a lavender sky. Our appetites burned at peak intensity. Tossing aside our manners, we helped ourselves to—and ate—the steaming food with our eager hands. I don't think any of us will ever forget the fresh, natural taste of it —the clams, tender, glazed with melted butter; the lobster, juicy and sweet; the chicken and corn, touched with a tang of salt and sea.

Why, I wonder, with seafood as incredibly good as ours, do we not eat a great deal more of it? Our biggest appetite is for shrimp; Americans consumed 393 million pounds of fresh and frozen shrimp in 1967. Among shellfish, crab ranks second, lobster third. After that, consumption of other shellfish and fish drops off dramatically. Yet we are envied by fish lovers the world over for the rich range of species that can be found in our coastal waters, in the warm Gulf of Mexico and in the chilly lakes, rivers and streams of inland areas. The country is so large that a fish plentiful in one region may be known only by reputation in another. Most Easterners have never had rex sole or petrale sole or sand dab, the last a moist little fish of the flounder family found off the state of Washington, but then again, a great many West Coasters have never eaten swordfish, now being caught all year long in the Atlantic. A trip around the United States can yield one new seafood treat after another. Try it some time: go down the East Coast and up the West, and see how many different kinds of clams and oysters alone there are to sample.

Each area not only has its own characteristic seafood, but its own way of cooking it. New England's way is simple. Why do more than boil or broil Maine lobster—except, perhaps, to make lobster Newburg (page 150)? There is, in all of eating, little that approaches the serene pleasure of having a whole lobster to oneself, picking out the nuggets of white meat from the red shell (page 147), dipping them in melted butter and washing them down with an agreeable white wine.

While New England's way of cooking seafood is simple, the cookery becomes more complex as you go south along the Eastern Seaboard. Maryland's crabs, for example, are prepared in many different ways, ranging from basic crab cakes, fried a golden brown, to crab imperial. H. L. Mencken once noted that in his hometown of Baltimore there were supposed to be at least 50 ways of preparing crabs. The shrimp of the Carolinas go into a broad spectrum of dishes—the most famous, perhaps, being pilau, a savory concoction of rice, diced peppers, tomatoes and spices. Florida's shrimp are often boiled in beer, a medium that enhances their flavor. In Louisiana shrimp may be cooked—as are crabs and crawfish—with a spice mixture known as crab boil, and this tingly blend of seasonings gets under the shell, to the enrichment of the firm flesh inside.

On the West Coast the pleasures of fish range from California's abalone in its opalescent shell and the tiny shrimp found off Eureka to the fantastic salmon of the Northwest. On the East Coast, there is only one oceangoing species of salmon, but there are five to be found in the Northwest: the Chinook, or king salmon (pages 142-143)—the world's biggest—and there, the most popular game fish; the coho, also a much-sought game fish; the sockeye; the chum, a prime source for canning; and the humpback. Whether smoked, poached, broiled, baked, served hot or cold, they all make delicious eating.

East Coast Clams and Oysters

The two species of clams found everywhere along the Atlantic Coast are quahog, or hard, clams and razor clams. Quahogs are called littlenecks or cherrystones when they are young and small, and at this stage should be served on the half shell. The larger quahogs are best for chowder. Razor clams on the Atlantic seaboard are steamed, fried or cooked in chowder. They should be eaten the day they are caught. Soft, longneck or steamer clams—the kind eaten at clambakes—occur along the Atlantic Coast as far south as North Carolina. In the same area, surf or hen clams—huge clams whose triangle-shaped shells are often used as ashtrays—are abundant. As with scallops, only the large, cylindrical adductor muscle is edible; it is eaten raw.

The Eastern, or American, oyster is found from Maine to the Gulf of Mexico. This oyster also has a variety of local names, such as Blue Point, Chincoteague and Cotuit. It may be eaten raw or cooked in the various ways in which any oysters are cooked. The small coon, or mangrove, oyster, which grows in clusters, is found along the seacoast from North Carolina to Florida. It is usually roasted, fried, or cooked in stews or soups.

For anyone making a seafood tour of the country, there will be some real surprises, along with all the anticipated pleasures. In Boston, sautéed codfish tongues and cheeks is an old favorite. In Baltimore, as in other places where hard crabs are sold, a mallet is the preferred utensil since the shell must be smashed to smithereens to get at the meat. Key West's stone crab, with its monster peach-colored claws tipped in black, requires every bit as direct an approach. Louisiana's buster crab—a rare treat—is, like Maryland soft-shelled crab, an easy thing to eat, so easy and so delicious, in fact, that it is a pity there are not more of them. But before a buster crab arrives at the table, a man must patiently watch for the precise moment when the crab is about to shed the shell and then remove it by hand; needless to say, this limits the supply. Washington's geoduck, an eight-inch clam that rests its two-foot-long neck, or siphon, on the beaches in languid poses, can shock on first sight; ground and used in chowder, it is passable eating. Anyone unprepared for the size of Washington's famed Olympia oysters may be amazed to discover that a couple, shucked, will fit into a thimble; 1,400 make a gallon. And Alaska's king crab *(page 66),* with its foot-long legs outstretched, when seen for the first time evokes images of a creature out of science fiction.

Yet, much as most of these specialties are appreciated in their own regions, we are still a meat-eating nation and do not properly appreciate fish. When good fish is available to us, we frequently ruin it by overcooking. We forget that, unlike almost all meat, fish is tender to begin with, and that by cooking it too much, we drive out the juices and flavor.

More than this, we have sadly neglected our great resource of fish. We let the Japanese, Russians and others make off with a large part of each year's catch in our offshore waters rather than go after it ourselves. In our sometimes smug acceptance of America's supposedly unlimited resources, we have done great damage to the habitats of many fishes. When we felled trees to clear land in the 19th Century, we left the soil exposed, and it washed into streams to silt over and destroy many spawning grounds. In this century we have poured wastes of many horrid sorts into our waters, in some areas killing not only the fish, but ruining the rivers themselves. From where I now sit writing this book, I can see the lovely Hudson, a majestic silver band sliding toward New York harbor; but I know from what I have read and seen that those are troubled waters. Once the Atlantic salmon rushed up the Hudson to spawn; but a salmon has not been seen there for a century. And while striped bass may yet be found in it and are plump, firm fish, they taste of oil and gasoline. So too do many of the shad, long one of New York's most popular seasonal fish. Farther north, in Boston, the picture is much the same. The Bostonians' regular July Fourth dinner used to be Atlantic salmon, broiled or poached. Now the only place in the United States where Atlantic salmon is found is Maine.

In spite of the carelessness and the neglect, things are beginning to look up a bit. The new method of flash-freezing fish—with a glaze applied in the last moment to seal in the essences—promises to improve the supply of fresh-tasting packaged fish. When it comes to buying the iced product, shoppers are displaying more awareness, daring to look a fish in the

West Coast Clams and Oysters

The tender little butter clam—also called the Washington clam and money clam—found on the Pacific Coast from Southern California to Alaska, is eaten raw. The long, narrow razor clam, native to the general area, is usually fried, while the huge horse clam—from the same section—is chopped up and cooked in chowder or in fritters. The Pismo clam, scattered all along the California coast, may not be caught until it measures 5 inches across. It is sautéed, baked or cooked in chowder. Another large clam, the geoduck (pronounced gooey-duck) is dug along the coast from southern Alaska to Northern California. The body of this giant clam is sliced and fried; its siphon, or neck, is ground up for chowder. The native oyster of the West Coast is the tiny Olympia, found from Alaska to Lower California. It may be eaten raw or cooked, while the larger Pacific oyster —which originated in Japan—is cooked before being eaten. This oyster goes by different names in different areas— Willapa Bay and Quilcene being two well-known variations.

eye to determine how fresh it is by the brightness of the pupil, poking the flesh with a finger to judge its firmness or lifting the gill covers to see whether they are red inside. (The oldest test of freshness, however, remains the surest—smell the fish. If it is truly fresh, there should be very little odor.)

American housewives are also beginning to realize that fish does not have to be cooked more than a few minutes. The Canadian Department of Fisheries has given us a nearly foolproof rule: measure a fish through its thickest part, and then give it about 10 minutes to the inch, whether you are poaching, broiling, baking or frying it. When cooked according to this timing method, a poached striped bass flaked at the touch of my fork, and its flesh was full of juice.

To what may this growing awareness be attributed? In part the credit belongs to good new cookbooks whose sound advice and foreign recipes encourage a great deal more experimentation than the simpler fish cookery of our ancestors. Credit should also go to the educational campaign of the Bureau of Commercial Fisheries. But I suspect that what is really at the root of this new appreciation is the national zest for sports fishing. Each year, more and more Americans are joining the ranks of those who already have enjoyed the thrill of catching their own fish, and are discovering something their forebears knew all along—just how good fish tastes when it is fresh from the water and grilled over the campfire, or pan-fried. The numbers of Americans out fishing today are truly staggering; there are some 30 million at present, and by 2000 there will be 50 million in all. In some regions overfishing is a distinct danger, as waters cannot be stocked fast enough to keep up with fishermen.

Yet while the fish population is threatened in certain areas, there are encouraging developments in other parts of the country. Occasionally, man's influence is beneficial. Perhaps the outstanding (although accidental) example of this is the appearance in Louisiana waters of large numbers of pompano. The oil rigs erected in the Gulf of Mexico became magnets for the pompano, drawing them from their wintering grounds off Florida to feed on fish around the pilings and take shelter under the platforms. Here they were soon found by anglers, and the once rare pompano *en papillote* (*page 150*)—pompano wrapped in parchment to preserve its steaming aromatic juices—now delights many New Orleans diners.

As our population continues to grow, there may be a real need in the future to turn to fish as a protein source. Of our current efforts to increase supplies of fish and shellfish, none is more fascinating, I think, than our attempts at "aquaculture." Although the Orientals have been raising fish in their paddies for centuries, it was only within the last few years that rice fields were put to off-season use as a home for channel catfish, and so successful was this experiment that today the fish are being raised in fields of their own. Now there is talk of farming shrimp in Louisiana and of increasing the amount of wetland being given over to the cultivation of crawfish and oysters. In Idaho, the Snake River Trout Ranch has successfully adopted a principle long employed by state fish hatcheries. Here rainbow trout are bred, fed and reared by the millions—not, however, in order to stock Idaho's icy streams, but to be sold all over the United

Opposite: Laden with quahog clams, New England clam chowder (*page 151*) awaits lunch guests in the dining room of a colonial home in Connecticut. The clams were dug along the New England coast, but any chowder clams may be used in this famous dish.

States. When they mature to delectable size, the fish are caught, killed, cleaned and frozen—a procedure taking half an hour.

In the past many kinds of American fish have been successfully transplanted from one area to another, and this work continues. Rainbow, brook and lake trout are all found today in waters far from their original homes. The tender, uniquely flavored striped bass, a commercial fish on the East Coast, has become a game fish on the West Coast since its introduction to the Pacific at the end of the 19th Century. Surely the most spectacular example of a fish taking hold in new waters is that of the Eastern shad, carried across country in 1871 and released into the Pacific. In the Northwest today, it is among the most common of fish, but shad lovers will be dismayed to learn that few Westerners eat it; they take out the roe, freeze or can it for shipment East, and turn the fish into catfood.

In Michigan—where, incidentally, no one lives farther than 75 miles from Lake Michigan's 3,200 miles of shoreline—what may well be the most ambitious fish transplantation attempt ever made is now underway. Twenty years ago Lake Michigan was hard hit by the lamprey, an eellike parasite that sucked the life juices out of the fish to which it attached itself with its round, rasping mouth. When a way to curtail the lamprey was found, the alewife population in the lake began to explode. Now alewives are the problem, dying by the thousands and piling up on the shores. The solution of the Michigan Department of Conservation has been to import eggs of the Chinook and coho salmon from the West Coast, hatch them and release the young fish into streams flowing into the lake. The hope is that they will not only feed on the alewives, but utilize the cool depths of the lake where few other species live—and thus tap a practically unused resource. Young cohos set loose in 1966 have already returned to the streams for spawning. This would seem to indicate that salmon, which ordinarily spend the greater part of their lives in the ocean, can thrive in a fresh-water lake. And to sports fishermen and cooks this will indeed be a boon.

I suppose it was only a matter of time before scientists began improving fish. They are, after all, among the most malleable of creatures. A single pair exhibiting only desirable characteristics will produce thousands of like offspring, and these in turn will yield thousands more. With selective breeding, the day of the superfish may not be far off. Indeed, a supersalmon has already been developed at the University of Washington in Seattle by Dr. Lauren H. Donaldson and his co-workers. The species used in the experiment was the Chinook, one of the most important of the commercial fishes in the Northwest. As early as 1949, Dr. Donaldson attacked the problem of developing a hardy breed of disease-resistant salmon. He succeeded beyond his wildest hopes. Normally Chinook require four to five years to reach maturity. Dr. Donaldson selectively bred the fish, fed them a high-protein diet and then released them to the ocean; some returned to reproduce a year earlier than expected. Moreover, these healthy fish were twice as big as others of their kind, and when the females spawned, they produced twice as many eggs. The American dream, once limited to a chicken in every pot, may soon be modified to include a salmon on every broiler—and a nice dream it is.

The Seafood Treasures of the Pacific Northwest

Seafood tastes best under an open sky near the sea with a tang of salt in the air. There is no better place to enjoy it than the Pacific Northwest, where the seafood and the scenery are unsurpassed—and where getting outdoors to enjoy both is a mass way of life. The picnickers on these pages held a Fourth of July outing on Puget Sound. They brought with them some of the region's great seafood specialties—steamer clams, Dungeness crab and a pair of king salmon—and added another treasure to their hoard by gathering Pacific oysters at Similk Beach *(above)* while the tide was low. Then they cooked a seafood feast, capping it with the king salmon prepared in two primeval, delicious ways *(pages 142-143)*.

Explaining the Mystery of the Oyster to a Curious Audience

For the children on the picnic the oysters at Similk Beach were a source of mystery and wonder. Bob Perry, a restaurant owner and experienced chef, showed them *(below)* how to pry an oyster open by inserting the point of an oyster knife at exactly the right spot. Then he let them see the watery, motionless creature on the pearly half shell. Later, when the picnickers had gathered all the oysters they wanted, they moved on to Skyline Beach, six miles away, and cooked the oysters *(opposite),* and everyone had a chance to taste this uniquely flavored food.

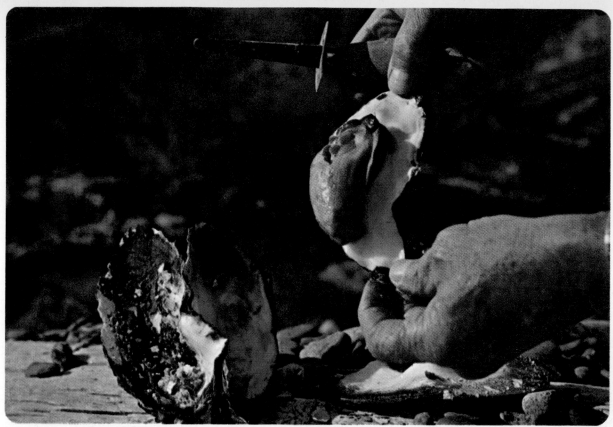

When the oysters were done their shells popped open, revealing the succulent specimens inside. Sprinkled with Worcestershire sauce, they made a fine hors d'oeuvre that passed the time for the picnickers while other food was being cooked.

The steaming clams, cooked in a Dutch oven, were flavored with dry vermouth. Chopped parsley and garlic powder were also added. The picnickers ate the tender clams as appetizers and sopped up the clam juice with French bread.

Roasted on a Plank

The picnickers cooked one of their salmon by ''planking'' it, the way the Indians used to prepare the fish. Bob Perry filleted the fish (this one weighed 12 pounds) with a sharp knife *(above left),* and rubbed it with butter, garlic and dill. Then he lashed it to a driftwood plank and propped it over a driftwood fire *(above).* While it was cooking, he watched carefully to see that the fire was hot enough at first to sear the flesh and seal in the juices. Then he let the fire burn low to cook the fish slowly and smoke it all the way through. When the fish was done *(left),* it was charred on the outside but succulent and moist, with a rich smoky flavor.

Well-stuffed Fish

The picnic's other main course was a 21-pound king salmon stuffed and then baked. Bob Perry made a savory mixture of chopped seaweed, salt, black pepper, mace, dry bread, turmeric, garlic, chopped onion, butter and egg. Next he slit the fish, stuffed it and tied the stuffing in tight. The salmon was then ready for the next step *(below, left)*.

To give it a salt flavor and keep it moist, the salmon was encased in kelp. Then, to protect it from ashes and keep it from cooking too fast, it was wrapped in foil.

To cook the salmon, Ray Eckmann *(right)* and Bob Alexander buried it in coals of charcoal and driftwood. They let it bake slowly for two and three quarter hours.

When the salmon was done, the cooks unwrapped it and savored its fragrant steam. Then they cut it up and served it to the picnickers with boiled Dungeness crab, a salad made of five beans (kidney, lima, canned green beans, *garbanzos* and wax beans), all accompanied by two kinds of white wine and French bread.

CHAPTER V RECIPES

Fried Smelts with Herb Butter

Cream the butter by beating it with a wooden spoon against the sides of a mixing bowl until it is smooth and fluffy. Beat in the ½ teaspoon of salt, a few grindings of black pepper, the parsley, chives, lime juice and Tabasco.

Place the herb butter on a sheet of wax paper about 3 feet long; fold the wax paper over it, and pat and shape the enclosed butter into a long, ½-inch-thick cylinder. Refrigerate it for at least an hour, or until the butter is firm.

Wash the smelts under cold running water and pat them thoroughly dry, inside and out, with paper towels. If the fish dealer has not removed the backbone, sever it from the head, and with the tip of a sharp knife gently lift it out, cutting it off at the base of the tail.

Sprinkle the fish generously with salt and a few grindings of pepper, dip it in flour on both sides and shake off the excess. Heat the shortening (it should be at least ½ inch deep in the pan) over high heat in a 10-inch heavy skillet until a light haze forms over it. Add as many of the fish, spread open, as the pan will hold comfortably, and cook them over moderate heat on both sides for 3 to 4 minutes each until they are crisp and brown. Remove them to a double thickness of paper towels to drain, and brown the remaining fish in the same fashion, adding more shortening to the pan if necessary.

Place the fish, spread open and skin side down, on a heated serving platter. Quickly, cut the chilled herb butter into approximately 1- to 2-inch lengths depending upon the size of the fish, and place a small cylinder, lengthwise, in the center of each fish. Serve at once before the butter has melted.

Artichokes Stuffed with Shrimp and Green Goddess Dressing

Trim the bases of the artichokes flush and flat so that they will stand upright without wobbling. Bend and snap off the small bottom leaves and any bruised outer leaves. Lay each artichoke on its side, grip it firmly and, with a large, sharp knife, slice about 1 inch off the top.

With scissors trim ¼ inch off the points of the rest of the leaves. Rub all the cut edges with lemon to prevent their discoloring. In an 8-quart enameled or stainless-steel pot (do not use aluminum; it will turn the artichokes gray), bring about 6 quarts of water and 3 tablespoons of salt to a boil. Drop in the artichokes and boil them briskly, uncovered, for about 30 minutes, turning occasionally. They are done when their bases show no resistance when pierced with the tip of a small, sharp knife. Drain them upside down in a colander. When they are cool enough to handle, spread their leaves apart gently, grasp the inner core of yellow, thistlelike leaves firmly and ease it out. Then, with a long-handled spoon, thoroughly scrape out and discard the fuzzy choke.

GREEN GODDESS DRESSING: In a small mixing bowl, beat into the 3

To serve 4 to 6

8 tablespoons softened butter (1 quarter-pound stick)
½ teaspoon salt
Freshly ground black pepper
1 tablespoon finely chopped fresh parsley
1 tablespoon finely chopped chives
1 tablespoon fresh lime juice
⅛ teaspoon Tabasco
18 smelts, with the backbones removed but the heads and tails left on
Salt
Flour
1½ to 2 cups vegetable shortening

To serve 6

Six 10- to 12-ounce artichokes
6 quarts water
3 tablespoons salt

GREEN GODDESS DRESSING
3 cups mayonnaise, freshly made, or a good, unsweetened commercial variety
1 tablespoon tarragon wine vinegar
1 teaspoon lemon juice
1 tablespoon finely chopped anchovies (6 to 8 flat anchovies canned in olive oil)
1 tablespoon chopped fresh tarragon or 1 teaspoon dried crumbled tarragon
¼ cup finely chopped scallions, including part of the green stems
¼ teaspoon finely chopped garlic
¼ cup finely chopped fresh parsley
⅛ teaspoon cayenne

2 pounds shelled, cooked and chilled tiny shrimp, preferably the West Coast or Alaskan variety
6 rolled, caper-stuffed anchovies (optional)
Lemon slices

An artichoke with shrimp and Green Goddess dressing—the latter named after a long-run play of the 1920s—makes a tempting appetizer.

cups of mayonnaise the vinegar, lemon juice, anchovies, tarragon, scallions, garlic, parsley and cayenne. Taste for seasoning and add a little salt if you think it needs it.

In a large mixing bowl combine the shrimp and 1½ cups of the dressing, stirring them gently until the shrimp are well coated. Fill each artichoke cavity with the mixture, mounding it slightly on the top. Arrange the anchovy, if you are using it, in the center of each shrimp mound and chill the stuffed artichokes until ready to serve.

To serve, place the artichokes on chilled plates and surround them with the lemon slices. Pass the remaining Green Goddess dressing separately.

145

Getting the Most and Best out of a Lobster

The lobster is a delicious but tantalizingly difficult food to enjoy. Yet with a lobster cracker and picks *(opposite)* and the proper approach—as explained below—the last tender morsel can be efficiently extracted.

1 Twist off the large claws *(top of page)* and crack them *(above)* with cracker, pliers or hammer.

2 Grip the lobster and separate the tail from the body by bending it up or down until it cracks.

3 Break off the fan-shaped flippers from the tail by bending them back until they snap free.

4 Hold the tail; insert a pick or fork in the flipper end and push meat out of the opposite end.

5 Pull off the shell. The body contains the tomalley, or liver, and, in some females, the roe.

6 Eat the small claws by sucking out the meat and juices as though you were sucking on a straw.

These popular East Coast fish—red snapper (pink fish in foreground), striped bass and pompano (white fish at center)—are excellent when baked with scallions, onions, green pepper, tomatoes and lemon juice, and accompanied by a dry white wine.

To serve 4

STUFFING:

2 tablespoons butter
2 tablespoons finely chopped scallions, including part of the green stem
2 tablespoons finely chopped green pepper
1 medium tomato, peeled, seeded and coarsely chopped
1 tablespoon finely chopped fresh parsley
Salt
Freshly ground pepper

A 2½- to 3-pound striped bass, eviscerated but head and tail left on (or other firm white-meat fish such as red snapper, pompano, haddock, cod, pollack, rockfish, whitefish or lake trout)
4 tablespoons melted butter
1 medium onion, peeled and thinly sliced
1 small green pepper, seeded and thinly sliced
6 sprigs fresh dill
½ cup dry vermouth
1 tablespoon lemon juice
Salt
Freshly ground black pepper

Baked Stuffed Striped Bass

For the stuffing, melt the 2 tablespoons of butter in a small skillet over moderate heat. When the foam subsides, add the chopped scallions and green pepper and cook, stirring constantly, for 2 to 3 minutes until the vegetables are wilted but not brown. Scrape into a small mixing bowl. Add the chopped tomato, parsley, salt and a few grindings of black pepper. Mix thoroughly.

Preheat the oven to 375°. Wash the fish inside and out under cold running water, and dry it thoroughly with paper towels. Fill the fish with the stuffing, sew the opening with thread or close it with small skewers and crisscross kitchen string around the skewers to secure them. Brush 2 tablespoons of the melted butter on the bottom of a shallow, flameproof baking dish attractive enough to serve from, and place the fish in it, surrounding it with the sliced onion, the green pepper and sprigs of fresh dill.

Combine the vermouth with the lemon juice and the rest of the melted butter, pour it over the fish and vegetables and bring it to a boil on top of the stove. Sprinkle the fish with salt and a few grindings of black pepper, and immediately transfer the baking dish to the middle of the oven.

Bake uncovered for about 30 minutes, basting the fish every 8 minutes or so with the pan juices. The fish is done when it is firm to the touch and flakes easily when prodded gently with a fork. Serve it immediately, from the baking dish.

Brook Trout

In a large, heavy skillet, cook the bacon over moderate heat until it has rendered all its fat and is brown and crisp. Transfer the bacon to paper towels to drain.

Wash the fish under cold running water and dry them thoroughly with paper towels. Sprinkle them inside and out with salt and a few grindings of black pepper, then dip them in the cornmeal, shaking them gently to remove any excess. Heat the bacon fat in the skillet over high heat until a light haze forms over it. Add the fish and cook them for about 5 minutes on each side, turning them over carefully with tongs. Regulate the heat so that the trout will brown evenly without burning. Remove them to a heated platter, arrange the bacon strips around them and serve at once.

To serve 4

8 strips of fat bacon
4 brook trout, about ¾ to 1 pound
   each, eviscerated but with heads
   and tails left on
Salt
Freshly ground black pepper
1½ to 2 cups white or yellow
   cornmeal

6 pompano fillets, about 7 inches
   long and weighing in all about 2½
   to 3 pounds
Salt
¾ cup thoroughly degreased chicken
   stock, fresh or canned
¼ cup dry white wine
2 tablespoons butter
2 tablespoons finely chopped shallots
   or scallions
3 tablespoons flour
2 tablespoons heavy cream
½ teaspoon lemon juice
½ teaspoon salt
⅛ teaspoon cayenne
6 teaspoons soft butter
1 cup coarsely diced cooked shrimp
1 cup coarsely diced crab meat, fresh
   or canned

6 tablespoons butter
3 cups cooked lobster, fresh or
   canned, cut into 2-inch pieces
⅓ cup Madeira or dry sherry
1½ cups heavy cream
5 egg yolks
¾ teaspoon salt
⅛ teaspoon cayenne
½ teaspoon lemon juice
6 patty shells, or 2 to 3 cups of
   steamed rice, or 8 to 12 buttered
   toast points
Paprika (optional)

Pompano Stuffed with Shrimp and Crab en Papillote

Preheat the oven to 250°. Wash the fillets quickly in cold water and dry them on paper towels. Salt them lightly and arrange them folded in half end to end in a shallow, lightly buttered baking dish large enough to hold them in 1 layer. Pour in the chicken stock and white wine, and add a little water if the liquid doesn't come halfway up the sides of the fish. Heat the baking dish on top of the stove until the liquid begins to simmer.

Then cover the dish loosely with a sheet of wax paper, a little larger than the dish itself, and poach the fish in the middle of the oven for about 6 minutes, or until the fillets are opaque and almost, but not quite, cooked through. Remove the fish from the pan with a large metal spatula and spread them open on a platter.

Strain the poaching liquid through a fine sieve into a small saucepan and, over high heat, boil it rapidly uncovered until it is reduced to 1 cup. Set aside. In another saucepan, melt the 2 tablespoons of butter over moderate heat.

When the foam subsides, add the chopped shallots or scallions and, stirring constantly, cook them for 2 to 3 minutes until they are soft but not brown. Stir in the flour and cook for a moment or two until it froths, then pour in the cup of reserved poaching liquid. Cook over moderate heat, stirring constantly with a whisk until the sauce is smooth and thick. Add the 2 tablespoons of cream, the lemon juice, salt and cayenne. Taste for seasoning.

Cut 6 sheets of parchment cooking paper or aluminum foil into 12-by-14-inch heart shapes. Brush each heart with a teaspoon of soft butter. Fold each heart in half lengthwise, then open it and lay a fillet alongside the center crease of each heart.

Put an equal amount of the shrimp and crab meat on the lower half of each fillet and moisten it with a tablespoon of the sauce. Then fold the other half of the fish over it, enclosing the stuffing. Pour the remaining sauce over each fillet, dividing it equally. Seal the hearts securely by crimping and rolling the edges of the halves firmly together.

Preheat the oven to 450°. Place the *papillotes* side by side on a lightly greased cookie sheet and bake them in the middle of the oven for about 8 minutes. The parchment paper will puff and brown. Serve the *papillotes* on individual heated plates and cut them open at the table.

Lobster Newburg

In a large enameled or stainless-steel skillet, melt the butter over moderate heat. When the foam subsides, add the lobster meat and, stirring constantly, cook for about a minute. Pour in the Madeira or sherry and 1 cup of the heavy cream and, stirring, bring it to a boil. Reduce the heat to its lowest point and, still stirring, cook for about 2 minutes. In a small bowl, beat the egg yolks into the remaining ½ cup of cream. Beat into them 4 tablespoons of the simmering lobster sauce, and then, in a slow stream, pour the mixture back into the skillet, stirring constantly. Cook over moderate heat until the sauce thickens, but under no circumstances let it come to a boil or it will curdle. Season with the salt, cayenne and lemon juice. Serve immediately in patty shells, on beds of steamed rice, or on hot buttered toast points, and sprinkle the lobster Newburg lightly with paprika if you like.

Oyster Fritters

Sift ½ cup of the flour and the salt into a mixing bowl. With a wooden spoon stir in the butter and the egg. Then pour in the beer gradually and mix only until the batter is fairly smooth. Don't overmix. Let the batter rest at room temperature for about an hour. When you are ready to fry the oysters, beat the egg white with a rotary beater or whisk until it is stiff enough to form unwavering peaks on the beater when it is lifted out of the bowl. Gently fold the beaten egg white into the batter and continue to fold until no streaks of white remain.

In a deep-fat fryer, heat the shortening or oil until it registers 375° on a deep-frying thermometer. The fat should be at least 3 inches deep. Dip the oysters in the remaining ½ cup of flour, shake off any excess and then dip in the batter. Let the excess batter drain off, then fry the oysters, 5 or 6 at a time, for 3 to 4 minutes until they are puffed and golden brown. Drain on paper towels and keep the fritters warm in a 200° oven until all the oysters have been fried. Serve at once with wedges of lemon.

New England Clam Chowder

Over high heat, fry the diced salt pork in a heavy 2-quart saucepan, stirring constantly for about 3 minutes until a thin film of fat covers the bottom of the pan. Reduce the heat to moderate, stir in the chopped onion and cook together for about 5 minutes longer, stirring occasionally. When the diced pork and onions turn a light golden brown, add 3 cups of water and the diced potatoes. Bring to a boil over high heat, then reduce the heat and simmer with the pan half covered for about 15 minutes until the potatoes are tender but not falling apart.

Add the chopped clams and their juices, the cream and thyme, and heat almost to the boiling point. Then taste and season with as much salt and pepper as you think it needs. Stir in the soft butter. Serve the chowder in large individual bowls with each portion dusted with a little paprika. Pilot crackers are the traditional accompaniment.

Deviled Crab

Preheat the oven to 350°. In a large mixing bowl, combine the celery, green pepper, scallions, parsley, crab meat (with all cartilage removed), 1½ cups of the crushed crackers, salt, mustard, a few drops of Tabasco, the cream and ½ cup of the melted butter. Mix together gently but thoroughly with a large spoon and taste for seasoning.

Spoon the mixture into a buttered 1½-quart casserole and sprinkle the remaining cracker crumbs evenly over the top. Dribble over it the remaining butter and bake the casserole in the upper third of the oven for about ½ hour, or until the crumbs are golden brown. Serve at once, directly from the casserole.

To serve 4 to 6

1 cup flour
½ teaspoon salt
1 tablespoon melted butter
1 egg, lightly beaten
½ cup beer
2 dozen fresh oysters, shucked, or 2 dozen frozen oysters, thoroughly defrosted
1 egg white
Vegetable shortening or vegetable oil for deep-fat frying
Lemon wedges

To serve 6 to 8

¼ pound salt pork, cut into ⅛-inch dice
1 cup finely chopped onion
3 cups cold water
4 cups potatoes, cut into ¼-inch dice
2 dozen shucked hard-shelled clams with their juice, coarsely chopped, or two 8-ounce cans chopped clams (about 2 cups)
2 cups heavy or light cream
⅛ teaspoon thyme
Salt
Freshly ground pepper
2 tablespoons soft butter
Paprika

To serve 4

½ cup finely chopped celery
⅓ cup finely chopped green pepper
½ cup thinly sliced scallions, including about an inch of the green stems
¼ cup finely chopped parsley
1 pound lump crab meat, freshly cooked, or the canned variety, thoroughly drained
1¾ cups coarsely crushed soda crackers
½ teaspoon salt
½ teaspoon dry mustard
Tabasco
¼ cup heavy cream
¾ cup melted butter

VI

Dairy Riches and Mountains of Snacks

"The cheese stands alone"
for a family portrait in
Wisconsin, the leading dairy state.
Reading generally from left
to right, and identified in
terms used by the Wisconsin
Cheese Foundation are:

 1 Favorite Style Cheddar
 2 Brick
 3 Ball Edam
 4 Cheddar
 5 Colored Münster
 6 Boccini
 7 Longhorn
 8 Parmesan
 9 Midget Longhorn
10 Block Swiss
11 Blue
12 Münster
13 Caraway Cheddar
14 Provolone
15 Spiced Gouda
16 Gouda
17 Wheel of Swiss

American dairying came over well ahead of the *Mayflower*—the first cows were led ashore by the Jamestown colonists in 1611—and it has done well for itself. Today every fourth sip or bite of nourishment we take is a dairy product, and all that milk, cream, sour cream, butter, cheese and ice cream goes down at the rate of 370 pounds per American consumer per year. Our collective annual bill for dairy products is $12 billion, which puts the business right up among the industrial giants.

This being so, many people may be as surprised as I was to learn that we are no longer the great nation of milk drinkers we have believed ourselves to be. I was all the more surprised because I feel that no country produces milk as uniformly excellent as ours, or takes its milk in such diverse forms: homogenized milk, skim milk, fortified milk, buttermilk, chocolate milk, strawberry milk, powdered and condensed milk, evaporated milk, malted milk, great shakes of milk. But as milk-quaffers the Finns—who lead all the rest—drink us under the table. They down about 75 gallons a person a year to our mere 35 gallons. Our herds of dairy cattle—once such a source of pride—have shrunk steadily from an all-time population peak of 25.5 million during World War II to only 13.5 million in 1967, and while the cows still may be as contented as ever, the dairy farmers are not.

Eating habits change; our consumption of milk has declined by about 10 per cent in a decade, and that of cream and butter by half. On the other hand, Americans are consuming more cheese than ever. The average American now eats over nine pounds a year, and the United States

The classic after-school snack eaten by generations of children consists of cookies and milk. The chewy oatmeal cookies shown here are quickly made —according to the recipe on page 168 —and quickly disappear.

has become the world's largest producer of this protein-loaded food, turning out twice as much as its nearest rival, France.

Americans have long held cheese in high regard, even though they have often been more impressed by muchness than goodness. Back in 1801, when Thomas Jefferson was inaugurated as President, a group of admirers from Cheshire, Massachusetts, gave him what was supposed to be the biggest cheese the world had known; it weighed 1,600 pounds, and it took three weeks to haul down to Washington on a sled. President Andrew Jackson was honored with a similar cheese, a 1,400-pound Cheddar. He kept it on display in the White House vestibule for almost two years, until it had ripened. Then, on Washington's birthday, he held open house—and the cheese was gone in two hours flat. "Cheese, cheese, cheese was on everybody's mouth," wrote a contemporary witness. "All you heard was cheese; all you smelled was cheese. Streams of cheese were going up the avenue in everybody's fist; balls of cheese were in a hundred pockets; every handkerchief smelled of cheese. The whole atmosphere for half a mile around was infected with cheese."

Today almost half of the cheese eaten in America is processed cheese, a bland mixture of natural cheeses of different ages, ground fine and blended by heating and stirring. The result is, more often than not, insipid. However, the trend—just barely perceptible at present, but a cause nevertheless for hope—seems to be away from processed cheese with an

154

attendant rise in popularity of cheeses of character and distinction. The best of those made here include a number of adaptations of classic European cheeses, and two vigorous cheeses of strictly American origin—Liederkranz and brick.

Among the oldest of our domestic natural cheeses is the ever-popular Cheddar, the familiar cheese that we eat in sandwiches and on apple pie. Much of it I find depressingly mild, but some excellent sharp Cheddars are produced in New York, Vermont and Wisconsin. An Oregon Cheddar, Tillamook, has gained favor all along the West Coast. Another fine Western cheese, sometimes described as Cheddar, is Monterey, a semisoft, mild white cheese that actually is only distantly related to Cheddar (a moister, more flavorful variety is known as Monterey Jack).

The popularity of numerous American cheeses copied from European originals reflects the influence of one nationality group or another. *Mozzarella*—pizza cheese—has gained wide acceptance in this country and is now produced commercially in large quantities. *Ricotta* is another Italian cheese of increasing popularity; it is akin to cottage cheese, but creamier, and is fine for baking and cooking. We even turn out an acceptable Parmesan and have been doing so for quite a number of years now; it is the product of Americans of Italian descent living in Fond du Lac, Wisconsin.

Occasionally, some of the American-made, foreign-inspired cheeses will taste as good as or better than the prototypes. Pennsylvania Bel Paese—creamy and tart—comes closest of any of our copied cheeses, perhaps, to the Italian original. People who know them (I don't) say that Warsawski and Kasseri, the one Polish, the other Greek, are finer here than at home.

Although most of our domestically produced copies of foreign cheeses vary considerably from the originals, this is not always to be regretted. A few can be interesting, if not downright delicious, departures. Our Port-Salut is milder than Europe's, but good in its own right. Our Camembert, though lacking the character of the French, may actually be the better buy, since it is the fresher cheese, and will not have passed its peak and shrunk up in the box by the time it is bought. Illinois produces an excellent Brie but still, alas, in small quantity. And Illinois, Ohio and Wisconsin make some good Swiss cheese.

Another important domestic cheese of foreign origin is Münster, which bears little resemblance to the Alsatian Münster, since it is far milder, with a lighter, fresher taste. But as Vivienne Marquis and Patricia Haskell, the co-authors of *The Cheese Book,* point out, Münster is "one of the best melting cheeses that we have." And when one considers the universal popularity of the grilled-cheese sandwich in the United States, that is saying a lot. Another domestic cheese quite similar to Münster is Wisconsin-made Fondutta —it differs only in being softer and more buttery.

While the cheeses just mentioned are derivative, two widely acclaimed cheeses—Liederkranz and brick—originated in America. And although Americans are supposed to prefer bland cheeses, both of these are strong. Liederkranz, a highly aromatic and slightly acid cheese, was the accidental discovery of Emil Frey, a cheese maker in Monroe, New York. Frey was attempting to duplicate the German cheese called Bismarck Schlosskäse when he hit upon Liederkranz. This bit of serendipity gave the world an

Overleaf: A dairy farm that has prospered in the face of the dairy industry's drop-off in recent years is this 250-acre establishment near Cedar Rapids, Iowa. Owner Glenn Boddicker has spent 27 years developing his farm, now tends it with the help of his wife and two hired hands. He owns 100 head of Holstein cattle, grows his own feed (alfalfa and corn), plows his earnings back into the farm—and by all these means, more than makes a go of it.

Continued on page 159

Homemade vanilla ice cream prepared in an old-fashioned, hand-cranked freezer is still one of America's best desserts.

even better cheese than the one he was trying to make, and he named his discovery Liederkranz, after the Liederkranz singing society in New York, to which he belonged (the word means "wreath of song"). In its wreath of odor, Liederkranz is almost the rival of Limburger. Brick, our only other native American cheese, is hardly known in the East or West, but it is much liked in the Midwest, having originated in Wisconsin. When new, it is quite mild, but it gains authority as it grows older, and well-aged brick tastes great with beer.

Any discussion of American cheeses, of course, would be incomplete without mentioning cottage cheese. It is the dieter's cheese par excellence. Yet another soft cheese of great popularity is, of course, cream cheese. (Neufchâtel is similar to cream cheese but is somewhat smoother and is advertised as having "30 per cent less fat.")

Along with cheese, a dairy product that continues to hold unmistakable popularity in America is ice cream. Cool, smooth, sweet and nutritious, it is served in an almost endless variety of flavors. (Who but Americans would have been so audacious as to combine nuts and cream to produce butter pecan?) The Italians may have got the idea for ice cream from the Chinese, and the French in turn from the Italians, but it was the American genius for mass production that put this perfect dessert within the reach of everyone. Ice cream has always been for us one of those necessary luxuries of life. George Washington had a "Cream machine for Making Ice," and so did Thomas Jefferson. Dolley Madison set a White House tradition, as well as a pattern for the country to follow, by serving to her guests one night, "high on a silver platter, a large, shining dome of pink Ice Cream." To Captain Frederick Marryat, the Englishman who wrote in such detail about our early customs, there was "one great luxury in America . . . the quantity of clear, pure ice . . . even in the hottest seasons, and ice creams are universal and very cheap." He was amazed to see common laborers sit down during the day for a dish of it. Making ice cream at home fell within everyone's province after 1846 when a woman named Nancy Johnson invented the hand-cranked freezer. The credit for it went, however, to William Young—but he merely did what the lady had neglected to do: he patented her machine.

After some initial resistance (so delicious a thing might, after all, be bad for you), ice cream became acceptable food even to those with a puritan outlook, and its uses, forms and flavors proliferated. The sundae takes its name from Sunday, when, without offense to God or man, it might safely be served. The ice-cream soda is similarly a product of virtue. It became the drink acceptable to those of the Women's Christian Temperance Union persuasion. And the soda fountain, in turn, became the one place to which ladies might repair for innocent refreshment.

Ice cream has been with us so long—and arrives so early in the lives of each of us—that there are few, from the very old to the very young, who are without some fond recollection of it. The old-fashioned ice-cream parlor may have vanished, but the nostalgia for it lives on, and today, among some decorators, its bentwood chairs and leaded-glass Tiffany-type lampshades are the very epitome of chic. Some of us remember feeling sophisticated when we went to the ice-cream parlor and ordered

Americans put into ice cream and ices almost every conceivable flavoring and fruit—even olallieberry, a variety of blackberry—as indicated by this sign at a Los Angeles ice-cream stand. The Howard Johnson restaurant chain is famous for its 28 flavors, and ice-cream parlors in some parts of the country go even further.

wicked flavors like Claret, Crème de Menthe and Champagne; others recall being convinced that we were serving man and country when, on the Fourth of July, we cranked the ice-cream freezer, an arduous chore that in the end always brought its own sweet reward.

Even the generations that have never tasted home-made ice cream *(page 35)* will not forget the pleasure dispensed in paper cups by good-humored men—with the picture of a movie star on every lid. Pops and Popsicles, frozen custards and soft ice creams, Fudgsicles, frappés, Eskimo pies and parfaits—those are the very names of our dreams. And then, of course, there is the most outlandish and flamboyant dairy preparation of all —the banana split. The thought of it makes me turn pale: the banana sliced lengthwise with enormous scoops of ice cream dumped on top of it; the river of chocolate syrup, the great gobs of whipped cream piled high and sprinkled with nuts and topped with cherries. Whoever orders one of these mountainous concoctions seems to be undertaking a feat like defying gravity or scaling Mt. Everest. But spoonful by heaping spoonful, cherries, nuts, whipped cream, ice cream and banana gradually disappear. And when it is finished a look of triumph spreads over the snacker's face, and it is clear that he feels superior to other mortals for this accomplishment.

The different flavors, shapes and sizes of all these dairy products reflect a deeply held national habit. At milk bars, roadside restaurants or standing like Dagwood before the refrigerator at midnight, Americans are the world's greatest snack eaters. The club sandwich—an American innovation upon which innovations are always being made—could well stand as the symbol of our culinary ingenuity, our deep and abiding pleasure in all the small but good things of eating. It has been estimated that we spend more than a billion dollars a year on potato chips, pretzels, crackers, corn chips, packaged nuts, cracker sandwiches, shoestring potatoes and other tidbits. And this figure, enormous as it is, does not include the money we spend on such other preferred snacks as candies, cakes, doughnuts, cookies, yoghurt, hors d'oeuvre, cheese dips and gourmet-type nibbling foods.

The most popular snacks, of course, are the hot dog and hamburger. Who among us has not sat in a ballpark on a sun-drenched afternoon, munched peanuts and enjoyed the juicy flavor of three or four hot dogs seasoned with mustard and washed down with ice-cold gulps of cola or beer? And who has not pulled into a drive-in restaurant, called an order into a microphone and seen a pretty, hip-swinging carhop materialize moments later bearing a tray laden with hamburgers or cheeseburgers?

No one really knows why Americans are such great nibblers. The habit goes way back and probably has something to do with our restlessness. The original American snack may have been milk and crackers—for crackers were an American invention. But snacking as a full-fledged national folkway probably got its impetus from the free-lunch counters set up on top of bars in the 1800s to encourage drinking—and to provide men in a hurry, as even Americans of the 19th Century could be, with a quick snack of raw oysters, salty ham or pretzels. "Gobble, gulp and go" was a motto of the day.

In modern times the supermarket has encouraged the habit as much as

A mechanical taffy puller at the Santa Cruz, California, amusement park cranks out 300 to 400 pounds of the tooth-jerking candy per day. Gooey wads weighing 26 pounds apiece are tugged and kneaded until the sugar, corn syrup, coconut oil, salt, butter, condensed milk, artificial flavoring and coloring that make it up reach the consistency favored by taffy fanciers.

anything, putting temptation on the shelves that are easiest to reach. The automobile no doubt has helped. "Let's pull up for a bite to eat" has so long been a national refrain that entrepreneurs have marred the landscape with roadside "eateries" of all shapes and sizes, including two-story tin pineapples and hot dogs as big as trucks. Largely as a result of motoring, many food fads have spread fast. The taco has worked its way up from the Southwest to Oregon and Washington, and even now this crisp-fried tortilla, its pocket filled with chili, cheese and chopped iceberg lettuce, may be heading east. Meanwhile, the pizza continues its boom. Few roads leading into our cities are not now perfumed by the warm odor of tomato, cheese and oregano; and the pie, small, medium or large, has wheeled out onto the superhighways in its conquest of America. And in restaurants and diners across the country *(pages 164-165)* motorists are cramming themselves this minute with hot dogs, fried clams, frozen custards—an almost limitless variety of snacks and dairy foods.

CORN DOG

Carnival Confections and Concoctions

Americans are forever stuffing themselves at carnivals, fairs and amusement parks, and the quantity and wild variety of foods they eat there would overload a troop of ravenous and iron-stomached elephants. For instance, at the Boardwalk amusement park in Santa Cruz, California *(opposite page)*, corn dogs—frankfurters dipped in cornmeal batter and deep-fried—are a brisk seller. And at the Iowa State Fair in Des Moines, cotton candy is a favorite *(above)*, along with frozen custard, popcorn, candied apples, slush floats and mountains of other snacks.

Overleaf: On every American road, advertisements exhort the passerby to sample the amazingly varied fare.

CORN BOIL
GALENA - SUNDAY, SEPT. 3

BREAKFAST
FOOD
BEER

No.2 10¢
SPUDS 39

EAT HERE CHUCK WAGON

FARM-STYLE
ROASTED
CORN-MEAL
MADE-WITH-NEW-CORN

IOWA KERNEL
POPCORN
HOT POPCORN • CARMEL CORN

LOCKER MARKET

SCHAAKES CHOICE
GRAIN FED
STEER BEEF

80
Varieties Cheese

COTTON
CANDY

HOLLYWOOD
DRIVE IN EAT IN YOUR CAR

FRESH
STRAWBERRY PIE

E BEST BREAKFAS
ON THE COAST

OUR SPECIALTY

Johnny's CAFE
TO GO
WILD BLACKBERRY PIE

OLD FASHIONED
HARD CIDER
HALF GALLON
$1.76 TAX PAID
FIFTH
79¢ TAX PAID
OLD BEER

FARM FRESH EGGS

OPEN

BREAKFAST
ANY TIME

VII

The Joy of Baking

America's versatile, hearty
corn can turn into this
luscious, crisp-crusted,
cornbread, sliced piping hot
and topped by butter. The
same recipe *(page 179)*
provides a full-flavored
stuffing for wild turkey.

Why, I wonder, recalling the incredibly delicious kitchen smells on the days when my wife and I bake bread, do not a great many other Americans bake their own as well? I think of baking, in all its many forms, as one of the most creative acts, and one that produces its own immediate reward in a far shorter time, say, than gardening—and it is certainly a lot easier than writing. Seeing the tan foam that yeast raises as it wakens in a little sugared water, watching the flour from the sifter build to a crumbling peak into which a spoon will sink with muffled sound, feeling the stickiness of the dough and then kneading it and knowing that it is alive—all these I count as pleasures. But none, of course, can compare to the final pleasure of throwing open the oven door to a warm gust of sweet yeast odor and finding browned loaves of bread, risen to perfection, inside.

But in spite of Liet's and my experience, the statistics tell a different story. Indeed, they are all too blunt. In 1900 about 95 per cent of the flour bought in the United States was for home use; today only about 15 per cent is. The cake and brownie mixes, the brown-and-serve rolls and breads, the refrigerated doughs and cookie batters, the frozen pies and cakes have all but taken over. I do not entirely lament this; they are easy, and they can be very good. But when I recall the perfume of our home on baking day, and the riches we enjoyed thereafter, breads and cakes and cookies, I grow hungry in a way no lid on a box, no cellophane wrapper, no aluminum pan, no computerized mix can ever make me.

Americans traditionally have been excellent home bakers. Some of our most original achievements in the kitchen have been in this line; indeed,

Oatmeal Cookies

To make 24 cookies

1 cup all-purpose flour
½ teaspoon baking powder
½ teaspoon salt
½ cup unsalted butter
¾ cup dark brown sugar
¼ cup granulated sugar
1 egg
1 teaspoon vanilla extract
1 tablespoon milk
1¼ cups uncooked oatmeal

Preheat the oven to 350° and lightly butter two 11-by-17-inch baking sheets. Sift the flour, baking powder and salt together into a mixing bowl. Cream the butter, the brown sugar and the granulated sugar together by mashing them against the side of another mixing bowl with a wooden spoon. Stir in the egg, the vanilla extract and the milk, continuing to stir until the mixture is smooth. Beat in the flour mixture, a little at a time, then add the oatmeal, stirring until the mixture is well blended. Drop the batter by the tablespoonful onto the baking sheets, leaving space between for the cookies to expand. Bake for 12 minutes, or until the cookies are lightly browned on top.

many American women have been better bakers than cooks. Hot breads, ranging from the basic roll through an array of biscuits, muffins and gems to the johnnycake of the North and the spoon bread of the South, are indisputably American. So, of course, is apple pie. And our cakes are special too. Using baking powder, we developed a whole new category of our own—the light, moist layer cake that we then proceeded to ice in so many different ways that frosting became yet another area of cooking in which American women could excel. Angel food is our invention and so, too, is chiffon cake. And as for American cookies—why do more than cite one, the ubiquitous toll-house cookie, with crunchy nuts and smooth nuggets of semisweet chocolate imbedded in its butter-rich batter *(Recipe Booklet)*? It is confectionery genius.

Americans became good bakers not just because they had to be in days when stores were poorly stocked or mostly out of reach in a largely rural society, but because they were blessed as no other people before them had ever been by overflowing harvests of grain, by abundant and inexpensive flours, and by mounds of creamy butter and loaves of cane sugar. White bread, long a luxury in many parts of Europe, acquired everyday status in America. Pie became a regular breakfast food, accompanied by steak; in New England, plates had their pie side and their meat side. Cake was served often enough after the big meal of the day to vie with pudding and ice cream as the national dessert, and there were cakes for every taste—chocolate, cornstarch, fig, coconut, fruit, marble, nut, orange, spice, and on and on. We even had the additional advantage of a completely new grain, corn, with which to develop a host of purely American foods.

Corn, of course, is a native of the Western Hemisphere. For a long time, it was our principal grain, and even today it stands at the very center of our cookery. It is both a seen and an unseen food—certainly we are eating it when we chew a piece of steak or pork from livestock that was fattened on it. And because of its importance to nutrition in general, corn remains one of our biggest crops. In the past it was a staple, eaten by some at least three times a day, mostly as bread, which they used as a sop for gravy and molasses. *The Nebraska Farmer* of January 1862 listed 33 different ways of preparing fresh or dried corn. These included, in addition to golden bread, corn muffins, corn cake and corn dodgers (made on a griddle), such cooked dishes as hominy and breakfast mushes like samp (coarsely ground dried corn) and hasty pudding (cornmeal boiled in water). All of these are still eaten in parts of the country—some, naturally, more often than others. Hominy, for example, remains an important food in the South, where it is prepared by soaking dried corn in lye to remove the hulls and then boiling the kernels in water. Hominy is not to be confused with hominy grits, or just plain grits, as they are more often called. These are grains of hominy, ground fine, cooked in water and eaten as a breakfast food—to the tune, in the Southeast, of over four pounds a person a year. Grits may also be baked, and a cheese and grits casserole is a delicious dish *(page 95)*.

While the popularity of some of the old and classic corn dishes is waning, one retains its strong hold on people everywhere, and that is cornbread *(page 179)*. I am amazed by the number of variations for it that

exist. But we have been using corn so long in our homes—and so many kinds of corn are available in America—that I suppose it was only natural that many different ways of making this basic bread should have sprung up. Hoecake, ashcake, johnnycake and corn pone all are forms of cornbread, cooked in different ways, and each has its own special quality. Johnnycake is at its best when made from the hard variety of corn called flint, which grows in the North; many Southern cornbreads call for dent corn, so named for the dents in the dry kernel. And spoon bread, the aristocrat of cornbreads *(Recipe Booklet)*, is always at its most delicious made from water-ground cornmeal (the millstones are water-driven).

Corn may be our native grain, but wheat—which we brought from Europe in the 17th Century—has also played an enormous role in nourishing the nation. While corn, so new at first to the settlers, quickly became an ordinary food, wheat long remained a luxury. George Washington grew it, and found milling an honorable profession; Mt. Vernon flour was famous for its high quality. To the pioneer, fed to the teeth on a diet of corn in all its many forms, wheat could spell most welcome variety. Wrote a Minnesota farmer in his diary for August 12, 1855: "Eat bread today made from wheat of our own raising ground. Though I have kept house for eleven years I have never eat wheat bread of my own raising. This seems an Epoch of some importance in my history, and realy seems quite a comfort."

In the latter part of the 19th Century, as more and more land was planted to wheat in the Midwest and improved methods of milling it were discovered, white flour became a commodity available to millions. Most of the flour went into loaves of homemade bread, and baking day—which involved the making of cakes and cookies as well—could be the busiest time in the week.

San Francisco's sourdough bread forms decorative patterns in the window of a bakery. The bread, which is made of fermented dough, was a favorite of Californian and Alaskan prospectors in gold-rush days: today's version, called French sourdough bread, goes everywhere, carried by airline travelers who find the loaves invitingly displayed at San Francisco's airport.

Continued on page 172

Pies, cakes and other baked goods have always been featured at that American institution, the church social. At the Universal Hagar's Spiritual Church in New York City the menu for a church spread included apple and cherry pies, coconut cake and poundcake, cornbread, rolls, fried chicken, roast beef, red rice (cooked with onions, green peppers and tomatoes), collard greens, potato salad and soft drinks. Members of the church take turns preparing these meals. The chief cook for this occasion was Leola Spencer, shown serving guests at left. Meals on these occasions cost only $1.25 (dessert and beverage are extra), and while the attendance is mostly from the members of the congregation, anyone is welcome.

171

A rich chocolate cake, chocolate frosted, is an easily made and immensely popular dessert. The delicious frosting is a simple mixture of melted chocolate and sour cream.

Many housewives had their own yeast preparation, or starter, on hand to use as a leaven (commercial yeast did not become available until 1868). They generally made it from hops, potatoes, sugar, salt, flour and water. Yeast cells, always present in the air, would settle on this broth, begin to multiply and set the starter to working—that is, fermenting. When women baked, they would mix a little of it with their flour and other ingredients to form dough. Those who found making their own starter too much trouble—or risky, since it was subject to such vagaries as temperature and light—often resorted to another method of leavening their bread, which involved combining cornmeal, water and sugar, and letting the mixture stand overnight to ferment. This was blended with flour, salt and other ingredients to yield the "salt-rising" bread mentioned so often in old cookbooks.

After the housewife went to all the trouble of making her own starter and nursing it along, she could be counted on to watch over it like a mother hen. But she rarely matched the cowboy cook for finickiness. His reputation depended on how good his sourdough biscuits were, and he coddled his starter like a child, taking it to bed with him to keep it warm through the long, cold night (a sudden drop in temperature might kill the yeast cells). The loss of a starter could take on the proportions of a disaster: creating a new one was no easy chore, and all but impossible in deepest winter. Besides, a new one might not impart as much good flavor to bread or biscuits as the old had (the strains of wild yeast vary from place to place). The cowboy cook made his starter by mixing up some flour and potato water in a keg and leaving it out in the sun to ferment—and then, after having got it going, he would as often throw it away, to begin again. The first mix had served merely to season his keg. Whenever he dipped up some starter to use in his biscuit dough, he made sure he returned to the keg exactly the amount of flour and water he had taken out. The yeast, as well as the boys, had to be fed. Similarly, the frugal New England housekeeper would scrape into the bowl where she kept her yeast preparation all the flour and dough that clung to her board after she finished kneading her bread.

Another leavening much used during the 19th Century was baking soda. It was known as saleratus, and it came in a bright-red package. Its advantage was that it combined quickly with the acid in sour milk or buttermilk, two ingredients readily available in the days before refrigeration, to release the carbon dioxide needed to make the batter rise. If the recipe called for sweet milk rather than sour, the cook had to add an acid—usually cream of tartar—to get the chemical reaction going. Things became a great deal simpler after the introduction of baking powder in 1856. This new product contained both baking soda and an acid salt, such as cream of tartar. When a liquid—either water or milk—dissolved the powder, the acid and soda started reacting, and carbon dioxide bubbled up in the batter. Soon baking powder and table salt were combined directly with flour by millers to yield the first of the "mixes," self-rising flour.

With a strong tradition of home-baked bread behind us, I have often been puzzled as to why we are so willing today to buy the plastic-wrapped loaves on the supermarket shelves. Whenever I compare American bread of this sort to European bread, I see ours as the 90-pound weakling, much in need of body building. There it sits in its glossy package, all wobbly slices and limp crust. People buy it, and bakers insist that this is what the public wants. They make it deliberately spongy so that the housewife squeezing it for freshness will feel its reassuring give. Those cowboys, who knew how to damn a thing they did not like, called baker's bread "gun waddin'" and "wasp's nest." President Ulysses S. Grant, who was never known for the delicacy of his manners, used to make tight little dough balls of it and fire them at his guests.

As early as 1869 two sisters, Catherine E. Beecher and Harriet Beecher Stowe (the latter known for her *Uncle Tom's Cabin*), in their book, *The American Woman's Home,* lamented the increasing popularity of store-bought bread and blamed its rise on those people who saw lightness as the only criterion of good bread. "How else can they value and relish bakers' loaves?" asked the agitated sisters. "Light indeed, so light that [the loaves] seem to have neither weight nor substance, but with no more sweetness or taste than so much cotton wool." Henry Ward Beecher, their reverend brother, joined the chorus of discontent in 1871, charging in a manifesto that the bleaching of flour, just then being introduced, was killing "the live germ of the wheat," and complaining bitterly that "what

Techniques for Melting Chocolate

Melting chocolate is a tricky business, for this ingredient is easily scorched. The safest way is to melt it in a pan or bowl over hot water, or in a slow oven. To melt it over direct heat, which takes less time, use a heavy pan. Stir the chocolate constantly and don't allow it to boil. In spite of all precautions, chocolate sometimes will "tighten" into a lumpy mass that cannot be broken up. If this happens, stir in 1 tablespoon of vegetable shortening for every 6 ounces of chocolate. It will then become fluid and manageable, ready for use in icings, candy, cake or cookie batter, soufflés, mousses or any recipe calling for melted chocolate.

Continued on page 176

Harvesting a Rare Grain

With a retail price of up to $10 a pound, wild rice may be the most expensive grain in the world. And when properly prepared as a side dish or stuffing, it is (to those who can afford it) worth every cent it costs. The Indians of Minnesota thought so too, and fought fierce wars for 150 years for control of the shallow waters where wild rice flourishes. Traditional harvesting methods are still used in gathering the crop. Working from canoes *(opposite)*, men bend the tall aquatic grasses (a different species from ordinary rice) and flail the heads with cedar sticks *(above, top)* until the grains fall into the boat *(above)*. After being parched, winnowed and threshed, the grain is ready for the epicurean market.

had been the staff of life for countless ages had become a weak crutch."

Actually, several factors contributed to the virtual annihilation of bread as something to make in the home. One was the increased mechanization of the bread-making process in the factory, with machines kneading great vats of dough faster than armies of bakers could have done it by hand. Another factor was the utter ease of buying the commercial product—baking bread, after all, was never a task to assume lightly (especially when the dough had to be kneaded 45 minutes to an hour, as an old recipe specified, without stop, as "any pause in the process injures the bread"). Yet another factor was the role the store-bought loaf came to play as a status symbol in some homes, no matter how bad it might be: why make your own when you can *afford* to buy it? And the final blow undoubtedly came when women, as during World War II, went to work: they had no time to bake bread. All too quickly the old recipes were shelved and the old skills forgotten. A young married woman I know had to teach herself by trial and error to make bread; when her mother and father came to visit her, she served them one of her yeasty loaves. Her father liked it so much he had the daughter teach her mother how to bake bread, and new love was thus breathed into an old marriage.

Flour is a tricky thing, and a great many serious home bakers know little about it, trusting to their skills or to chance to make everything turn out right, rather than proceeding from the confidence instilled by knowledge. Too often the white flour that we use in our baking is treated as though it were *just* flour, a consistently white powder, the same all over the country and the world, which, of course, it is not. Bakers and millers have long known that allowance must be made for the *kind* of flour that is used, although most recipes pay only lip service to this principle when they urge that the dough for a particular bread be kneaded for 10 minutes or that biscuit batter be handled as little as possible—without ever explaining why.

The two basic categories of white flour—hard and soft—can be distinguished by their "feel"; hard flour—made from hard wheat—actually feels hard between the fingers, while soft flour seems silky. Hard flour contains a higher percentage of protein, and since it is protein that gives body to dough, this flour is used most often to bake bread. When moistened, the protein forms gluten, and kneading the dough helps develop the gluten. The gluten may be visualized as spirals: as the dough is kneaded and folded over again and again, the spirals begin to flatten out and overlap in three-dimensional patterns. In the "cage" thus formed are trapped the bubbles of gas produced by the living yeast cells; these make the dough rise. When the dough is smooth and elastic, the gluten is considered well developed and the bread may now be set aside to rise.

The popular "all-purpose" flour sold in stores today is, as its name suggests, a blend of hard and soft flours, calculated to meet as many baking requirements as possible. Ideally it should work well for all, and it often does. But only one milling company puts out an all-purpose flour that is identical in formula no matter where it is purchased in the country. At least one of the giants of the industry deliberately tailors its product according to the region in which it is to be sold. For example, the flour it

sells in the Southeast (where the per capita consumption of flour is higher than in any other part of the United States) is made up of a greater proportion of soft than hard, and for a simple enough reason—the company knows that more biscuits than bread are going to be baked in the Southeast. Biscuits are best made from soft flour; indeed, they may be a Southern specialty not because people originally preferred them to bread, but because the wheat Southern farmers grow yields soft flour. For breadmaking, all-purpose flour can be reinforced with high-gluten flour, to be found sometimes in specialty shops or health-food stores. Better yet is bread flour, also known as baker's flour. It can usually be bought directly from a local baker.

I would like to think that home baking is about to undergo a renaissance, hankering as so many of us do today for more complete satisfaction from our foods. I am not calling for a return to the cakes of yesteryear—the Prince of Wales, the Minnehaha, the Silver Ribbon, the Election Cake—with their all too casual employment of eggs and butter, their devil-may-care attitude toward custard fillings and sticky icings. Delicious though these have been, they undoubtedly would be too rich for our tastes. But all cakes need not therefore be forsaken. There are less extravagant ones for us to make, like the chocolate layer cake with chocolate-and-sour-cream topping shown on page 172, for which there is a recipe on page 182. And bread recipes remain as basic and good as ever *(page 178)* and need only to be tried again. "The true housewife," we are reminded by the Beecher sisters, who were thought very wise in their day, "makes bread the sovereign of her kitchen."

Pancakes topped with butter and swimming in maple syrup quiet the appetites of millions of hungry Americans. The variety and quantity of pancakes eaten in the United States is almost limitless. The menu of a popular restaurant chain lists the following kinds of pancakes: apple, banana nut, blueberry, boysenberry, buckwheat, buttermilk, chocolate chip, corn, French, German, pecan, potato, strawberry and Swedish.

American White Bread

To make one 9-inch loaf

1 package dry yeast
1 cup lukewarm milk
1½ tablespoons sugar
2½ to 3 cups all-purpose flour or
    bread flour
4 tablespoons soft butter
1 teaspoon salt

GLAZE
1 egg, lightly beaten with 1
    tablespoon milk

Sprinkle the yeast into a half cup of the lukewarm (110° to 115°) milk. Add 1 teaspoon of the sugar and stir until thoroughly dissolved. Place the mixture in a warm, draft-free place—such as an unlighted oven—for 5 to 8 minutes, or until the yeast has begun to bubble and almost doubled in volume.

Then pour it into a large mixing bowl, add the remaining ½ cup of milk and stir until the yeast is dissolved. With a large spoon, slowly beat into the mixture 1 cup of the flour and continue to beat vigorously until smooth. Still beating, add the butter, remaining sugar, salt and 1½ more cups of flour. Transfer the dough to a lightly floured surface and knead it by folding it end to end, then pressing it down, pushing it forward and folding it back for at least 10 minutes, sprinkling the dough every few minutes with small amounts of as much of the remaining flour as you need to prevent the dough from sticking to the board. When the dough is smooth and elastic, place it in a large, lightly buttered bowl. Dust it with a sprinkling of flour and cover the bowl loosely with a kitchen towel. Let the dough rise in a warm, draft-free place for 45 minutes to an hour, or until the dough doubles its bulk and springs back slowly when gently poked with a finger. Then punch the dough down again with one blow of your fist to reduce it to its original volume. Let it rise 30 to 40 minutes until it again doubles in bulk.

Preheat oven to 375°. Lightly but thoroughly butter a 9-by-5-by-3-inch loaf pan. Shape the dough into a compact loaf, somewhat high and round in the center, and place it in the pan. Cover with a towel and let the dough rise in the same warm place (about 25 minutes) until it reaches the top of the pan. Thoroughly brush the top of the loaf with the egg and milk glaze. Bake in the lower third of the oven for 30 to 40 minutes, or until the loaf is golden brown and a toothpick inserted in its center comes out clean and dry. Invert the bread on to a cake rack and cool before slicing.

Clover Leaf Rolls

To make 24 rolls

1 recipe for American white-bread
    dough (*see above*)
1 tablespoon soft butter
2 tablespoons melted butter

Prepare the dough as described in the white-bread recipe above up to the point where it has risen for the second time. With a pastry brush, lightly but thoroughly grease each cup of two 12-cup muffin tins with 1 tablespoon of soft butter. Pinch off small pieces of the dough and shape them into small balls, rolling them between your palms until they are about ½ inch in diameter. Arrange 3 balls closely together in each muffin cup, cover the tins with a dry kitchen towel and let the dough rise in a warm place (about 25 minutes) until each roll reaches the top of the pan.

Preheat the oven to 425°. Brush the dough with the melted butter and bake in the middle of the oven for 10 to 15 minutes until the rolls are golden brown. Test for doneness by inserting a toothpick in a roll; it should come out dry and clean. Remove the rolls from the tins and serve them while they are still hot and crusty.

Strawberry Shortcake

Preheat the oven to 450°. Sift the flour, sugar, baking powder and salt together into a large bowl. Add the butter, and, with your fingertips, rub the dry ingredients and butter together until most of the lumps disappear and the mixture resembles coarse meal. Pour in the cream and mix thoroughly until a soft dough is formed. Gather it into a compact ball and place on a lightly floured board. Knead the dough for about a minute by folding it end to end and pressing down and pushing forward several times with the heel of your hand. Roll the dough out into a circle about 1 inch thick. With a 3-inch cookie cutter, cut out 6 circles. Cut the remaining dough into 6 2½-inch circles. (If there isn't enough dough, gather the scraps, knead briefly and roll out again.) Arrange the 3-inch circles on a lightly buttered cookie sheet. Brush each with a teaspoon of melted butter; top with a smaller circle. Bake in the middle of the oven for 12 to 15 minutes until firm to the touch and golden brown.

Meanwhile, chop half the strawberries coarsely, reserving the most attractive ones for the top. Separate the shortcakes. Spread a layer of chopped strawberries on the bottom circles, sprinkle with sugar and gently place the smaller circles on top. Garnish with the whole strawberries. Strawberry shortcake is traditionally served with heavy cream.

To make 6 small shortcakes

4 cups all-purpose flour
6 tablespoons sugar
5 teaspoons baking powder
2 teaspoons salt
12 tablespoons butter (1½ quarter-pound sticks) chilled and cut into bits
1½ cups heavy cream
6 teaspoons melted and cooled butter
2 pints of fresh, ripe strawberries
1½ teaspoons sugar
1 pint heavy cream for topping

Leola's Cornbread

Preheat the oven to 400°. Sift into a mixing bowl the cornmeal, flour, sugar, salt and baking powder. Beat the eggs lightly, add the melted butter and shortening, and stir in the 1½ cups of milk. Pour into the bowl of dry ingredients and beat together for about a minute, or until smooth. Do not overbeat. Lightly butter an 8-by-12-inch shallow baking pan and pour in the batter. Bake in the center of the oven for about 30 minutes, or until the bread comes slightly away from the edge of the pan and is golden brown. Serve hot.

NOTE: If you wish you may bake the cornbread in a 9-by-5-by-3-inch loaf pan. Increase the baking time to 45 minutes.

To make one 9-inch loaf

1½ cups yellow cornmeal
1 cup all-purpose flour
⅓ cup sugar
1 teaspoon salt
1 tablespoon baking powder
2 eggs
6 tablespoons melted and cooled butter
8 tablespoons melted and cooled vegetable shortening
1½ cups milk

Griddle Cakes

Sift the flour, baking powder, sugar and salt together into a large bowl. Make a well in the center of the flour and pour in the eggs and milk. With a large spoon mix only long enough to blend; stir in the melted butter. Do not overmix; the pancakes will be lighter if the batter is not too smooth. Heat a griddle or heavy skillet over moderate heat until a drop of water flicked onto it evaporates instantly. Grease the griddle or skillet very lightly with oil; continue to grease when necessary. Pour the batter from a pitcher or ladle into the hot pan to form pancakes 4 inches in diameter. Cook 2 to 3 minutes until small, scattered bubbles have formed—but have not broken—on the surface. Immediately turn with a spatula and cook for a minute until the other side is golden brown. Stack on a heated plate and serve with melted butter and maple syrup.

NOTE: One cup of thoroughly drained, fresh, canned or thoroughly defrosted and drained frozen fruit may be added to the batter before frying.

To make 18 to 20 pancakes

2 cups all-purpose flour
2 teaspoons baking powder
2 teaspoons sugar
1 teaspoon salt
3 eggs, lightly beaten
2 cups milk
¼ cup melted butter
¼ cup vegetable oil

Home-baked sticky buns, Texas Royal Ruby Red grapefruit and hot coffee make a satisfying breakfast.

Sticky Buns

To make 12 buns

Sprinkle the yeast and a pinch of sugar into the lukewarm water. Let the mixture stand for 2 to 3 minutes, then stir it to dissolve the yeast. Set the container in a warm, draft-free place, such as an unlighted oven, for 5 to 8 minutes, or until the solution has begun to bubble and has almost doubled in volume.

Pour the milk into a heavy 1-quart saucepan and warm it over medium heat until bubbles form around the edge of the pan. Turn the heat to low and add 4 tablespoons of the butter and ¼ cup of the sugar. Stir constantly until the sugar dissolves, then cool to lukewarm and combine with the yeast mixture.

Sift the flour and salt into a deep mixing bowl. Make a well in the flour and pour into it the yeast and milk mixture, the egg yolks and the teaspoon of lemon rind. With your hands or a large wooden spoon, work the flour into the other ingredients until they become a medium-firm dough.

On a lightly floured surface, knead the dough by folding it end to end, then pressing it down and pushing it forward several times with the heel of your hand. Sprinkle the dough with a little extra flour whenever necessary to prevent it from sticking to the board. Repeat the kneading process until the dough becomes smooth and elastic. This will take about 10 minutes.

Shape the dough into a ball and put it in a large, lightly buttered bowl. Dust the top of the dough lightly with flour, cover with a kitchen towel and set in a warm, draft-free spot (again, an unlighted oven is ideal). In 45 minutes to an hour, the dough should double in bulk.

Punch the dough down with your fist, then transfer from the bowl to a lightly floured board and knead again briefly. Roll it out into a rectangle 12 inches long and ¼ inch thick. Brush the dough with 3 tablespoons of the remaining melted butter and sprinkle the combined ¼ cup of sugar, the cinnamon and currants or raisins over it evenly.

In a small, heavy saucepan, combine the ½ cup of water, the brown sugar and 4 tablespoons of butter. Stir until the sugar dissolves and bring to a boil over high heat. Reduce the heat to moderate and cook the syrup for about 10 minutes until it has the consistency and color of maple syrup.

Let the syrup cool slightly, then dribble half of it over the surface of the dough. With your hands, roll the dough into a tight cylinder about 2 inches in diameter and cut it crosswise into 1-inch rounds. Grease a round 10-inch cake pan with the remaining 1 tablespoon of melted butter. Pour into it the other half of the syrup and sprinkle it evenly with the chopped walnuts. Arrange the rounds, cut side down, in a circle around the edge of the pan; continue the pattern with the remaining rounds until the pan is full. Let them rise in a warm, draft-free place for about 25 minutes, or until they are double in bulk. Meanwhile, preheat the oven to 350°.

Bake the buns in the middle of the oven for about ½ hour. When the buns are golden brown and firm to the touch, remove them from the oven and invert them onto a cake rack. Separate the buns and serve warm or at room temperature.

1 package active dry yeast
Pinch sugar
½ cup lukewarm water (110° to 115°)
1 cup milk
8 tablespoons melted butter (1 quarter-pound stick)
½ cup sugar
3½ cups all-purpose flour
¼ teaspoon salt
2 egg yolks
1 teaspoon grated lemon rind
1 teaspoon cinnamon
½ cup currants or raisins
½ cup water
1½ cups brown sugar, packed down
4 tablespoons butter
½ cup coarsely chopped walnuts

To make one 9-inch cake

Six 1-ounce squares of unsweetened
　　chocolate
12 tablespoons unsalted butter
　　(1½ quarter-pound sticks),
　　softened
2¼ cups sugar
4 eggs
1 teaspoon vanilla
2 cups all-purpose flour
1½ level teaspoons baking powder
¼ teaspoon salt
1½ cups milk

CHOCOLATE SOUR-CREAM FROSTING
Three 6-ounce packages semisweet
　　chocolate bits
¼ teaspoon salt
1½ cups sour cream
12 to 15 shelled walnut halves

To make one 9-inch pie

2½ cups all-purpose flour
8 tablespoons chilled vegetable
　　shortening or lard
4 tablespoons chilled butter, cut into
　　¼-inch pieces
¼ teaspoon salt
6 tablespoons ice water

FILLING
1½ cups dried pitted prunes
1½ cups dried apricots
1 cup shelled walnuts, coarsely
　　chopped
½ cup sugar
1 teaspoon grated lemon rind
1 teaspoon vanilla
8 tablespoons (½ cup) melted
　　butter, plus 1 tablespoon
1 cup heavy cream, whipped
　　(optional)

Three-Layer Chocolate Cake

Preheat the oven to 375°. Break the chocolate into small pieces, place in a small saucepan and melt over moderate heat, stirring constantly with a spoon. Do not let it boil. Cool to room temperature. In a large mixing bowl, cream the butter and sugar together by mashing and beating it with a large spoon until it is light and fluffy. Beat in the eggs, one at a time, then beat in the melted chocolate and vanilla. Sift the flour, baking powder and salt together into another bowl. Beat ¼ cup of the dry ingredients into the chocolate mixture, then beat in ¼ cup of milk. Continue adding the flour and milk alternately in similar amounts, beating until the batter is smooth.

Butter and flour three 9½-inch circular cake pans. Invert the pans and rap them on the edge of the table to knock out any excess flour. Divide the batter equally among the three pans and bake them in the center of the oven for 15 to 20 minutes, or until the cakes come slightly away from the edge of the pan and are firm to the touch. A knife inserted in the center of the cakes should come out dry and clean. Turn the cakes out on cake racks to cool.

Spread the top of each cake with about ¼ inch of the chocolate sour-cream frosting and place the layers one on top of another on a cake plate. With a long metal spatula or knife, thoroughly coat the sides of the cakes with the remaining frosting, and add more frosting to the top of the cake if you wish. Decorate the top with the halved walnuts.

CHOCOLATE SOUR-CREAM FROSTING: In the top of a double boiler, melt the chocolate over boiling water. With a whisk or spoon, stir into it the salt and the sour cream. Ice the cake while the frosting is still slightly warm.

Prune and Apricot Pie

In a large mixing bowl, combine the flour, vegetable shortening or lard, butter and salt. Working quickly, use your fingertips to rub the flour and fat together until they look like flakes of coarse meal. Pour 6 tablespoons of ice water over the mixture, toss together, and press and knead gently with your hands until the dough can be gathered into a compact ball. Dust very lightly with flour, wrap in wax paper and chill for at least ½ hour.

Lightly butter a 9-inch pie plate and divide the ball of dough into 2 parts, one a third larger than the other. On a floured surface, roll out the larger half of dough into a circle about ⅛ inch thick and 13 to 14 inches in diameter. Lift it up on the rolling pin and unroll it over the pie plate. Be sure to leave enough slack in the middle of the pastry to enable you to line the plate without pulling or stretching the dough. Trim the excess pastry with a sharp knife, so that the pastry is even with the outer rim of the pie plate. Roll the smaller half of the dough into a rectangle 12 inches long and about ⅛ inch thick. With a sharp knife or pastry wheel, cut it into 6 strips about 1 inch wide. Refrigerate both the pie shell and the pastry strips while you make the filling.

Place the prunes and apricots in a small enameled or stainless-steel saucepan, and pour in enough water to cover them by about an inch. Bring the water to a boil. Boil rapidly for 4 to 5 minutes, then drain in a

A rich and gaudy climax for any meal is provided by prune and apricot pie with a latticework crust and fluted edge.

sieve. Dry the fruit with paper towels, and cut each prune and apricot into 4 pieces. Combine them in a mixing bowl with the walnuts, sugar, grated lemon rind and vanilla. Add the melted butter and, with a large spoon, mix together thoroughly. Spoon the filling into the pie shell. Arrange the reserved 3 strips of dough ¾ of an inch apart across the top of the pie and crisscross the other 3 strips of dough over them. With your fingers, tuck the ends firmly under the rim of the pie plate to secure them.

Preheat the oven to 350°. Brush the crisscross strips of pastry with the 1 tablespoon of melted butter and bake the pie in the middle of the oven for about 1 hour, or until the pastry is golden brown and the fruit is tender.

Serve warm or at room temperature, accompanied by unsweetened whipped cream if you like.

VIII

Two Hundred Years in the Kitchen

America's contribution to world cooking has been tremendous—after its fashion. If our recipes have not been widely copied by people everywhere, our kitchens and their appliances and gadgets have been—and so, of course, have our supermarkets. The American influence extends to food processing as well, and "convenience food" is no longer the disdained term abroad that it used to be. Behind this culinary revolution modestly stands the American woman. She helped launch it when she began to protest her domestic servitude a century ago, and her battleground became the kitchen. All the labor-saving devices (and labor-saving foods) she uses there today, all the fine cookbooks she owns, she more than deserves. Not one to rest on her laurels, she is busily applying much of the time and energy she has thus gained to improving her cooking—learning how to cook not just well, but superbly, even going to school *(opposite)* and adventuring into realms where only chefs have trod before. It is ironic, therefore, that she should be looked upon as lazy and spoiled by so many overseas who know nothing of her long struggle and who have already benefited so greatly from her hard-won battle.

Our heroes are generally thought of as men. After delving into the cooking lore of the last two centuries, I would like to see credit given to some unsung heroines—those anonymous women who labored in primitive kitchens from dawn to sunset at the never-ending task of feeding their husbands and children. It was they, really, who carried this country on their backs through all the formative stages of its growth. The democratic experiment, as the American way of life was called then, was no experiment to

The intense interest in cooking among American women and men is evidenced at a class in Philadelphia. As the students watch, Mrs. Julie Dannenbaum, a well-known cooking instructor, shows how to put the finishing touches on hors d'oeuvre.

them: it was a harsh reality. They were equals among equals, expected to put their shoulders to the wheel. They worked as hard as their menfolk, and often they functioned at the edge of despair. In my great-grandmother Rosaltha Neal's diary for 1875 there is this entry, a small, feeble outcry, penned and unpunctuated on April 10 when even spring had failed to lift her spirits: "Baked and mopped/twisted a ball of yarn/made some boxes/and sowed tomato seeds/I feel sad and lonely/Oh dear."

Most women labored by themselves in their kitchens; if they had any help, it usually came from their children, who could be counted on to bring in firewood, take out the ashes, stack the cookies—and get underfoot. To be sure, there were occasionally some maiden aunts helping out, and there were servants in America, too, paid or slave, but something in the whole idea of service went against the American grain. Waiting on people (even being waited on) seemed beneath the dignity of a democratic people. It was a steppingstone to something better, and when it was done, it was often done begrudgingly; servants were the great saboteurs of the rich, and among the slaves in the South slopping the soup or breaking the china was one way of "talking up."

Independent of outlook and perfectionist by nature, American women may have actually preferred to work unaided. They were motivated by love of their families, and they cooked and cleaned with a devotion no servant could ever have mustered. If they took time off, it was to have a baby, or to lay up a little credit in the next world by attending prayer meetings or deciding moral issues—"Question: Is the liquor dealer the biggest scoundrel in the world? Affirmative, carried."

It is easy to forget how different—how very hard—things used to be in the kitchen. In the early days, a woman was less a cook than a processor of foodstuffs, and her stove, her worktable, her pantry, the dairy where she kept her pans of milk and slabs of butter were all integral parts of a factory over which she was sole boss. No one knew better than she that woman's work is never done. She was keeper of the fires, guardian of the chickens, milker of the cows; she was butcher, baker, dairymaid; she was doctor, nurse, druggist, dispenser of homemade elixirs, embrocations and physics. She corned beef and salted pork; she picked hops and made beer. And she was supposed to smile. If she faltered or collapsed in her round of chores, she could expect little pity. One shrew who called herself Aunt Sophronia felt constrained to remind the frazzled what going mad or dying would mean: "If a wife dies of overwork, a housekeeper will cost $5 per week plus . . . and if a wife goes to an asylum, let her consider the expenses. Or, if she dies, her husband takes another wife and her children become mere step-children. Don't be a dead hawk tied to the pole of a scarecrow."

As a cook and processor of foods, the American housewife possessed many tools, but some of the utensils that she owned sound more fitted for foundry use than kitchen. Among the "conveniences you cannot do without," wrote one cookbook author of the 1850s, were "a meat knife and a saw, a steak pounder and board, a potato-jammer, two wooden bowls, one for mashing turnips and squash and the other for draining your dishes in, a pair of steelyards, and a giggering iron."

Back in the 17th Century, at the very dawn, so to speak, of American cookery, kitchen equipment had been, of course, more basic. In many homes it consisted of a handful of clumsy utensils and an iron pot. The colonial housewife's first convenience was probably a crane on which to hang the pot.

When pieces and kinds of equipment began to multiply, one item that almost everyone was sure to have was a "tin kitchen," or Dutch oven (not the iron pot with tight-fitting lid called that today, but a metal box with one side open, which stood on the hearth). A small fowl would be put in it, and heat reflecting off the back wall would help cook the bird. But the Dutch oven must have been little comfort to the cook who had to cope with cumbersome and heavy utensils—pots weighed as much as 40 pounds. And all that went up the chimney was not smoke from the logs; sometimes it came from the lady of the household's skirt, ignited by the fire as she stood stirring porridge, or boiling vegetables.

The introduction of the iron stove and range in the second quarter of the 19th Century (which American women took to in a way European women did not) was little help to the housewife. The iron monster—hotter than any fireplace had ever been—had always to be fed, and before she could prepare a decent meal on it she had to master all the ins and outs of its complicated system of flues and ventilators. Recipes that had worked well for fireplace cookery did not do for range cookery, and had to be revised or abandoned entirely. Gone, and missed, was the old brick oven and its mellow heat, in which a succession of foods was baked— bread, beans, pies, biscuits and cookies. Forty years went by before, in the 1870s, a range appeared that was adaptable to cooking's many needs.

The amount of information an American woman of the 18th or 19th Century needed to know in order to go about the business of cooking was formidable. We turn on a stove, but she started a fire—and that was by no means all. She knew which woods yielded the best heat, and which wood best suited which food. If she planned to roast beef in the fireplace, she made sure to start a fire early, so that it would burn down to coals. Sometimes she kindled the fire with pine cones, preferably dry ones, because these had "the most burning juice in them." She avoided hemlock and chestnut, since they snapped, and instead used hickory or oak, which yielded white-hot embers. And she judged how far from the fire to put the meat by the feel of the heat on the back of her hand.

When stoves and ranges came into use, determining the temperature of the oven took considerable bravery. One test was simply to stick your hand into the oven. If it had to be removed after 20 ticks of the clock, the oven temperature was in the vicinity of 450°. Another test involved sprinkling flour on a pie tin and placing the tin in the oven. If when three minutes were up the flour was black, then the temperature was 450°. A medium filbert brown indicated a moderate oven, a light brown a slow oven.

Knowing how long to cook something was often purely a matter of guesswork. Before clocks became cheap enough for most people to buy them, many women relied on the sun as a timer to tell them when a dish was done. Some kitchens had marks painted on their floors, from which

Hudson's Rocking Table Apple Parers.

Kitchen gadgets for almost every chore appeared in great profusion in the 19th Century. This hand-cranked apple peeler, patented in 1812, was designed to speed the housewife's task of peeling bushels of apples for canning, for pies and for apple butter.

187

the hours could be read as though from a sundial. Robert P. Tristram Coffin, in his book, *Mainstays of Maine*, tells how his mother "timed a cake by the sunbeam creeping across the floorboards." This woman, who had never used a cookbook in her life, trusting to experience instead, would put her ear to her bread and "if it was still singing to itself," she would clap it back into the oven and give it another 10 minutes. Cakes sang too —and may still—but who harkens to them now? The sound came from the batter or dough as it dried out in the heat of the oven. It announced the approaching moment when a broom straw might be inserted safely into a cake without causing the cake to fall.

Many women cooked purely from memory, needing, like Mrs. Coffin, no assistance from the printed word. But others valued and treasured cookbooks, or set down their recipes in collections of their own. To leaf through one of these yellowed-manuscript cookbooks, with faded, spidery handwriting and 150-year-old food stains summoning up the past on every page, is an eerie experience. And between the pages of these there usually turn up three or four clipped recipes, from old magazines and newspapers, or from that ephemeral source, the tin can. ("Even the cookbook may yet be obsolete," rejoiced one housewife, "for every can of prepared food has a label with directions how to cook.") The real fun, however, is to dip into books that had fairly wide distribution. They are quaint and wonderfully naive ("Home advice, with whispers to epicures." "By a Lady, with notes for dyspeptics." "By a physician."). And they paint a beautiful picture of changing patterns of American life.

Cookbook publishing has been a flourishing industry in this country for a couple of hundred years. The first truly American cookbook appeared in 1796, a thin but popular work by Amelia Simmons. She called herself "an American orphan" on the title page, and she seemed motivated by envy as well as self-pity, when she wrote in her preface, "It muft ever remain a check upon the poor solitary orphan, that while thofe females who have parents, or brothers, or riches, to defend their indifcretions, that the orphan muft depend upon *character*." Poor Amelia. Her character was nearly defamed by the person she had employed to help her prepare her book for publication. This scoundrel "(with a defign to impofe on her, and injure the sale of the book) did omit several articles very effential in some of the receipts, and placed others in their stead, which were highly injurious to them, without her confent—which was unknown to her, till after publication. . . ." Thus she had to append an errata sheet to the book, correcting errors as grievous as the one that marred the recipe for rice pudding—"for 14 eggs read 8."

But in spite of such gaffes, *American Cookery* sold briskly. It was the first book of its kind designed solely with an American audience in mind (all others were reprints of English works). Its success, however, may have had as much to do with the sound shopping advice it offered as it did with its imprecise recipes for "cramberry" sauce and "pompkin" pie ("One quart of milk, 1 pint pompkin, 4 eggs, molaffes, allfpice and ginger in a cruft, bake 1 hour"). The tips for buying fish are still valid today, and those for meat, poultry and game also have applicability—although to be sure, veal no longer comes to market "flouncing on a fweaty horfe." Either Miss Simmons was excessively suspicious, or the American merchant a conniver, for she warns often of fraud. (Not until 1906 would the food and drug laws provide the housewife with some protection.) The gills of fish might be peppered, moistened with blood or even painted, all in order to give them a false look of freshness. And cheese —beautiful to behold—might be something else again to eat, colored with "hemlock, cocumberries, or saffron, infufed into the milk."

Old cookbooks like Miss Simmons' confirm again how difficult the housewife's day-to-day existence must have been. The concentrate called "veal glue" corresponds to our bouillon cube, but the 18th Century housewife had to start from scratch to make it—preparing her own broth, reducing it, letting it cool and jell, and then putting it on a cloth to dry out. "This will harden," says an old recipe, "and may be carried in the pocket without inconvenience." When some boiling water was added to the glue, a good, strong soup resulted. William Byrd of Westover, Virginia, found this pocketable soup so handy he urged foresters to take it into the woods with them. "One pound . . . wou'd keep a Man in good Heart above a Month," he wrote, "and is not only nourifhing, but likewife very wholefome."

Heaven help the poor woman who wanted to serve a gelatin dessert or rennet pudding, today two of our simplest dishes. She generally got her gelatin by boiling down calves' feet, and she obtained her rennet in one of two inconvenient ways. She might take chicken gizzards, peel away the inside skins and wash and dry these; then, to make a chocolate cream, a two-woman operation, she would lay the gizzard skins in a napkin and rub them with a spoon while her assistant poured cream over them. The rennet and cream thus blended would pass through the napkin, and the process would be repeated four times. Or, following the advice of Mary Randolph in *The Virginia Housewife* (1824), the first of our regional cookbooks, the cook could take the stomach of a calf, hang it in a dry, cool place for several days, turn it inside out and slip off "all the curd nicely with the hand."

Early cookbooks were never just cookbooks: they were encyclopedias of household knowledge, and treated topics as unrelated as manners and medicine. "Avoid all unnecessary noise or motion," advised *The Skillful Housewife's Book* (1852). "Lean not your chair aginst the wall or furniture. Spit not upon the carpet or floor." Another cookbook of the early 19th Century told what to do for a toothache, first offering a few soothing words: "To all, a toothache is an intolerable torment, but what an overcoming agony it must be to a Grand Gourmand when [it] deprives him of food, the grand solace for all his sublunary cares. When this affliction befalls, the following specific is recommended: R. Sal volatile, 3 parts; laudanum, 1 part; mix and apply." (Laudanum is opium.)

Some idea of the wide scope of the old cookbooks can be gauged from the contents of a single one, *The Universal Receipt Book or Complete Family Directory,* published in 1814 by a society of gentlemen in New York. The first recipe is for bologna, the second is a remedy for jaundice, and the third tells how to clarify and preserve butter. Among its pages are directions for dyeing cloth and leather, making perfume and the Armenian

The Mosteller Automatic Lemon Squeezer

Patented in 1901, this kitchen gadget was the complete lemon juicer. It cut the lemon, squeezed the juice out of it, separated the seeds and removed the peel—all in one operation.

Continued on page 192

Fast and Fancy Desserts

These desserts would appear to require the arduous and time-consuming handiwork of a master chef. But with today's kitchen appliances, all three of them can be prepared easily and quickly by the busiest housewife. The recipe for the Nesselrode pudding at left called for puréed chestnuts; canned puréed chestnuts were used. The frozen cranberry mousse (*center*) was made with canned berries and bottled cranberry juice, and the cold orange soufflé at right was flavored with frozen orange-juice concentrate. The cream used in all three recipes (*pages 200-201*) was whipped with an electric mixer, and each of these desserts was chilled or frozen in a refrigerator.

method of jewel-setting. There are also prescriptions: "Doctor Macbride's Single Remedy for the Stone," the "Tonquinese Remedy for the Bite of a Mad Dog," and a "Remedy for the Staggers in Horses, which has been found effectual in repeated trials. By a Gentleman in North Carolina." The book's more exotic recipes include the "Incomparable Method of Salting Meat as Adopted by the late Empress of Russia," "Turkish Rouge, or the Secret of the Seraglio" and "An Excellent Catsup which will keep good more than 20 years."

All such books tended to be advertised as practical, and made great claims for themselves, like the one that promised a "receipt, by which meat, ever so stinking, may be made as sweet and wholesome, in a few minutes, as any meat at all." But most, I suspect, left a great deal to be desired. *Ladies' Indispensable Assistant* (1851) had "directions for managing canary birds." And *The Practical Housekeeper and Young Woman's Friend* (1855) told how coffee could be made from burnt crusts ("If you happen to burn your bread or cake, cut off the burnt crusts and save them for coffee; put them in a pitcher and pour over boiling water."). In the same book was printed—as a novelty, one hopes—the recipe for "Empress of France Bride's Cake—Weight 320 pounds." This called for 24 pounds of butter, 84 pounds of sugar, 30 pounds of currants, 32 eggs, 40 lemons and a great deal more. Even the "Good Common Wedding Cake" called for three pounds of butter, 24 eggs and half a pint of brandy.

Frugality was another notion much underscored by cookbook authors of the 19th Century. Mrs. Lydia Maria Child titled her work *The Frugal Housewife* (1829) and dedicated it "to those who are not ashamed of economy." She recommended that children be put to work at an early age, weeding the garden or picking berries ("In this country, we are apt to let children romp away their existence till they get to be 13 or 14."). Mrs. Child felt that a family of four could get by in the city on $600 a year. Maybe they could—in midcentury America calf's liver sold for two cents a pound, beef liver a penny, and rump for five cents a pound.

Then, as now, what ultimately helped sell cookbooks was their soundness. Undoubtedly for this reason and none other, Eliza Leslie's *75 Receipts for Pastry, Cakes and Sweetmeats* (1827) became the most popular cookbook of its day. By 1851, it had gone through 38 editions and sold 40,-000 copies. (Amelia Simmons' book went through 11 editions, and Mrs. Mary Randolph's *The Virginia Housewife* [1824], through nine.)

Reading the old cookbooks—even those calling themselves frugal and practical—can leave the distinct impression that many ingredients we consider rare or expensive today were so common a century ago as to be taken for granted. The enormous number of recipes calling for oysters makes this bivalve sound as though it were the most plentiful of God's creatures and the cheapest. There were oyster sauce, essence of oysters, oyster pie; there were raw oysters, baked oysters, fried oysters, fricasseed oysters. Oysters were used in stuffings, in chicken pies, on top of steaks. The old cookbooks also contain a preponderance of recipes for baked goods and preserves, including pickled nasturtium seeds, and catsup crops up so often it is hard to imagine any table ever being without it. But homemade catsup was quite a different condiment from the commercial product of

 Continued on page 196

Early kitchens, like this one in North Carolina, also served as dining rooms; cooking was done in the fireplace.

Nickel Plate Rail Guard.

Artistic Design.

Substantial Construction Throughout.

Great Fuel Saver.

Plate Holder.

Roll Back Door.

Roomy Warming Oven.

Mirror Finish Nickel.

Silver Nickel Brackets.

Draft Regulator.

LARGE WHITE ENAMEL WATER TANK

Lift Up Top Section.

Lift Off Tea Pot Stand.

Ring Co for Sma Pots.

Handy Oven Dampe

Guard Rail or Drying Rod.

Poker Door.

Draft Registers.

Wood Feed Door.

Airtight Riveted U-SO-NA Iron Body.

Massive Floor Base.

Sanitary Oven Rack.

Rust-Proof Casing.

Reservoir Damper.

"Never Fail" Baking Oven.

Nickel Oven Door.

U-SO-NA Rust-Resisting Body

Always Cool Alaska Wire Handle.

Flue Clean Out

Large Double Handle Ash Pan.

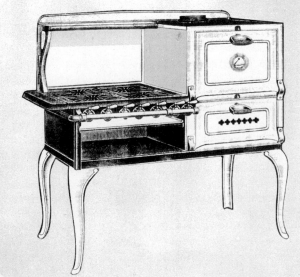

Evolution of the Stove

The contraption above was the latest thing in cookstoves in the 1911 Sears, Roebuck catalogue. It was a coal burner, but its design differed little from that of the more widely used wood burners. This coal burner, made of cast iron and trimmed with nickel plate, had a warming oven at the top and a reservoir at the right for heating water, features that were left out of the stove's descendants. One of these (left), a popular porcelain-enameled gas range with nickel trim, is shown as it was offered in the 1924 Sears catalogue. Gas ranges like this one made possible cleaner and cooler kitchens.

The "counter that cooks" *(below)* shows what the kitchen stove has come to in modern times. The heating elements in the foreground are completely covered with a glass-ceramic material that is easily wiped clean of spills. To complement this sort of range top, a wall oven must be separately installed.

today: for one thing, it was never just tomato. Oysters, walnuts, goose-berries, cranberries, mushrooms, grapes were all reduced through slow simmering to spicy essences and bottled.

Even the most cursory investigation of the old cookbooks reveals something startling—the way the authors freely borrowed, in fact, plagiarized, from each other. (Amelia Simmons and Eliza Leslie copied many of their recipes directly from English sources.) If the authors' own personalities poked through at all, it was most often in the introductions to their books. These abounded with gratuitous information, especially on how to run a home. System, said Mrs. M. L. Scott, in the introduction to *The Practical Housekeeper* (1855), was the great secret of good housekeeping. Piling on the chores, she wrote, "You may think it is a difficult matter to bring about all these things, but I can assure you that you will find it easier for yourself to do all the labor for six persons with system for your guide, than to do the labor for ten, with the aid of two servants and no system. I speak what I know."

If housewives were left satisfied, amused, confused, irritated, frustrated or bored by all the various information the different cookbooks pretended to give them, they were to be jounced right off their rocking chairs by the food faddists, whose numbers steadily grew as the 19th Century wore on. This strange group of men and women, with their even stranger ideas, were to have far-reaching effect on the American diet and eating habits. Sylvester Graham (1794-1851), whose last name is memorialized today on a sack of flour, can be looked upon as the first of these crusaders. When he launched his attack on the American diet, sometime around 1830, dyspepsia (severe indigestion) was so widespread as to seem a national disease. Thus his ideas for improving digestion (and elimination) fell on fertile ground. Imagine the housewife's consternation when he revealed to her that all the meat she so innocently served her husband and children actually inflamed tempers and induced sexual excesses. And what could her reaction have been when Sylvester Graham told her that condiments—the pepper and mustard she used to season her food, the bottle of catsup she placed so casually on the table—could induce insanity?

Graham saw health and salvation in bran, the outer portion of the wheat kernel, which was being sifted from flour by millers anxious to produce as purely white a product as possible. Dyspepsia could be cured, bodies purged and souls purified, he argued, if only bran were put back into flour. What he could not have known is that bran contained minerals and vitamins essential to health; what he did know is that as an irritant of the bowels it had a laxative effect. Graham bread, Graham crackers, Graham gems—all made with Graham flour containing a high percentage of bran—were his contribution to American cooking.

Graham's views were to be picked up and modified by other food faddists. Even God was brought into the cult, handing down his ideas on proper nutrition through an oracle, Mother Ellen Harmon White (1828-1915), spiritual leader of the Adventist Church. God-given health and happiness are yours, she promised, provided you eat two meatless meals a day, drink only water, avoid salt, spices and spirits, and do not smoke. High on her list of heavenly foods was Graham bread. In 1866 she founded the Western Health Reform Institute at Battle Creek, Michigan, and several years later hired Dr. John Harvey Kellogg (1852-1943) to manage it for her. Dr. Kellogg was not only to run the Institute: he was to take it over. He changed its name to the Battle Creek Sanitarium (it became known as the San) and he made it, as Ronald M. Deutsch has said in *The Nuts among the Berries,* "a veritable fountainhead of faddism." Here the sick and the neurotic, the underweight and the overweight went for complete overhauling. "Bran does not irritate," said the good doctor. "It titillates!" And bran was on every tongue. In addition to being titillated, his patients were put on strange diets, suited, the doctor assured them, to their own special needs. The skinny were plied with 26 feedings a day, forced to remain motionless in bed with sandbags on their bellies to increase absorption of nourishment, and not allowed even to brush their teeth, since any expenditure of energy might deprive them of a valuable calorie or two. Patients suffering from high blood pressure were served nothing but grapes; they were obliged to swallow 10 to 14 pounds of grapes a day. Foolish as such ideas may have been, Dr. Kellogg's influence crept right into the American home.

Out of one of Dr. Kellogg's pet theories—that people needed to chew dry, brittle food to keep their teeth in shape—came dried cereal. Part of the regular regimen of the San had been the endless munching of zwieback, but when a woman complained of breaking a tooth on it, the doctor vowed to provide a substitute, and he thereupon launched "experiments to produce toasted or dextrinized cereals in a form which, while dry and crisp," could be offered to people with artificial teeth, sore teeth or diseased gums. Actually, the cereal his experiments yielded was suspiciously like another faddist's product, Granula; Kellogg dared call his product Granola, but then thought twice about it when he was sued and quickly changed the name to Granose. In its very first year he managed to sell 100,000 pounds of Granose, and sales went on climbing ever afterward (today the breakfast-cereal industry in the United States is a $660-million-a-year business).

Among the many thousands Dr. Kellogg treated at the San was Charles Post. Although the diet and the ablutions that were a part of his life at the San for nine months did Post no good, he survived with the determination to succeed as Kellogg had. In 1895 he invented Postum, and three years later, Grape Nuts. Post's success—and his fortune—soon rivaled Kellogg's. It was partly thanks to the industries such men founded that the American breakfast, once a ponderous yet thoroughly nourishing meal of meat and pie, eggs and sausage, mush and syrup, coffee and cocoa, dwindled to the ultra-convenient, almost instant meal it is in most American homes today.

As ideas of what constituted a proper diet whirled around inside her head, the housewife was beginning to receive from outside the home some real, emancipating help. She had found a defender of her rights—someone who understood how hard she was obliged to work in the kitchen—in the aforementioned Catherine Beecher (1800-1878), whose books on domestic science shed needed light on a dark area. But more importantly, Miss Beecher dared ask probing questions—"In what respects are women

Gone with the two-cent price are some of the utensils in the 1914 Sears, Roebuck catalogue. Sears no longer carries wooden butter scoops (*center right*); it does, however, sell pie tins like the one shown at top left—for more than 50 times that amount.

subordinate? Wherein are they superior and equal in influence?"—and she posed bold answers. She saw the home as a power base for women, and housekeeping as an honorable profession. Out of her democratic view of society, she envisioned a servantless home that could be easily run. "A moderate style of housekeeping, small, compact and simple domestic establishments must necessarily be the general order of life in America," she wrote. And to achieve this, she called for the exclusion "from the labors of the family all that can be . . . excluded"—in short, for a simplification and an organization of the work process. What Catherine Beecher did, in a sense, was draw up a bill of rights for housewives.

In proposing that the kitchen be made a more efficient and cheerful place in which to work, she took for her model the ship's compact galley. Miss Beecher was way ahead of her time: when at last the kitchen was redesigned, in the 1920s, architects got their inspiration from another efficient unit, the galley of the railroad car. As much as she lamented the passing of the fireplace, with its brick bake oven, she settled for the fire-breathing range and called for its gradual improvement. In regarding housework, especially cooking, not as demeaning but uplifting work, a respected career for women, she bestowed dignity on it and she gave pride to downtrodden souls. But perhaps the most subtle service she rendered was in the realm of recipes. She helped bring order and coherence to an area of cooking where heretofore there had been almost none. And she set an example for all cookbook authors to follow by seeing to it that her recipes were not only readable, but workable. Unlike a great many other women of her day who were reluctant to part with their cooking secrets and smilingly passed out misinformation instead, Miss Beecher divulged hers straight-faced, straightforwardly.

Toward the end of the 19th Century, cookbooks began noticeably to improve. Among these were the *White House Cookbook* ("Every recipe has been *tried* and *tested,* and can be relied upon as one of the *best* of its kind"); *Miss Parloa's Kitchen Companion* ("Taken for all and all, canned foods, especially fruits and vegetables, are a great blessing, and as safe as most of the foods that we use"); and *The Buckeye Cookbook,* a remarkable work, according to those who own it and still use it. Curiously, all three books came out in 1887. Another excellent work was *Mrs. Rorer's Cookbook* by Mrs. Sara T. Rorer, a woman with sound ideas about eating but shaky notions of nutrition. And, then, of course, there was *The Boston Cookbook* by Mrs. Mary J. Lincoln, the great Fannie Farmer's predecessor at the Boston Cooking School and a woman to whom Miss Farmer owed a much greater debt than she acknowledged.

In the wake of all these pioneers, it remained only for Fannie Farmer (1867-1915) in her famous cookbook (which is still being used today) to do away with, once and for all, those meaningless terms that were an affliction of all American recipes—"a lump of butter the size of a walnut," "a fistful of flour," "a pinch of salt" or "cook until done"—and to substitute for them the level measure, the precise and accurate cooking time.

With a growing awareness of what good cooking could be also came notions of sophistication. Many women first wakened to the pleasures of French cooking as they listened to Monsieur Pierre Blot, a colorful chef who traveled across the country and lectured to them, often in their own living rooms. In his footsteps others were to follow. Among these was Jessie Marie De Both, remembered for the flamboyant courses she conducted in theaters and meeting halls to the amusement and edification of her audience. Along with such spreaders of culinary knowledge came the new encyclopedic and accurate cookbooks of the 1930s and 1940s. At least one of these, *The Joy of Cooking,* a work suffused with the personality of the author, Mrs. Irma Rombauer, remains a bestseller.

More important perhaps than the recipes and ideas that flowed into the home through cookbooks and magazines (only a dozen years ago fewer than 40 per cent of American women actually owned cookbooks) were the conveniences that began more and more to appear in the kitchen. First it was the icebox (in summer fresh meat no longer had to be eaten up in a day to keep it from spoiling, nor chickens cooked four hours after slaughter). Next it was running hot water, along with the cold. Then it was the gas stove, a frightening apparatus for the uninitiated— and then, just as soon as mastery of its dials and heat had been achieved, along came the electric stove to sow confusion again. The icebox gave way to the refrigerator and the freezer. And out of Clarence Birdseye's observation that Eskimos in Labrador froze their meat and fish evolved the quick-freezing of various foodstuffs, a revolution of the first order in American cooking.

As women woke up to their rights, not just at the polling place but in the home, the dream of Catherine Beecher was gradually fulfilled. Woman's work was at last organized and simplified—and men were to help her not just at the drawing board but in the kitchen, where they took a wider and wider role, some becoming excellent cooks. Time-and-motion studies showed just how much energy housewives had been wasting in their labors, and kitchens were made over to suit their needs. Appliances underwent streamlining, and all but the refrigerator became standardized in height to provide uniform working surfaces. The stove came down off its cabriole legs *(page 194)* and squatted on the floor, and ovens that had been at chest level now sank below the waist—forcing the cook to her knees and to the realization that perhaps the designer-engineers had gone too far. But things have a way of coming full circle, especially in the American kitchen, and today many ovens are back up at their old height—and some have even been set right into the wall.

Perhaps it could be said that the housewife, who used to be more a processor of foods than a cook, is today more a technician than a cook— working with push-button ease, utilizing ready-prepared foods, waiting for her timer to announce when dinner is ready. But that would be overstating it, and it would be ignoring the elaborate kinds of dishes the housewife is now attempting as American cooking becomes increasingly a cuisine. Moreover, love is still a requisite of good cooking, the guarantee that the food will turn out well. And even in the future—when we all will partake of freeze-dried fruits and vegetables, radiation-preserved meats and "flesh" that is not flesh at all, but spun soybean fibers—the criterion of good cooking will still be the same old one, taste. The palate, like the faithful heart, does not change.

The final recipes in this book are desserts made possible by modern refrigeration. Each of these dishes must be chilled in a refrigerator or freezer.

Frozen Cranberry Mousse

To make about 2 quarts

8 egg yolks
1 cup bottled cranberry juice, or juice from drained cranberries plus enough bottled juice to make 1 cup
Two 16-ounce cans whole cranberries (about 4 cups), drained, or 4 cups freshly cooked cranberries, cooled and drained
1 tablespoon grenadine
4 egg whites
½ cup sugar
1 cup heavy cream, chilled

Beat the egg yolks with a whisk or a rotary or electric beater until they are thick and lemon yellow, then beat in the cranberry juice. Transfer the mixture to a small saucepan and cook over moderate heat, stirring constantly until it thickens enough to coat the spoon heavily. Under no circumstances allow this to boil or the eggs will curdle. Stir in the cranberries and grenadine, and pour into a bowl. Chill in the refrigerator for about ½ hour until it thickens slightly.

Beat the egg whites until they foam, then gradually beat in the sugar. Continue to beat until the whites form unwavering peaks on the beater when it is lifted out of the bowl. In another bowl whip the chilled cream until it holds its shape softly. With a rubber spatula, fold the cream gently but thoroughly into the thickened cranberry mixture, then fold in the egg whites, folding until streaks of white no longer show. Pour into refrigerator trays, or a 2-quart decorative mold or soufflé dish. Cover with foil and freeze until firm. The cranberry mousse may be served in scoops like ice cream, unmolded on a plate, or served directly from a soufflé dish.

Cold Orange Soufflé

To serve 6

2 envelopes unflavored gelatin
1 cup cold water
8 egg yolks
Two 6-ounce cans frozen orange juice concentrate, thoroughly defrosted but with no water added
8 egg whites
1 cup sugar
1 cup heavy cream, chilled
3 tablespoons sugar
½ cup heavy cream, whipped

Sprinkle the gelatin into the cup of cold water and let it soften for about 5 minutes. Meanwhile, with a whisk or a rotary or electric beater, beat the egg yolks until they are thick and lemon yellow. Beat in the softened gelatin.

Then cook the mixture in a small enameled or stainless-steel saucepan over moderate heat, stirring constantly, until it thickens enough to coat a spoon lightly. Do not let it come near a boil or it will curdle. Remove the pan from the heat and quickly stir in the defrosted orange juice. Transfer the mixture to a large mixing bowl and chill in the refrigerator for about ½ hour, or until it thickens to a syrupy consistency.

Beat the egg whites until they begin to froth, then pour in the sugar slowly and beat until the whites form unwavering peaks on the beater when it is lifted out of the bowl. In another bowl, whip the chilled cream until it holds its shape softly, then beat into it the 3 tablespoons of sugar. With a rubber spatula, fold the cream gently but thoroughly into the orange mixture (if it has set too firmly and formed lumps, beat gently with a whisk or rotary beater until smooth), then fold in the egg whites, folding until no streaks of white show. Tie a wax-paper collar around a 1½-quart soufflé dish. It should rise about 2 inches above the rim of the dish. Pour in the soufflé mixture up to the top of the collar, smooth the top with a spatula and chill in the refrigerator for at least 4 hours, or until firm. Carefully remove the collar and pipe decorative swirls or rosettes of whipped cream through a pastry bag on top of the soufflé.

Nesselrode Pudding

To serve 6

Soak the currants and raisins in the rum for at least 15 minutes, then drain and reserve the rum and the fruit separately. Beat the egg yolks with a whisk or a rotary or electric beater for about a minute, then beat in all but 3 tablespoons of the cup of sugar. Continue to beat until the yolks are thick and fall slowly back into the bowl in a ribbon when the beater is lifted up. Heat 2 cups of the cream in a small saucepan until small bubbles begin to form around the edge of the pan. Slowly beat the hot cream into the egg yolk mixture, then return to the pan. Cook over moderate heat, stirring constantly, until the mixture thickens enough to coat a spoon lightly. Do not let the mixture come near a boil or it will curdle. Remove from the heat and stir in the chestnut purée, rum, vanilla, currants and raisins. Chill for about ½ hour.

Whip the remaining cup of chilled cream until it thickens slightly, then add the reserved 3 tablespoons of sugar and whip until the cream forms firm peaks on the beater when it is lifted out of the bowl. Fold it into the Nesselrode mixture with a rubber spatula, making sure the two are well combined. Brush a 1½-quart mold, preferably a charlotte mold, with the teaspoon of oil. Invert to drain any excess oil, then fill the mold with the Nesselrode mixture. Cover the top of the mold securely with foil and freeze the pudding for at least 6 hours until firm.

To unmold, run a knife around the inside edge of the mold, dip the bottom briefly in hot water and wipe it dry. Place a chilled serving platter on top of the mold, invert and rap it once on the table to dislodge it.

Fit a pastry bag with a small star tip, fill the bag with the whipped cream, and pipe rosettes on the top and a decorative border around the bottom of the pudding. Place a small candied chestnut on each rosette.

½ cup currants
¼ cup raisins
½ cup dark rum
4 egg yolks
1 cup sugar
3 cups heavy cream
An 8¾-ounce can unsweetened
   chestnut purée
1 teaspoon vanilla
1 teaspoon vegetable oil

GARNISH
½ cup heavy cream whipped with 1
   tablespoon confectioners' sugar
Candied chestnuts

Maple Mousse

To serve 6 to 8

Sprinkle the gelatin into the ½ cup of cold water and let it soften for about 5 minutes, then set the cup in a shallow pan of simmering water, and stir until the gelatin has dissolved and is clear. Combine with the maple syrup. In a large mixing bowl, beat the egg yolks with a whisk or a rotary or electric beater for 2 or 3 minutes until thick and lemon yellow. Beat into the yolks the maple syrup mixture and pour it into a small saucepan. Cook over moderate heat, stirring constantly, until the mixture thickens enough to coat the spoon heavily. Do not let it boil or the eggs will curdle. Remove from the heat, stir in the brown sugar and mix thoroughly. Transfer to a large bowl and cool to room temperature.

Meanwhile, beat the egg whites until they form unwavering peaks on the beater. In another bowl, whip the chilled cream until it holds its shape softly. With a rubber spatula, fold the cream gently but thoroughly into the maple syrup mixture, then fold in the egg whites, folding until streaks of white no longer show. Rinse a 1½-quart mold, preferably a charlotte mold, in cold water. Shake out the excess water and pour in the mousse mixture. Chill in the refrigerator for at least 4 hours, or until firm.

To unmold, run a knife around the inside edge of the mold, dip the bottom briefly in hot water and wipe it dry. Place a chilled platter on top of the mold, invert and rap it on the table. Chill until ready to serve.

1 envelope plus 2 teaspoons
   unflavored gelatin
½ cup cold water
1 cup pure maple syrup
4 egg yolks
½ cup brown sugar
4 egg whites
2 cups chilled heavy cream

To serve 6 to 8

2 tablespoons soft butter
4 egg whites
Pinch of salt
¼ cup sugar
4 egg yolks
½ teaspoon vanilla
½ cup flour
1 cup orange marmalade or apricot
  preserves
1 to 2 tablespoons orange juice
  (optional)
1 quart vanilla ice cream, slightly
  softened

THE MERINGUE
8 egg whites at room temperature
Pinch of salt
¾ cup superfine sugar

Baked Alaska

Brush a tablespoon of soft butter over the bottom and sides of an 11-by-16-inch jelly-roll pan. Line the pan with a 22-inch strip of wax paper and let the extra paper extend over the ends of the pan. Brush the remaining butter over the paper and scatter a small handful of flour over it. Tip the pan from side to side to spread the flour evenly. Then turn the pan over and rap it sharply to dislodge the excess flour.

Preheat the oven to 400°. In a mixing bowl, beat the egg whites and salt until they form soft, wavering peaks. Add the sugar, two tablespoons at a time, and beat until the whites cling to the beater solidly when it is lifted out of the bowl. In another small bowl, beat the egg yolks for about a minute, then add the vanilla. Mix a large tablespoon of the whites into the yolks, then pour the mixture over the remaining egg whites. Fold together, adding the ½ cup flour, two tablespoons at a time.

Pour the batter into the jelly-roll pan and spread it out evenly. Bake in the middle of the oven for about 12 minutes, or until the cake draws slightly away from the sides of the pan, and a small knife inserted in its center comes out dry and clean. Turn the cake out on a sheet of wax paper, then gently peel off the top layer of paper. Let the cake cool and cut it in half crosswise. Spread one layer with the cup of marmalade or apricot preserves (if it is too thick to spread, thin it by beating into it 1 or 2 tablespoons of orange juice) and place the second layer on top. Mold the softened ice cream on a sheet of aluminum foil into a brick the length and width of the cake. Wrap in the foil and freeze until solid.

About 10 minutes before serving, make the meringue. First, preheat the broiler to its highest point. Then, beat the egg whites and salt until they form soft peaks. Still beating, slowly pour in the sugar, and continue to beat for about 5 minutes, or until the egg whites are stiff and glossy. Remove the ice cream from the freezer and place it on top of the cake on a flat, ovenproof baking dish. Mask the cake and ice cream on all sides with the meringue, shaping the top as decoratively as you like. Slide the cake under the broiler for 2 to 3 minutes, and watch it carefully; it burns easily. The meringue should turn a pale, golden brown in 2 to 3 minutes. Serve at once before the ice cream begins to melt.

To make 1½ pints

¾ pound large sugar cubes
3 medium navel oranges
2 cups water
¼ cup fresh lemon juice
Small bunch fresh mint

Lemon-Orange Ice

Rub about 10 sugar cubes over the skins of the whole oranges to saturate them with the orange oil. Then squeeze the oranges. If they do not produce 1 cup of juice, use another orange. In a 1½ or 2-quart saucepan, bring the water and all of the sugar cubes to a boil over high heat, stirring until the sugar dissolves. Timing from the moment when it begins to boil, let the mixture boil briskly, without stirring, for 5 minutes. Immediately remove the pan from the heat and cool the syrup to room temperature. Stir in the orange juice and lemon juice, and pour into 2 ice-cube trays. Freeze for 3 to 4 hours at least, beating the ice after a half hour to break up the solid particles that will form on the bottom and sides of the tray. Continue to beat every half hour until the ice has a fine and snowy texture. Serve on chilled dessert plates or in sherbet glasses and garnish with the mint.

Tips on Outdoor Cooking

Cooking certain foods over coals gives them a unique, smoky flavor. Of the three common fuels—nonresinous wood, charcoal and briquets—the latter are the cleanest, most dependable and easiest to work with.

If you are using a grill or brazier, as most outdoor cooks do, first line the box or bowl with heavy aluminum foil to catch the drippings. Then, make a fire base about an inch deep of gravel or one of the commercial fire bases. Use enough to provide an ample level surface for the fire.

The easiest way to start a fire is with an electric fire starter, but if you do not have an electric starter, fill a tin can with briquets and pour starter fluid over them. Cover the can tightly, and let it stand long enough for the briquets to be saturated. Pile a few of these "marinated" briquets in a heap, pour more fuel over them and light them. Then add fresh briquets.

Most cooks make larger fires than they need. In a small portable grill, you may begin with one or two dozen briquets. If you need to add fuel later, lay the fresh fuel around the burning coals and rake it in as it ignites. The fire will be ready about half an hour after it has been lit, or when all briquets are ignited and a little white ash begins to show.

Before starting to cook, spread the coals evenly with a poker, creating a flat surface slightly larger than that of the food to be cooked. Start the cooking with the meat as high as possible above the coals and bring it closer as the fire cools. (If your grill is not adjustable, regulate the heat by spreading the coals or sprinkling them with a little water.)

Grilling (Broiling)

Relatively low temperatures are best for all cooking over coals, but the fire should be hotter for broiling than for spit roasting. A grill thermometer is helpful. It should register about 325° at grill level before broiling starts.

BEEF, PORK AND LAMB: Any meat that can be fried, oven- or pan-broiled can be broiled on an outdoor grill.

POULTRY: Small broiling chickens should be split and the backbones removed to make them flat. Larger ones should be cut into pieces. Small chickens will cook in 30 minutes, larger ones in 50 minutes. Ducklings, halved or quartered, should be broiled 45 to 60 minutes and turned occasionally.

SEAFOOD: Fish should be cooked in a grill basket for easy flipping. Whole fish weighing 5 to 6 pounds can be grilled in 20 to 45 minutes. They are done when the internal temperature reaches 150°. Small fish may be wrapped in a double thickness of aluminum foil and roasted in the coals. They will be done in 15 to 20 minutes. Fish steaks will cook on a grill in 7 to 15 minutes. Fillets will be done in 5 to 7 minutes.

Charcoal-broiled lobsters are delicious. A 1¼-pound one will take about 12 to 14 minutes. Split the lobster after it is done, remove the stomach and fill with butter.

Oysters grilled in the shell have a unique, smoky flavor; cook them until the shells pop open.

Shrimp to be broiled should first be dipped in oil or butter, or marinated for a couple of hours. They will cook in 3 to 5 minutes.

FRUITS AND VEGETABLES: Whole apples may be wrapped in foil and baked in the edge of the coals, or they may be cored and filled with sugar, cinnamon and butter before they are wrapped and cooked in the same way. They will be done in about 30 minutes in either case.

To cook corn on the cob, pull back the husks, remove the silk, put the husks back in place and tie them with a string. Then soak them in water for at least 30 minutes so they will be tender and moist. Corn will roast on a grill in 10 to 15 minutes over a hot fire.

Potatoes will roast in about 45 minutes buried in the coals.

KABOBS: Food cooked on skewers is usually cut into 1½- to 2-inch cubes. It may be beef, pork, lamb, veal, fish, shellfish, poultry, fruits or vegetables, alone or in any of several combinations.

The skewers may be ready-made ones of metal or bamboo, or they may be improvised from wire or green twigs.

String meat cubes close together to cook them rare—farther apart if you want them well done. Meat kabobs will cook in 10 to 16 minutes.

Rotisserie or Spit Roasting

Cooking roasts, whole poultry or game birds over coals requires a rotisserie or hand-turned spit and a meat thermometer. Most outdoor roasting today is done on electrically turned rotisseries.

For roasts to cook properly on a rotisserie, they must be perfectly balanced on the rod and should turn easily with it. The rod must pass as nearly as possible through the center of gravity of the meat. If the meat is not balanced the spit will turn jerkily and its motor may even stop. Therefore, it is advisable to buy roasts that are boned, rolled and tied.

The thermometer should be inserted at a slight angle so that the tip is in the center of the roast but not resting in fat or against the rod or a bone.

Before starting to cook anything on a rotisserie, make a trough of aluminum foil about 3 or 4 inches wide. (A metal ice-cube tray is ideal for this purpose.) Bank the coals to the rear of the trough and position the trough to catch the drippings, thus preventing flareups from burning fat.

Only the leaner and tenderer cuts of meat should be cooked on a rotisserie. Here are some suggested cuts, approximate cooking times for the weights given and the temperature the thermometer should reach.

BEEF: Rib-eye or Delmonico, 4 to 6 pounds: rare, 20-22 minutes per pound, 120°; medium, 22 to 24 minutes per pound, 145°. Sirloin tip, 3½ to 4 pounds: rare to medium, 35 to 40 minutes per pound, 120°-145°. Rolled rib, 5 to 7 pounds: rare, 18 to 20 minutes per pound, 140°; medium, 30 to 35 minutes per pound, 150°.

PORK: Boned rolled shoulder, 4 to 5 pounds: 20 to 22 minutes per pound. Loin roll, 3 to 5 pounds: 20 to 25 minutes per pound. Leg, boned, 7 to 10 pounds: 20 to 25 minutes per pound. Fresh ham, 10 to 12 pounds: 20 to 25 minutes per pound. (All pork roasts should reach a temperature of 170°.)

LAMB: Rolled leg, 4 to 5 pounds: 18 to 22 minutes per pound, 140°. Shoulder roll, 3 to 5 pounds: 18 to 22 minutes per pound, 140°.

POULTRY: Chicken, 3 to 5 pounds: 20 minutes per pound, 165°. Duckling, 4 to 5 pounds: 18 minutes per pound, 165°. Goose, 12 to 15 pounds: 12 to 15 minutes per pound, 160°. Turkey, 12 to 15 pounds: 18 to 20 minutes per pound, 160°.

FISH: Whole fish, 5 to 6 pounds: 20 to 45 minutes, 150°. A small whole fish cooks in 15 minutes.

Marinades and Bastes

A marinade is a liquid mixture in which food is soaked before it is cooked. It usually contains wine or lemon juice to tenderize the flesh.

A baste is brushed or sprinkled on the food while it is cooking. It is designed to add a distinctive flavor on the outside and to moisten the food. Most marinades can be converted to bastes by adding oil to them.

Some meats, poultry and fish to be cooked over coal should first be marinated. Some should be basted as they cook. Others do not need marinades or bastes. Avoid indiscriminate use of "barbecue" sauces that do nothing but disguise natural flavors. An all-purpose marinade and baste, one that may be used with any meat, game or poultry, can be made by combining equal parts of dry Italian or French vermouth and olive oil.

For less tender cuts of beef and for game, combine 2 cups of red wine, ¼ cup of vinegar or lemon juice, 1 sliced onion, ¼ cup each of chopped onion and carrot, a few peppercorns and an herb bouquet consisting of bay, parsley and thyme. (Add one cup of oil to make a baste.)

For poultry, shellfish, beef or pork, combine equal parts of soy sauce, sherry or whiskey and oil. This may be seasoned with garlic.

To make a highly seasoned barbecue sauce for meat and poultry, combine one 8-ounce can of tomato sauce, 1 teaspoon each of dry mustard, sugar and salt, 1 tablespoon each of Worcestershire sauce and vinegar, ½ cup of red wine, 1 clove of finely chopped garlic. Add Tabasco to taste. Simmer 10 minutes and strain. For a baste, add ½ cup of oil.

To make pepper barbecue sauce for steaks, chops and hamburgers, combine one 8-ounce can of tomato juice with ¼ cup each of olive oil, chopped green pepper and chopped green onion. Add 3 cloves of finely chopped garlic, 1 tablespoon or more of chili powder and salt to taste. Simmer 10 minutes and strain. For a baste, add ½ cup of oil.

Recipe Index

NOTE: An R preceding a page refers to the Recipe Booklet. Size, weight and material are specified for pans in the recipes because they affect cooking results. A pan should be just large enough to hold its contents comfortably. Heavy pans heat slowly and cook food at a constant rate. Aluminum and cast iron conduct heat well but may discolor foods containing egg yolks, wine, vinegar or lemon. Enamelware is a fairly poor conductor of heat. Many recipes therefore recommend stainless steel or enameled cast iron, which do not have these faults.

Soups

Black bean soup	R7
Cheddar cheese soup	R5
Cold split pea soup with mint	60; R6
Crawfish bisque	96; R4
Cucumber bisque	64; R8
New England clam chowder	151; R2
Pumpkin soup	61; R9
Seafood gumbo	R3

Fruits and Vegetables

Avocado-tomato cocktail	104; R24
Baked apples	53; R26
Boston baked beans	91; R17
Bread and butter pickles	11; R25
Buttermilk fried onions	58; R16
Cabbage in white wine	58; R14
Caesar salad	63; R22
Celery Victor	63; R14
Corn oysters	R16
Cranberry-orange relish	33; R26
Creamed onions and peas	33; R11
Grandmother Brown's rhubarb marmalade	18; R27
Hashed brown potatoes	R18
Mashed potatoes	34; R19
Mushrooms and onions in sour cream	59; R12
Old-fashioned apple butter	77; R27
Pennsylvania Dutch fried tomatoes	91; R10
Potato salad	59; R20
Spiced acorn squash	33; R12
Spinach ring	59; R13
Spinach salad	65; R23
Three-bean salad	99; R24
Tomato aspic	64; R21
Wild rice with mushrooms	58; R15

Meat

Baked bourbon-glazed ham	121; R33
Barbecued spareribs	98; R35
Braised short ribs of beef	127; R37
Chile con carne	99; R41
Crown roast of lamb with peas and new potatoes	120; R29
Crown roast of pork with sausage-apple stuffing	R31
Fried rabbit with sour cream gravy	105; R43
Ham balls	R36
New England boiled dinner	90; R39
Red-flannel hash	90; R40
Roast beef	R38
Roast lamb shanks and lentils	130; R28
Roast mint-stuffed leg of lamb	R30
Roast saddle of venison with cream sauce	130; R42
Stuffed pork chops	121; R32
Sweetbreads and ham under glass	124; R34

Poultry

Broiled Long Island duckling	120; R52
Broiled squab with lemon-soy butter	R55
Chicken salad	R49
Duck in orange aspic with orange and onion salad	126; R50
Fried pheasant with cream gravy	R58
Old-fashioned chicken pie	R48
Roast dove or pigeon	102; R56
Roast pheasant with applejack cream sauce	125; R54
Roast quail on toast	R57
Roast Rock Cornish game hens with pine-nut stuffing	R53
Roast wild turkey with cornbread stuffing	32; R44
Smothered chicken with mushrooms	R47
Southern fried chicken with cream gravy	95; R46

Fish and Shellfish

Artichokes stuffed with shrimp and Green Goddess dressing	144; R70
Baked stuffed striped bass	148; R60
Barbecued shrimp	R69
Barbecued swordfish	R61
Broiled shad	R64
Brook trout	149; R63
Cioppino	102; R72
Clam hash	R74
Deviled crab	151; R71
Dilled salmon soufflé	R59
Fried smelts with herb butter	144; R65
Frogs' legs, roadhouse style, with tartar sauce	R73
Jambalaya	97; R68
Lobster Newburg	150; R76
Oyster fritters	151; R78
Pacific oyster stew	98; R77
Palace Court salad	105; R66
Pompano stuffed with shrimp and crab en papillote	150; R62
Scalloped clams	R76
Scallops remoulade	R75
Sautéed shad roe	R64
Shrimp mousse	R67

Eggs and Cheese

Blender hollandaise	R81
Blender mayonnaise	R80
Chiles rellenos	98; R82
Eggs Benedict	R81
Grits and cheddar cheese casserole	95; R79
Macaroni, ham and cheese casserole	R80

Breads, Rolls and Breakfast Cakes

American white bread	178; R84
Baking powder biscuits	R85
Clover leaf rolls	178; R85
Griddle cakes	179; R88
Leola's cornbread	179; R87
Popovers	R88
Snipdoodle	R83
Spoon bread	R89
Sticky buns	181; R86

Desserts

Apple pie	35; R96
Baked Alaska	202; R104
Banana cream pie	R98
Black bottom pie	R100
Butterscotch brownies	R112
Cheesecake	R94
Cherry cobbler	R93
Chocolate brownies	R112
Cold orange soufflé	200; R109
Deep-dish peach pie with cream cheese crust	R95
Frozen cranberry mousse	200; R108
Key lime pie	94; R103
Lemon-orange ice	202; R106
Lemon pie	R99
Maple mousse	201; R107
Nesselrode pudding	201; R110
Oatmeal cookies	168; R111
Old-fashioned vanilla ice cream	35; R106
Orange-walnut torte	R92
Pecan pie	94; R101
Pineapple roll	R105
Prune and apricot pie	182; R102
Pumpkin pie	34; R97
Strawberry shortcake	179; R90
Three-layer chocolate cake	182; R91
Toll-house cookies	R111

Abalone, 67, 88, *89*

Advertisements for food, *164-165*

African influence on American cookery, 74

Agriculture, 37; Luther Burbank's influence, 56-57; West Coast truck farms, 86; westward movement and regional specialization, 48-49

Alaska, *66;* cookery, 68, 70-71

Ambrosia, 56

Andouilles (sausage), 116

Animal husbandry, 57

Antelope, 119

Apple butter, 73, 77

Apple trees, *12-13,15*

Apples, 15, *54-55;* baked, 53; in Pennsylvania Dutch dishes, 72, 73

"Aquaculture," 137-138

Artichokes, *45;* chilled, with shrimp, *145*

Aschaffenburg, Mr. and Mrs. Lysle, 80

Avocados, 56

Bacon, 118

Bagels, 74

Baking, 166-177

Baking powder, 173

Baking soda, 173

Bananas Foster, 80

Barbecue, 111. *See also* Outdoor cooking.

Bass, striped, 138, *148-149*

Beans: baked, 70; red beans, 109

Beard, James, 28

Beecher, Catherine E., 173, 177, 197-198, 199

Beecher, Henry Ward, 173

Beef, 52, 107-111; barbecued, 111-112; preferred cuts, 107-108; gravy, 10

Beer, 15

Bel Paese cheese, 155

Berries, *12-13,* 28, *57,* 73; preserving, 24; served with maple sugar, 18

Beverages: alcoholic, 42, 50-51, 79, 84; Border Buttermilk, 84; *café brûlot,* 80, *83;* chocolate, 50; coffee, 50; lemonade, 25; sazeracs, 79; wines, 54, 56, 68

Biscuits. *See* Breads.

Bismarck Schlosskäse (cheese), 155

Blackberries, 18-19; pie, 13

Black-eyed peas, 77

Blot, Pierre, 198

Blue cheese, *152*

Boccini cheese, *152*

Boddicker, Glenn, *156-157*

Bohemian influence on American cookery, 73

Boiled dinner, 67

Bouillon cubes: "veal glue," 189

Bread-and-butter pickles, 11

Breads, 167, 168-169; cornbread, *166,* 168-169; garlic, 28; hot, 75; johnnycake, 11; oatmeal muffins, 11; "salt-rising," 172; sourdough, 68; sourdough biscuits, 109, 172-173; sourdough French bread, 86, *169;* spoon bread, 168, 169; steamed brown bread, 70; store-bought, 173-176

Breakfasts: New Orleans, 80; Southern, 76, 77, 78; Texas, *180*

Brennan, Ella, 80

Brick cheese, *152,* 155, 159

Brie cheese, 155

Broccoli, 40

Brunswick stew, 119

Buffalo meat, 119

Burbank, Luther, 56-57

Butterscotch pie, 22

Cabrito, 82

Caesar salad, *62*

Café brûlot, 80, *83*

Cajun cooking, 80-82

Cakes, 168; angel food cake, 73, 168; chocolate, 22, *172,* 177; Lady Baltimore, 78; Tropic Aroma, 23

California: agriculture, *44-45,* 49; cookery, 68

Cambria Pines, California, 86-88

Camembert cheese, 155

Canned foods, 52, 56

Canvasback duck, 52-53, 56

Carrots, glazed, *14,* 18, 26

Catfish, 67; cultivation of, 137

Catsup, 192-196

Cattle: diet for, 112-113; Texas Longhorns, 108-109; transporting to market, 108-109

Cedar Rapids, Iowa, *156-157*

Cereal, 197

Chapman, William, 78

Charcoal for outdoor cooking, *110,* 116, *117, 203*

Charleston, South Carolina, 76-78

Chaurice (sausage), 116

Cheddar cheese, *152,* 155; caraway Cheddar, *152*

Cheese, *152,* 153-159. *See also* Edam, Swiss, etc.

The Cheese Book, 155

Cheesecake, 27, 74

Chenango County, New York, 20

Cherries, 22

Cherry tomatoes, 52

Chesapeake Bay, 75

Cheshire, Massachusetts, 154

Chestnuts, roast, with turkey, *30-31*

Chicken, 118; chopped chicken livers, 74; fried, 73, 75; in Pennsylvania Dutch dishes, 72; roast, 25; soup, 24

Chiffon cake, 168

Child, Mrs. Lydia Maria, 192

Chili, 82-84, *100,* 161; chili peppers, 83, 84, *87;* chili powder, 83

Chinese cooking, 21

Chives, 40

Chocolate, 177; beverage, 50

Chopped chicken livers, 74

Church suppers, 11, *170-171*

Cioppino, 86, *103*

Citrus fruits, *44-45,* 56; introduction into California, 49

Clams, 134; chowder, 27, *136;* clambakes, *92-93,* 133-134

Cobblers, fruit, 22

Codfish, 135

Coffee, 50

Coffeecake, 73

Coffin, Robert P. Tristram, 188

Cole slaw, 27

Collard greens, 77

Colonial America, 37-40, 187

Cookbooks: *American Cookery,* 188-189; *The Boston Cookbook,* 198; *The Buckeye Cookbook,* 198; *The Frugal Housewife,* 192; *The Joy of Cooking,* 199; *Ladies' Indispensable Assistant,* 192; local, 11; modern, 22; *Miss Parloa's Kitchen Companion,* 198; *The Practical Housekeeper and Young Woman's Friend,* 192, 196; *Mrs. Rorer's Cookbook,* 198; *75 Receipts for Pastry, Cakes, and Sweetmeats,* 192; *The Skillful Housewife's Book,* 189-192; *The Table,* 52; *The Universal Receipt Book or Complete Family Directory,* 189-192; *The Virginia Housewife,* 189; *White House Cookbook,* 198

Cookies: Norwegian, 73-74; oatmeal, *154,* 168; sugar, 28; toll-house, 168

Cooking schools, *184,* 185

Cooking utensils, 10, 187, *197*

Corn, 25, 42, 168-169; chowder, 73; on the cob, 38, *39;* cornbread, 168-169; cornbread dressing for turkey, *30-31;* cornmeal, 21; in Pennsylvania Dutch dishes, 72

Cottage cheese, 159

Cotton candy, *163*

Cowboys, 109-111, *172-173*

Crab, 135; "crab boil," 85; king-crab legs, *66;* king-crab salad, *66;* Maryland, 134; she-crab soup, 79; stuffing for flounder, 77

Cranberries: catsup, *66;* mousse, *190-191;* cranberry-orange relish, *30*

Crawfish, 80-82; bisque, 96

Cream cheese, 159; hard sauce, 22; with bagels and lox, 74

Creole cooking, 69, 79-80, 97

Crêpes Fitzgerald, 80

Cuban influence on American cookery, 69

Cucumbers; for pickles, 10

Currant cassis, 28

Czech influence on American cookery, 8, 73

Dairy industry and products, 152-160

Dandelion greens, 72, 115

Dannenbaum, Mrs. Julie, *184*

Daube, 79

De Both, Jessie Marie, 199

Deer, 119, *129*

Des Moines, Iowa: State Fair, *162-163*

Desserts, *190-191. See also* Cakes, Cookies, etc.

Deutsch, Ronald M., 197

Donaldson, Dr. Lauren H., 138

Doughnuts, 18, *19*

Dressing, cornbread, *30-31*

Duck, *115,* 118; canvasback, 52-53, 56

Dutch influence on American cookery, 28-29, 42, 73

Edam cheese, *152*

Eggs, how to cook, 119

English influence on American cookery, 8, 74

Ephrata, Pennsylvania, 72

European visitors to U.S., 26-27, 49-50

Family reunions, 11-14

Farm cooking, 8-10, *14*

Farmer, Fannie, 198

Ferns, fiddlehead, *66,* 70-71

Filippini, Alessandro, 52-53
Finger bowls, 76
Fish, 133-138; cooking time, 137; cultivation of, 137-138; freshness, 137; frozen, 135-138; and water pollution, 135. *See also* Bass, Trout, etc.
Florida cookery, 69
Flounder stuffed with crab, 77
Flours, 167-168, 169, 176-177, 196
Fond du Lac, Wisconsin, 155
Fondutta cheese, 155
Food supply in the U.S., 37, 49
Fowler, Wick, 82-84
French influence on American cookery, 74; and Thomas Jefferson, 41-42
Frey, Emil, 155
Frozen foods, 56, 199; fish, 135-138; turkey, 52
Fruit, fresh, *36, 57*. *See also* Apples, Cherries, etc.
Fudge, 22

Galesburg, Illinois, 73
Game meats, 41, 51, 52-53, 56, 68, 69, 80, 110, 119, *128-129*
Gardens: in colonial Virginia, 39; Thomas Jefferson's, 41, 43-48; victory gardens, 24-25
Gelatin desserts, 20, 189
Geoduck, 135
George VI, King of England, 27
German influence on American cookery, 8, 21, 69, 71, 73
Gouda cheese, *152;* spiced Gouda, *152*
Graham, Sylvester, 196
Graham flour, 196
Grains, 167-168. *See also* Corn, Oatmeal, etc.
Grapefruit, *180*
Grapes: Concord, *29;* introduction into California, 49; introduction into Virginia, 48
Gravy, dried beef, 10
Grits, 78, 168
Grouse, ruffed, *128*
Gumbo, *79-80*

Ham, 113-115; glazed, *122-123;* Pennsylvania Dutch, *72;* Smithfield, 75; with sweetbreads, *124*
Hamburgers, 111, *117,* 160
Harper's Weekly, 108
Harrison, William Henry, 111

Hash, red-flannel, 67
Haskell, Patricia, 155
Hawaiian cookery, 68
Health foods, 196-197
Henry, Patrick, 42
Herbs, 24
"Higdom," 10
Hominy, 78, 168
Hors d'oeuvre, *184*
Hot dogs, 115, *117,* 160; "corn dogs," *162*
Howard Johnson restaurant chain, *159*
Huguenots, 74

Ice cream, 159-160; flavors, *159;* homemade, *158;* with tequila, 84
Idaho, 137
Immigrants to U.S.: influence on cookery, 8, 21, 49, 69, 70-74
Indians: influence on American cookery, 8, 21; in New York, 19
Indonesian food, 28-29
Iowa State Fair, *163*
Italian influence on American cookery, 8, 21, 24-25, 42

Jackson, Andrew, 154
Jambalaya, 67, 79, *97*
Javelina, 119
Jefferson, Maria, 43
Jefferson, Patsy, 42, 43
Jefferson, Thomas, 40-43, 48, 49, 154, 159
Jerusalem artichokes, 40
Jewish influence on American cookery, 74
Johnnycake, 11, 168, 169
Johnson, Nancy, 159

Kasseri cheese, 155
Kellogg, Dr. John Harvey, 197
Kentucky burgoo, 119
Key lime pie, 75
King crab, *66,* 135
Kitchens: labor-saving devices, 185, 186, *187, 189,* 199; in New York farmhouses, 14-15; North Carolina, *193;* stoves, *194-195*

Lady Baltimore cake, 78
Lafayette, Marquis de, 42
Lake Michigan, 138
Lamb, 116-118; crown roast, *106;* lamb shanks and lentils, *131*
Leaven for breads, 172-173
Lemaire, Julien, 42

Lemon juicer, *189*
Lemon meringue pie, 22
Lemonade, 25
Lentils with lamb shanks, *131*
Leslie, Eliza, 192
Levitt, William, 119
Liancourt, Duc de, 50
Liederkranz cheese, 155, 159
Limburger cheese, 159
Lincoln, Mary J., 198
Liver dumplings, 23
Lobsters, 38, 92, *146-147;* Maine, 28, 134; lobster Newburg, 52, 134
Long Island duckling, *115,* 118
Long Island Sound, clambakes, 133-134
Longhorn cheese, *152;* Midget Longhorn, *152*
Los Angeles, California, Farmer's Market, *36,* 86
Louisiana Purchase, 48
Lox, 74
Luau (Hawaiian feast), 68

McAllister, Ward, 53, 56
Madison, Dolley, 43, 159
Madison, James, 43
Maine lobster, 28, 134
Maple syrup and syrup making, 15-18, *20,* 23, 43; with acorn squash, *9*
Marinades for outdoor cooking, 203
Markets, *36, 46-47, 86*
Marmalade: rhubarb, 11, 18; wild orange, 75
Marquis, Vivienne, 155
Marryat, Capt. Frederick, 50, 51-52, 159
Martineau, Harriet, 49
Maverick, Maury, Jr., 84
Mazzei, Philip, 48
Meat: 107-119; in American diet, 50, 52, 107-108. *See also* Beef, Pork, etc.
Meat loaf, 108
Melon balls, *57*
Menus, 19th Century, 53. *See also* Breakfasts.
Mexican influence on American cookery, 68, 82
Michaud, Mr. and Mrs. Aimé, 89
Milk, 153
Mint, 40
Mirliton, 75
Monroe, New York, 155
Monterey cheese, 88, 155
Monticello, Virginia, 41, 43, 48

Mount McKinley, *66*
Mousse, cranberry, *190-191*
Mourning dove, *128*
Mozzarella cheese, 155
Münster cheese, *152,* 155
Mutton, 52

Nacho, 84
Neal, Ella, 14, 15, 20, 21, 22, 29
Neal, Rosaltha, 186
Nesselrode pudding, *190-191*
Neufchâtel cheese, 159
New England cookery, 67-71
New Haven, Connecticut, *110*
New Orleans, 78-80, 82; Bon Ton restaurant, 82; Brennan's restaurant, 80, *83;* Corinne Dunbar's, 79; "crab boil," *85;* Pontchartrain Hotel, 80
New York City: cookery, 74; Delmonico's restaurant, 52, 53-56
New York State, *12-13;* Chenango County, 20; epitaphs from country graveyards, 19; Indians, 19; 19th Century cuisine, 52; settlement, 10, 11

Oatmeal, 21; cookies, *154,* 168; muffins, 11
Okra, in gumbo, 79-80; soup, recipe for, 78
Olive trees, introduction into California, 49; into U.S., 48
Onions, 92, 112; creamed, 20; pie, 24
Opossum, 119
Oranges, *44-45, 57;* in ambrosia, 56; wild orange marmalade, 75; cold orange soufflé, *191*
Otselic Valley Grange, 11
Outdoor cooking, 111, 203; clambakes, *92-93,* 133-134; oysters, *140-141;* salmon, *142-143;* seafood, *139;* steaks, *110, 113, 116, 117;* trout, *132*
Oysters, 86, 134, 135, *140-141,* 192; gathering, *139;* roast, 76-77; soup, 80

Paella, 79
Pancakes, *177;* potato, 23
Papashvily, George and Helen, 86-88
Parmesan cheese, 42, *152,* 155
Partridge, chukar, *128*
Pastries, 73-74
Peaches, 22, 49

Peas, black-eyed, 69, 77
Pecan pie, 78, *81*
Pecan trees, 43
Peccary, 119
Pennsylvania Dutch cookery, 71-73
Pepper pot, 67
Perry, Bob, *140*
Petit (maître d'hôtel to Thomas Jefferson), 42
Pheasant, ringneck, *128*
Pickles, *72;* chunk, 10; one-day bread-and-butter, 11; Pennsylvania Dutch, 72-73; sour, 17
Pie: apple, 27; blackberry, 13; butterscotch, 22; currant, 12; Key lime, 75; lemon meringue, 22; pecan, 78, *81;* prune and apricot, *183*
Pigeon, 119
Pilau, shrimp, 134
Pilgrims, cooking, 21
Pineapple, *57*
Pizza, 161
Plauché, Jim, 79
Pojoaque, New Mexico, 87
Polish influence on American cookery, 73
Pompano, 137, *148-149*
Popovers, 22
Pork, 71-72, 113-116; in early American diet, 50
Port-Salut cheese, 155
Portuguese influence on American cookery, 69
Post, Charles, 197
Potatoes, 40; baked, 28; pancakes, 23; roast, 203; sweet potatoes, 18, 26, 77
"Potherbs," 24
Poultry, 118-119. *See also* Chicken, Duck, etc.
Preservation of foods, 52, 56-57. *See also* Frozen foods.
Processed cheese, 154
Protein in American diet, 50
Provolone cheese, *152*
Puddings: bread, 82; hasty, 21; Nesselrode, *190*
Puget Sound, *139*
Pumpkins, *40-41;* soup, *61*

Quail, *128;* roast, 80

Rabbit, cottontail, *129*
Randolph, John, 39
Randolph, Mary, 189
Raspberries, *46;* sauce, 28

Red snapper, *148-149*
Regional cookery, *map* 68-69
Reindeer salami, 66
Relishes and preserves, *72;* berry, 24; cranberry catsup, *66;* cranberry-orange, *30;* green tomato, 10; Pennsylvania Dutch, *72;* rhubarb marmalade, 11, 18
Rennet, preparing, 189
Rhubarb marmalade, 11, 18
Rice: Piedmont, 43; wild, *174-175*
Ricotta cheese, 155
Rock Cornish hen, 119
Rockfish, Chesapeake Bay, 75
Rogers, Will, 99
Rombauer, Irma, 199
Roosevelt, Franklin D., 27
Rorer, Sara T., 198
Rotisseries for outdoor cooking, 203
Rye, 70

Salad dressing, Green Goddess, *145*
Salads, 27; Caesar, *62;* dandelion greens, 72; king crab, *66;* Palace Court (seafood), 86, *104;* spinach, *65;* and Thomas Jefferson, 42; three-bean, *100-101*
Salmon, 74, 86, 134-135, 138; kippered, 75; in Lake Michigan, 138; planked, *142-143*
Salt pork, 115
San Antonio, Texas: Koehler's restaurant, 111-112
San Francisco: Palace Court restaurant, *103*
Sand dab, 134
Sandwiches, 160
Santa Cruz, California, *162*
Sauerbraten, 21
Sausage: *Kielbasa,* 73; Pennsylvania Dutch, 72; pork, 115; reindeer salami, 66
Scallops, 27-28
Scandinavian influence on American cookery, 73-74
Schnitz un knepp, 72, 73
Scrapple, 71
Sears, Roebuck, 194, 197
Seattle: Pike Place Market, *46-47,* 86
Shad, 138
She-crab soup, 79
Sheep-herders, 117
Shellfish, 88; abalone, 67, 88, *89;* clam chowder, *136;* clambakes, *92-93,* 133-134; clams, 134, 135;

consumption of, 134; crabs, 134, 135; "crab boil," *85;* crawfish, 80-82; crawfish bisque, *96;* lobster, *146-147;* oysters, 86, 134, 135, *140-141;* shrimp, 78, 79, 134. *See also* Lobster, Shrimp, etc.
Short, William, 42
Shortcake, 18
Shrimp, 78, 79, 134; with chilled artichoke, *145*
Similk Beach, Washington, *139, 140*
Simmons, Amelia, 188-189
Skyline Beach, Washington, 140
Smithfield, Virginia, 75
Snacks, 160-161
Snake River Trout Ranch, 137
Sole: petrale, 134; rex, 134
Soufflé, cold orange, *191*
Soups: clam chowder, 27, *136;* corn chowder, 73; crawfish bisque, 82, *96;* oyster, 80; okra, 78; pumpkin, *61;* she-crabs, 78, recipe for, *79;* split pea, chilled, *60*
Sourdough, 68; biscuits, 109, 172; bread, *169*
South Otselic, New York, 11
Southern cookery, 69, 75-82, 114-115
Spanish influence on American cookery, 79
Spencer, Leola, *170-171*
Spinach salad, *65*
Split pea soup, 60
Squash, 78; acorn, *9;* butternut, 20; zucchini, 24
Squirrel, 119
Starter for bread, 172-173
Steak, 28, 73, 108, 109; cooked outdoors, *110, 113,* 116, *117,* 203
Stew, 110; Brunswick stew, 119
Sticky buns, *180*
Stockbridge, Massachusetts, 49
Stoves, 187, *194-195*
Stowe, Harriet Beecher, 173, 177
Strawberries, 28, 57; wild, 18
Succotash, 43
Supermarkets, 56, 160-161
Swedish influence on American cookery, 73
Sweet potatoes, candied, 18, 26, 77
Sweet Springs, Tennessee, 49
Sweetbreads and ham, *124*
Swiss chard, 25
Swiss cheese, *152,* 155

Tacos, 161
Talkeetna, Alaska, 66

Tamales, 86
Tequila, 84
Terrapin, 51, 69
Texas: barbecues, 111; cookery, 82-84
Texas Longhorn cattle, 108-109
Thanksgiving dinners, 19-21, *30-31*
Thyme, 24
Tillamook cheese, 155
Toll-house cookies, 168
Tomatoes, 24, 52, 78; in cream sauce, 73; in Pennsylvania Dutch food, 72-73; relish, 10
Trout: brook, 17; cutthroat, *132;* rainbow, 137
Turkey, 20, 52, 57, *114,* 118; cornbread stuffing for, *31;* wild, *30-31, 129*
Turtle, 111

U.S. Department of Agriculture, 57
University of Washington, 138

Veal, 116-118
Vegetables. *See* Artichokes, Carrots, etc.
Venison, 119
Victory gardens, 24-25
Virginia, 38-40, 75-76, 113-114

Warsawski cheese, 155
Washington, George, 21, 159, 169
Water pollution, and fish, 135
Watercress, 40
Watermelons, *51*
Western Health Reform Institute, 197
Westward movement, 48-49
Wheat, 169
White, Mother Ellen Harmon, 196
White House cookery in Thomas Jefferson's era, 43
Whitefish, planked, 73
Wild turkey, *30-31, 129*
Williamsburg, Virginia, 39, 75-76
Wine, 20, 21, 28, 68
Wolfe, Thomas, 160
Wood for cooking, 187
Woodcock, *128*
Wyoming, *113, 132*

Yeast, 172-173
Young, William, 159

Zanesville, Ohio, 111
Zisman, Sam, 111

Credits and Acknowledgments

The sources for the illustrations in this book are shown below. Credits for the pictures from left to right are separated by commas, from top to bottom by dashes.

All photographs by Mark Kauffman except: 4—Charles Phillips except top left Majorie Pickens. 12, 13, 16, 17, 20, 29—Dale Brown. 14, 23—Dana Brown. 54-55—Charles Phillips. 66—Joseph S. Rychetnik. 68, 69—Maps by Lothar Roth. 87—Joern Gerdts. 92—Richard Meek. 93—Drawings by Matt Greene—Richard Meek. 128, 129—Drawing by Ed Young. 165—Top center Charles Moore from Black Star. 187, 189—The Bettmann Archive. 193—Bruce Roberts from Rapho Guillumette. 194—Sears, Roebuck and Co. 195—Camera Associates. 197—Sears, Roebuck and Co. from the New York Historical Society Collection.

For their help in the production of this book the editors wish to thank the following: Arkansas Game and Fish Commission, Little Rock, Ark., William Mathers; Lysle Aschaffenburg, New Orleans, La.; Audubon Society, New York; The Right Reverend Alfred Bailey, New York; Berliner & Marx Meat Market, New York, William F. Berliner; Boone and Crockett Club, Pittsburgh, Pa.; Borden Co., New York; Adelaide and Ella Brennan, New Orleans, La.; British Information Services, New York; Mr. and Mrs. Albert Brown, Westport, Conn.; Canadian Department of Fisheries, Ottawa, Pauline Klosewych; Jane Carson, Williamsburg, Va.; Mr. and Mrs. William Chapman, Charleston, S.C.; Corning Glass, Corning, N.Y.; Bette Davis; Department of Conservation, Lansing, Mich., Dr. Ronald Rydicki; Finnish Consulate, New York, Mikho Immonen, Consul; Fleischmann Laboratories, Stamford, Conn.; Wick Fowler, Austin, Texas; General Mills, Minneapolis, Minn., Dr. Arthur Odell; Hammacher Schlemmer, New York; Dr. and Mrs. Ed Harvey, Astoria, Ore.; International Shrimp Council, New York, Frances Smith; Jean's Silversmiths, Inc., New York; Mr. and Mrs. Alan Johnson, Tempe, Ariz.; Dr. Frank V. Kosikowski, Ithaca, N.Y.; Laboratory of Radiation Biology, Seattle, Wash., Dr. Lauren R. Donaldson, Dr. Bonham Kelly; William Levitt, Alta, Utah; Long Island Duck Farmers Cooperative, Eastport, Long Island; Louisiana Wild Life and Fisheries Commission, Baton Rouge, La., Peter Juno; Mr. and Mrs. Paul Martin, New Orleans, La.; Maryland Market, New York, Milton Kaufman; Mr. and Mrs. Maury Maverick, San Antonio, Texas; Mr. Foster Shops, New York; National Apple Institute, Washington, D.C., Fred P. Corey, New York, Demetria Taylor; National Dairy Council, Chicago, Ill.; National Live Stock and Meat Board, Chicago, Ill., Reba Staggs, Don Walker; National Shooting Sports Foundation, Riverside, Conn.; National Trust for Historical Preservation, Washington, D.C., Helen D. Bullock; National Turkey Federation, Mount Morris, Ill., M. C. Small; New York Public Library; Norwegian Consulate General, New York; Mr. and Mrs. Byrne O'Connor, Lowville, N.Y.; Mr. and Mrs. George Papashvily, Cambria, Calif.; Pillsbury Company, Minneapolis, Minn.; James Plauché, New Orleans, La.; Poultry and Dairy International Sales Corp., New York; Alice Powell, Talkeetna, Alaska; RMH International, Inc., New York; Sears, Roebuck and Co., Skokie, Ill.; Mr. and Mrs. George Seaton, Los Angeles, Calif.; Tony Simon, Jackson Hole, Wyo.; State of Minnesota Department of Conservation, Division of Game and Fish, St. Paul, Minn., Dr. John B. Moyle, Research Coordinator; Dr. Karl F. Stephens, Brookline, Mass.; Mr. and Mrs. Earl Stiles, Albany, N.Y.; Sunkist Growers, Inc., Los Angeles, Calif.; Tiffany & Co., New York; Johnny Turner, Jackson Hole, Wyo.; United Fresh Fruit & Vegetable Association, Washington, D.C., R. A. Seelig; U.S. Bureau of Commercial Fisheries, San Pedro, Calif., Dr. Paul D. Fulham; Joseph Ledner, New York; Judith Shaw, New York; Victor Samson, Seattle, Wash.; U.S. Department of Agriculture, Economic Research Service, Washington, D.C., Anthony Mathis; U.S. Department of Agriculture, Washington, D.C., Donald Seaborg; Wheat Flour Institute, Chicago, Ill.; Mr. and Mrs. Thomas J. Williams, San Francisco, Calif.; Wisconsin Cheese Foundation Inc., Madison, Wis.; Sam Zisman, San Antonio, Texas.

Sources consulted in the production of this book include: *The History of the United States of America during the Administrations of Jefferson and Madison*, Henry Adams; *Come an' Get It*, Ramon F. Adams; *Grandmother in the Kitchen*, Ruth L. Adamson; *The American Heritage Cookbook*, Editors of *American Heritage*; *Standard Cyclopedia of Horticulture*, L. H. Bailey; *Thomas Jefferson's Garden Book*, Edwin Betts, ed.; *Helen Brown's West Coast Cook Book*, Helen E. Brown; *The Complete Book of Outdoor Cookery*, Helen E. Brown and James A. Beard; *The Williamsburg Art of Cookery*, Helen Bullock; *TheSod-House Frontier*, Everett Dick; *New England Cookbook*, Eleanor Early; *Edible Plants of Eastern North America*, Merritt L. Fernald and Alfred C. Kinsey; *Mr. Jefferson's Ladies*, Gordon Hall; *The Atlantic Migration, 1607-1860*, Marcus L. Hansen; *American Regional Cookery*, Sheila Hibben; *Economic Botany*, Albert F. Hill; *Upland Game Hunter's Bible*, Dan Holland; *The Pennsylvania Dutch Cook Book*, Ruth Hutchison; *Mechanization Takes Command*, Siegfried Giedion; *Over the Counter and on the Shelf*, Laurence A. Johnson; *The Art of Creole Cookery*, William I. Kaufman and Sister Mary Ursula Cooper, O.P.; *Jefferson, the Scene of Europe, 1784-1789*, Marie Kimball; *Thomas Jefferson's Cook Book*, Marie Kimball; *American Cookery Books*, Waldo Lincoln; *Jefferson and His Times*, Dumas Malone; *Society in America*, Harriet Martineau; *Society as I Have Found It*, Ward McAllister; *Wondrous World of Fishes*, National Geographic Society; *Jefferson at Monticello*, Rev. Hamilton Wilcox Pierson; *About Lobsters*, T. M. Prudden; *The First Forty Years of Washington Society*, Margaret Smith; *Hunter's Encyclopedia*, Stackpole Books; *The Original Picayune Creole Cookbook*, The Times-Picayune Publishing Co.; *Cattle and Men*, Charles W. Towne and Edward N. Wentworth; *Economic and Social History of New England, 1620-1789*, William B. Weeden; *We Who Built America*, Carl F. Wittke.